Negotiating with Terrorists

This edited volume addresses the important issue of negotiating with terrorists, and offers recommendations for best practice and processes.

Hostage negotiation is the process of trying to align two often completely polarized parties. Authorities view hostage-taking as unacceptable demands made by unacceptable means. However, terrorists view their actions as completely justified, even on moral and religious grounds. If they are to try and reconcile these two sides, it is essential for hostage negotiators to understand terrorist culture, the hostage-takers' profiles, their personality, their view of the world and also the authorities, their values and their framing of the problem raised by the taking of hostages.

Although not advocating negotiating with terrorists, the volume seeks to analyze when, why, and how it is done. Part I deals with the theory and quantifiable data produced from analysis of hostage situations, while Part II explores several high-profile case studies and the lessons that can be learnt from them.

This volume will be of great interest to students of terrorism studies, conflict management, negotiation, security studies, and international relations in general.

Guy Olivier Faure is Professor of Sociology at the Sorbonne University, Paris V, and a member of the Steering Committee of the Processes of International Negotiation (PIN) Program at the International Institute of Applied Systems Analysis (IIASA) in Laxenburg, Austria. He has served as an adviser on hostage negotiations. He has authored and co-authored fifteen books on negotiation and conflict resolution. His works have been translated into twelve languages. **I. William Zartman** is the Jacob Blaustein Distinguished Professor Emeritus of International Organization and Conflict Resolution and former Director of the Conflict Management and African Studies Programs at the Paul H. Nitze School of Advanced International Studies, Johns Hopkins University, Washington, DC. He is a member of the Steering Committee of the Processes of International Negotiation (PIN) Program at the International Institute of Applied Systems Analysis (IIASA) in Laxenburg, Austria. He is author or editor of over twenty books on negotiation, conflict, and mediation.

Cass series on political violence
Series editors: Paul Wilkinson and David Rapoport

This series contains sober, thoughtful and authoritative academic accounts of terrorism and political violence. Its aim is to produce a useful taxonomy of terror and violence through comparative and historical analysis in both national and international spheres. Each book discusses the origins, organizational dynamics and outcomes of particular forms and expressions of political violence.

Aviation Terrorism and Security
Edited by Paul Wilkinson and Brian M. Jenkins

Counter-terrorist Law and Emergency Powers in the United Kingdom, 1922–2000
Laura K. Donohue

The Democratic Experience and Political Violence
Edited by David C. Rapoport and Leonard Weinberg

Inside Terrorist Organizations
Edited by David C. Rapoport

The Future of Terrorism
Edited by Max Taylor and John Horgan

The IRA, 1968–2000
An analysis of a secret army
J. Bowyer Bell

Millennial Violence
Past, present and future
Edited by Jeffrey Kaplan

Right-wing Extremism in the Twenty-first Century
Edited by Peter H. Merkl and Leonard Weinberg

Terrorism Today
Christopher C. Harmon

The Psychology of Terrorism
John Horgan

Research on Terrorism
Trends, achievements and failures
Edited by Andrew Silke

A War of Words
Political violence and public debate in Israel
Gerald Cromer

Root Causes of Suicide Terrorism
Globalization of martyrdom
Edited by Ami Pedahzur

Terrorism versus Democracy, second edition
The liberal state response
Paul Wilkinson

Countering Terrorism and WMD
Creating a global counter-terrorism network
Edited by Peter Katona, Michael Intriligator, and John Sullivan

Mapping Terrorism Research
State of the art, gaps and future direction
Edited by Magnus Ranstorp

The Ideological War on Terror
Worldwide strategies for counter-terrorism
Edited by Anne Aldis and Graeme P. Herd

The IRA and Armed Struggle
Rogelio Alonso

Homeland Security in the UK
Future preparedness for terrorist attack since 9/11
Edited by Paul Wilkinson et al.

Terrorism Today, second edition
Christopher C. Harmon

Understanding Terrorism and Political Violence
The life cycle of birth, growth, transformation, and demise
Dipak K. Gupta

Global Jihadism
Theory and practice
Jarret M. Brachman

Combating Terrorism in Northern Ireland
Edited by James Dingley

Leaving Terrorism Behind
Individual and collective disengagement
Edited by Tore Bjørgo and John Horgan

Unconventional Weapons and International Terrorism
Challenges and new approaches
Edited by Magnus Ranstorp and Magnus Normark

International Aviation and Terrorism
Evolving threats, evolving security
John Harrison

Walking away from Terrorism
John Horgan

Understanding Violent Radicalisation
Terrorist and Jihadist movements in Europe
Edited by Magnus Ranstorp

Terrorist Groups and the New Tribalism
Terrorism's fifth wave
Jeffrey Kaplan

Negotiating with Terrorists
Strategy, tactics, and politics
Edited by Guy Olivier Faure and I. William Zartman

Negotiating with Terrorists
Strategy, tactics, and politics

**Edited by Guy Olivier Faure and
I. William Zartman**

Routledge
Taylor & Francis Group
LONDON AND NEW YORK

First published 2010
by Routledge
2 Park Square, Milton Park, Abingdon, Oxon OX14 4RN

Simultaneously published in the USA and Canada
by Routledge
270 Madison Ave, New York, NY 10016

Routledge is an imprint of the Taylor & Francis Group, an informa business

© 2010 Selection and editorial matter, Guy Olivier Faure and I. William Zartman; individual chapters, the contributors

Typeset in Times by Wearset Ltd, Boldon, Tyne and Wear

All rights reserved. No part of this book may be reprinted or reproduced or utilized in any form or by any electronic, mechanical or other means, now known or hereafter invented, including photocopying and recording, or in any information storage and retrieval system, without permission in writing from the publishers.

British Library Cataloguing in Publication Data
A catalogue record for this book is available from the British Library

Library of Congress Cataloging-in-Publication Data
Negotiating with terrorists: strategy, tactics and politics/edited by Guy Olivier Faure and I. William Zartman.
p. cm.
Includes bibliographical references.
1. Terrorism. 2. Negotiation. 3. Hostage negotiations. 4. Crisis management. I. Faure, Guy Olivier. II. Zartman, I. William.
HV6431.N45 2010
363.325'16-dc22

2009037318

ISBN10: 0-415-56629-0 (hbk)
ISBN10: 0-203-85559-0 (ebk)

ISBN13: 978-0-415-56629-2 (hbk)
ISBN13: 978-0-203-85559-1 (ebk)

To André Akoun, an outstanding mind and an incomparable mentor

Contents

List of figures	xi
List of tables	xii
Notes on the contributors	xiv
Acknowledgments	xv
The PIN Program at the IIASA	xvi
Introduction: negotiating with terrorists – who holds whom hostage? GUY OLIVIER FAURE AND I. WILLIAM ZARTMAN	1
PART I **How to negotiate: kidnapping the kidnappers**	29
1 Guidelines for negotiating with terrorists LAURENT COMBALBERT	31
2 Quantitative and qualitative aspects of kidnapping and hostage negotiation ALEX P. SCHMID AND P. FLEMMING	47
3 Supping with the Devil DAVID PINDER	69
PART II **Practical/tactical: freeing the hostages**	85
4 Terrorist negotiation strategy in Lebanon KAREN A. FESTE	87
5 Negotiating in Beslan and beyond ADAM DOLNIK	125

6	**Negotiating visible and hidden agendas**	148
	VICTOR KREMENYUK	
7	**Negotiating the grand swap in Kandahar**	163
	P. SAHADEVAN	
	Conclusion: lessons for action	197
	GUY OLIVIER FAURE AND I. WILLIAM ZARTMAN	

References 214
Index 226

Figures

1.1 Analysis of the context indicators 36
1.2 The organization of a negotiating team 41
2.1 Hostage incidents, 1968–2005 48

Tables

1.1	Terrorist types	32
2.1	Type of international hostage incidents, 1968–2005	47
2.2	Definitions of kidnapping and hostage-taking, with examples	51
2.3	Some diplomatic kidnappings of the 1960s and 1970s	52
2.4	Types of immediate victims of international hostage incidents, 1968–2005	52
2.5	Duration of incidents, 1978–2005	53
2.6	Ransoms reportedly paid for Western hostages in Iraq	54
2.7	Hostage-taker behavior, 1978–2005	55
2.8	Deadlines allowed to pass, 1978–2005	55
2.9	Deadlines where threats were carried out, 1978–2005	55
2.10	Types of government response, 1978–2005	56
2.11	Demands for media coverage, 1978–2005	56
2.12	Demands for political change, 1978–2005	56
2.13	Prisoner release demands, 1978–2005	57
2.14	Safe haven demands, 1978–2005	57
2.15	Safe passage demands, 1978–2005	57
2.16	Hostages' fate, 1978–2005	58
2.17	Hostage-taker negotiation success, 1978–2005	59
2.18	Three main negotiation tactics in kidnapping situations	59
2.19	Kidnapping negotiation tactics and good practice	60
2.20	International "best practice" in dealing with hostage-taking situations: key objectives	61
2.21	Typology of hostage-takers	61
2.22	Tasks of the negotiation team	62
2.23	Profile of a (Dutch) negotiator	62
2.24	The three phases of a hostage situation	63
2.25	Basic principles for dealing with hostage situations	64
2.26	Typical terrorist demands	65
2.27	Verbal tactics of hostage negotiators	66
2.28	Predictors of how negotiations are progressing (I) positive signs	66
2.29	Predictors of how negotiations are not progressing (II) negative signs	67

2.30	Common wisdoms on hostage negotiations	67
4.1	Anti-American terrorist events of Iran–Lebanon linkage, November 1979–November 1991	98–99
4.2	US punitive acts against Iran, October 1977–July 1988	107–110
4.3	The fate of American hostages and US assets returned to Iran, 1984–1992	112–114
7.1	The negotiation process	189

Contributors

Laurent Combalbert is a professional hostage negotiator and trainer in Paris, France, and author of the PACIFICA method.

Adam Dolnik is a research associate at the International Centre for Political Violence and Terrorism Research at the Institute of Defence and Strategic Studies, Nanyang Technical University, Singapore, and professor at the University of Wollongong, New South Wales, Australia.

Guy Olivier Faure is Professor of Sociology at the University of Paris V Sorbonne, France, and a member of the PIN Steering Committee at IIASA, Austria.

Karen A. Feste is Professor of International Relations and Graduate Director of the Conflict Resolution Institute in the Graduate School of International Studies at the University of Denver, Colorado, USA.

P. Flemming is an independent scholar associated with the International Terrorism: Attributes of Terrorist Events (ITERATE) project.

Victor Kremenyuk is Deputy Director of the Institute for US and Canada Studies, Russian Academy of Science, Moscow, Russia, and retired member of the PIN Steering Committee at IIASA, Austria.

David Pinder is a professor in the Peace Studies Programme at the University of Bradford, UK.

P. Sahadevan is Associate Professor of Political Science at the Jawaharlal Nehru University, New Delhi, India.

Alex P. Schmid is Director of the Centre for the Study of Terrorism and Political Violence (CSTPV) at the University of St Andrews, Scotland.

I. William Zartman is the Jacob Blaustein Distinguished Professor Emeritus of International Organization and Conflict Resolution at the School of Advanced International Studies (SAIS) of the Johns Hopkins University in Washington, DC, USA, and a member of the PIN Steering Committee at IIASA, Austria.

Acknowledgments

We are grateful for the support of the Smith Richardson Foundation for this project of the Processes of International Negotiation (PIN) Program at the International Institute of Applied Systems Analysis (IIASA) and to IIASA itself for underwriting the PIN Program. We are also grateful for Jeroen Gunning and David Rapoport for their encouragement, and to Isabelle Talpain-Long for carefully monitoring the manuscript.

I.W.Z.
G.O.F.

The PIN Program at the IIASA

Since 1988 PIN, at IIASA in Laxenburg, Austria, has been conducted by an international Steering Committee of scholars and practitioners, meeting three times a year to develop and propagate new knowledge about the processes of negotiation. The committee conducts a book workshop every year devoted to the current collective publication project and involving analysts and diplomats from a wide spectrum of countries, in order to tap a broad range of international expertise and to improve the understanding and the practice of negotiation. It also offers mini-conferences (road shows) on international negotiation in order to disseminate and encourage research on the subject. Such road shows have been held at the Argentine Council for International Relations, Buenos Aires; Beijing University; the Center for Conflict Resolution, Haifa; the Center for the Study of Contemporary Japanese Culture, Kyoto; Geneva Center for Strategy and Policy; the Netherlands Institute of International Relations, Clingendael, The Hague; the Swedish Institute of International Affairs, Stockholm; the University of Cairo; University Hassan II, Casablanca; the University of Helsinki; School of International Relations, Tehran; Nanjing-Johns Hopkins Universities; Harvard University; Carleton University; the University of Warsaw; and the UN University for Peace, San Jose, Costa Rica.

The PIN Program publishes a semi-annual newsletter, *PIN Points*, and sponsors a network of over 4,000 researchers and practitioners in negotiation. The program has been supported by the William and Flora Hewlett Foundation, the Smith-Richardson Foundation, and the US Institute of Peace. Contact: pin@iiasa.ac.at.

Members of the PIN Steering Committee: Rudolf Avenhaus, German Armed Forces University, Munich; Mark Anstey, Michigan State University in Dubai; Franz Cede, University of Budapest/Austrian Foreign Ministry; Guy Olivier Faure, University of Paris V, Sorbonne; Paul Meerts, Netherlands Institute of International Affairs, Clingendael; Valerie Rosoux, Catholic University at Louvain; Gunnar Sjöstedt, Swedish Institute of International Affairs; I. William Zartman, Johns Hopkins University; and Ariel Macaspac Penetrante, University of Vienna, administrator.

Selected publications of the PIN Program

Negotiating with Terrorists: Strategy, tactics and politics, edited by Guy Olivier Faure and I. William Zartman, 2010. Routledge, Abingdon.

Engaging Extremists: Negotiating Ends and Means, edited by I. William Zartman and Guy Olivier Faure, 2010. US Institute of Peace, Washington, DC.

Negotiated Risks: International Talks on Hazardous Issues, edited by R. Avenhaus and G. Sjöstedt, 2009. Springer, New York.

Escalation and Negotiation, edited by I. William Zartman and Guy Olivier Faure, 2005. Cambridge University Press, Cambridge.

Peace versus Justice: Negotiating Backward- and Forward-looking Outcomes, edited by I. William Zartman and V. Kremenyuk, 2005. Rowman & Littlefield, Lanham, MD.

Negotiating European Union, edited by P. W. Meerts and F. Cede, 2004. Palgrave Macmillan, Basingstoke.

Getting it Done: Post-agreement Negotiations and International Regimes, edited by B. I. Spector and I. William Zartman, 2003, United States Institute of Peace Press, Washington, DC.

How People Negotiate: Resolving Disputes in Different Cultures, edited by Guy Olivier Faure, 2003. Kluwer, Dordrecht.

Professional Cultures in International Negotiation: Bridge or Rift?, edited by G. Sjöstedt, 2003. Lexington Books, Lanham, MD.

Containing the Atom: International Negotiations on Nuclear Security and Safety, edited by R. Avenhaus, V. A. Kremenyuk, and G. Sjöstedt, 2002. Lexington Books, Lanham, MD.

International Negotiation: Analysis, Approaches, Issues, second edition, edited by V. A. Kremenyuk, 2002. Jossey-Bass, San Francisco.

Preventive Negotiation: Avoiding Conflict Escalation, edited by I. William Zartman, 2001. Rowman & Littlefield, Lanham, MD.

Power and Negotiation, edited by I. William Zartman and J. Z. Rubin, 2000. University of Michigan Press, Ann Arbor, MI.

International Economic Negotiation: Models versus Reality, edited by V. A. Kremenyuk and G. Sjöstedt, 2000. Edward Elgar, Cheltenham.

Introduction
Negotiating with terrorists – who holds whom hostage?

Guy Olivier Faure and I. William Zartman

Hostage negotiation is not something new under the sun, but modern forms of terrorism have their own specifics. What has dramatically changed is the extension of terrorist practice and of its effectiveness. After almost four decades of experience in the domain of practice, it is time for conceptual reconsideration. A number of attributes make hostage negotiation, especially in its political/ideological version, extremely specific – dramatic stakes, emotional arousal, political anxiety, enormous gap between values systems, denegation of the legitimacy of the other as a negotiation counterpart (Faure, 2003; Taylor and Donohue, 2006).

The situation is complex, with hostage-takers holding their captives within an unfriendly environment. Each side may be defined as the hostage of the other. For the victims, the nature of the relation is clear: they are detained by force. But the perpetrators too have made themselves hostages by their action. Be they in an airplane, a building, a ship, even a train, they are surrounded by official authorities and are not free to move. In a formal way, they can be framed as prisoners, or voluntary prisoners with some bargaining leverage for having with their hostages a currency of exchange.

Substantively, on the negotiators' side, the terrorist poses unacceptable demands by unacceptable means. On the terrorist side these two aspects are viewed as perfectly justified even on moral or religious grounds. Thus, there is not much room for negotiation. However, in fact the very situation calls for negotiation, not surrender. What is essential is to understand the process by which what is impossible becomes possible. For that purpose, it is essential to better know this new terrorist culture, the hostage-takers' profiles, their personality, their view of the world, of the authorities, their values, and their framing of the problem raised by the taking of hostages. Concerning the negotiation process itself, under which conditions can it be carried out, by what logic, with what terms of trade? And when to abandon negotiation and switch to the "tactical option"?

Terrorism and hostage-taking

The current literature addressing this most peculiar type of negotiation, which involves dealing with the worst possible negotiation counterparts, can be divided into two main categories: analytical works and practical advice. The analytical literature explores the conditions making such negotiation possible, the specific elements of the negotiation process, the potential outcomes, the psychological profile and motivations of the terrorists, and their usual strategies and tactics (Baldwin, 1976; Dolnik, 2006; Dolnik and Fitzgerald, 2007; Donohue and Taylor, 2006; Faure, 1988, 2002, 2003, 2008; Hayes, 2002; Miller, 1980; Miller, 1995; Nesser, 2006; Oettgen and Spinazzola, 1987; Waugh, 1982; Wilson, 2000; Zartman, 1990, 2006).

Drawn from field experience, technical manuals have been produced to provide advice for practitioners and negotiators on the ground. These guidelines deal mostly with the methods and tactics to be applied to different types of situation. Basic principles are outlined, such as avoiding verbal conflict, actively listening, avoiding deadlines, gaining time, lowering expectations, giving nothing away but always making trade-offs, understanding that lies and deception are acceptable in such critical matters, paying attention to external accomplices or terrorist members hidden among the hostages, detecting listening devices installed by terrorists, diverting the captors' attention away from the hostages, reassuring hostage-takers that the site will not be attacked, minimizing the seriousness of the crime, trying to build at least a minimal level of trust, avoiding the word "hostages," traumatizing language or value-laden formulas, not suggesting exchanging oneself for hostages, and not exposing oneself physically (Adang and Giebels, 1999; Bolz et al., 2002; Bolz and Hershey, 1980; Clutterbuck, 1987; Cooper, 1981; Davidson, 2002; Faure, 2006; Hammer et al., 1997; Hammer, 2007; Lanceley, 1999; MacWilson, 1992; McMains and Mullins, 2001; Pearson and Radli, 1999; Poland and McCrystle, 1999; Thomson, 2001).

Modern terrorism is both part of and a reaction to the huge movement that is globalization and at the same time reacts against and benefits from this new development. Terrorist groups are set up on transnational bases with no territorial reference. Borders are no longer obstacles and the extension and sophistication of hi-tech has greatly contributed to the development of organizations characterized as informal, decentralized, where communication is fast, anonymous and effective. It is no longer necessary to have a territorial base even if situated for instance in a country with a collapsed state. The field of action of terrorism is a civilian context, where spotting a group is most difficult and the actions potentially most deadly. In addition, the law often drastically limits defense capacities implemented by the authorities. Terrorism is also a reaction against globalization, the inexorable spread of modern social and economic norms and actions that threatens traditional cultures and societies. In more specific cases, such as the terrorist actions in Sri Lanka or Palestine, its focus is more centered on a geographic area, but it still takes advantage of the anti-globalization reaction.

Terrorism is far from being a new practice. Intimidation is not even an activity limited to the human species, as many animals tend to use it to dominate one another. Russian terrorism in the nineteenth century rooted in mysticism, nihilism or revolutionary ideologies amounted to over 18,000 attempts. Bulgarians, Macedonians, and Armenians opposed the Ottoman power by adopting terrorist methods. Palestinians after 1948 have taken up again the same methods against the Hebrew state. A break with the classical model took place with Irish and Palestinian terrorists, who moved the field of their fight outside the concerned territory, spreading death for the former in the United Kingdom and the latter in the entire world. The point is not even as previously done to hit symbolic monuments, kill personalities or even simple people who belong to the enemy community. Any individual, whoever he is, could be a physical victim and feel the impending threat any time. This is one of the particularities of the fourth wave in modern terrorist history (Rapoport, 2006). Furthermore, new ideological movements generate considerable numbers of candidates to martyrdom. The deterritorialization of terrorism contributes to its durability, for nobody knows where these groups will strike. In addition, they cannot be easily spotted, which makes classic military measures ineffective.

The term "terrorism" yields varying definitions, heavily loaded with political and emotional implications. The UN Security Council (Resolution 1373) defines terrorism as violent or criminal acts designed to create a state of terror in the general public and by the US government as premeditated, politically motivated violence perpetrated against noncombatant targets by sub-national groups or clandestine agents, usually intended to influence an audience. A widely accepted academic characterization presents terrorism as:

> an anxiety-inspiring method of repeated violent action, employed by (semi-)clandestine individual, group or state actors, for idiosyncratic, criminal or political reasons, whereby – in contrast to assassination – the direct targets of violence are not the main targets. The immediate human victims of violence are generally chosen randomly (targets of opportunity) or selectively (representative or symbolic targets) and serve as message generators. Threat and violence-based communication processes between terrorist organization, imperiled victims, and main targets are used to manipulate the main target (audience(s)), turning it into a target of terror, a target of demands, or a target of attention, depending on whether intimidation, coercion, or propaganda is primarily sought.
>
> (Schmid, 1988)

It is a violent aggression against noncombatants by non-state actors aimed at influencing a target audience to serve the interests of the terrorists rather than achieve specific political goals (Victoroff, 2005). The calculated use of violence against civilians is basically done for purposes of intimidation or coercion: Weapons of the weak against the strong and of the desperate against the authorities. A number of tactical means are used, such as hi-jacking, assassination, car bombing, suicide bombing, kidnapping, and threats of these actions or even threats of possible use of chemical, biological, and nuclear weapons. Terrorism is understood as an attempt to provoke fear and intimidation in the target audience which is often disproportionate in regard to the real danger. Terrorist actions are therefore designed and deliberately timed to attract wide publicity and cause public shock, fear, anxiety, dismay, social disorder, even panic. Terrorists usually intend to achieve political or religious goals that go beyond their personal interests. Thus, gangsters would not be classed as terrorists even if spreading fear through organized crime or rackets.

Guerrilla warfare and "freedom fighters'" actions are sometimes confused with terrorist acts, as a relatively small force attempts to achieve large goals by using organized violence against a larger force. The confusion was highlighted in a speech by Yasir Arafat at the United Nations (1974) in which he stated that "The difference between the revolutionary and the terrorist lies in the reason for which each fights." In fact, the UN definition exclusively considers the target, and not the motive, as the differentiating variable, which is combatants or noncombatants. So, if these groups commit acts of terrorism, such as killing innocent civilians, even because of so-called good reasons, they still fall under the terrorist classification. Frequently, guerilla actions aim at military targets. Thus, guerrilla warfare tends to be considered as part of a military strategy rather than terrorism, although terrorism and guerrilla warfare are both forms of asymmetric warfare.

Several themes characteristic of a terrorist act appear recurrently in the claims made by the perpetrators, such as the reference to the ideals of the group, implying that those ideals justify the actions; for example, Hamas's demands that the whole territory they consider as Palestine only belongs to the Palestinians. Historical memory is reactivated (Faure and Rubin, 1993) and old grievances are again put forward, such as the oppression suffered by an ethnic or religious group; for example, the Tamil Tigers' reference to subjugation of the Tamils by the Singhalese. Claims for punishment for specific acts are also made such as for the occupation of Iraq by a foreign power. Specific demands are made as a justification of what is perpetrated; for example, al-Qaeda's demand that all non-Muslims be driven away from Saudi Arabia.

Victims and targets

Almost 50,000 individuals worldwide were either killed or injured by terrorist attacks in 2008. Based upon a combination of reporting and demographic analysis of the countries involved, well over 50 percent of the victims were Muslims, and most of them were victims of attacks in Iraq, Pakistan, and Afghanistan. Open source reporting identifies approximately 65 percent of the almost 50,000 casualties of terror as simply civilians

In 2008 approximately 11,800 terrorist attacks against noncombatants occurred worldwide, resulting in over 54,000 deaths, injuries and kidnappings according to the National Counter-Terrorism Center (NCTA, 2008). The largest number of terrorist attacks occurred in the Near East, mainly Iraq, but South Asia with Afghanistan, Pakistan, and India had the greatest number of fatalities. These two regions were also the locations for 75 percent of the 235 high-casualty attacks (those that killed ten or more people). Violence against noncombatants in Africa, especially due to the prevailing chaos in Somalia and the Democratic Republic of the Congo, resulted in a total of about 2,200 fatalities.

A great variety of actions can be undertaken by terrorists to serve their purpose. The WITS database (Worldwide Incidents Tracking System) refers to the following activities: armed attack, arson/firebombing, assassination, assault, barricade/hostage, bombing, CBRN, crime, firebombing, hi-jacking, hoax, kidnapping, near miss/non-attack, theft, and vandalism. Terrorist use of hostage-taking or kidnappings for ransom increased significantly in 2008. Over 1,200 people died because of that type of practice. The number of kidnappings in South Asia rose by 45 percent. The number of kidnappings in Pakistan rose sharply by 340 percent and in Afghanistan by about 100 percent, while in India the number rose by 30 percent (NCTA, 2008).

Western countries in Europe and North America are not the prime targets of jihad terrorism, as demonstrated by the vast gap in the numbers of casualties in the Middle East compared with the West. The September 11 drama and the ensuing "war on terror" have first contributed to a "clash within one civilization," turning this part of the world into an epicenter of terrorism. However, Europe is also a quite vulnerable battlefield. It has become over a number of years the main base of some terrorist support groups. This process has been facilitated by the growth of Muslim communities, the increasing tensions with the local populations, and the relative freedom with which radicals could organize themselves in mosques, charitable and cultural organizations. Ideological and religious indoctrination have been provided by militants who came to these countries as religious heads. In addition, a common phenomenon is happening all over the world: the radicalization of the second generation of immigrants, thus providing new human resources for more jihads.

A changing actor: the terrorist

Since there is no such thing as "war on terrorism," there is no negotiation with terrorism but simply a possible negotiation with terrorist organizations. In fact, one cannot negotiate with an ideology or with a method for gaining power but only with people, whoever they are. Over 150 groups or clandestine agents who have been connected to a terrorist attack in various ways have been listed (NCTC database on terrorist incidents, NCTA, 2008). A third of them are well known terrorist organizations. The Taliban, more than any other group, claimed credit for the largest number of attacks and the highest fatality totals. Al-Shabab al-Islamiya (Muslim Youth) was the second deadliest group. Considering the overall available data, the deaths by perpetrator category put Islamic extremists ranking first with a number of 8,284, followed by secular/political/anarchists, 2,513, and Christian extremists, 932. The methods used in attacks are armed attack, 5,993, then bombing, 4,131, then kidnapping, 1,125, then suicide, 405 (NCTA, 2008).

The leading instigators of suicide attacks were the Tamil Tigers in Sri Lanka, a group that based its actions on strictly political values. This group committed seventy-six of the 315 incidents recorded until now, more than Hamas (fifty-four) or Islamic Jihad (twenty-seven). Secular Muslim groups like the Kurdistan

Workers' Party, the Popular Front for the Liberation of Palestine and the Al-Aqsa Martyrs Brigades account for more than a third of suicide attacks in the Muslim world.

On a more qualitative stand, investigations have shown that there is no clear correlation between poverty and terrorism. Poverty does not cause terrorism and prosperity does not cure it. In the world's fifty poorest countries there is little or no terrorism at all. At the same time, structural causes such as poverty do indirectly form the basis for terrorist actions and motivations. Terrorists see themselves as events-takers, not events-makers, in a globalizing world or in unequal societies within a single nation; they seek self-determination and self-improvement within the global or national society. In contrast, the link between terrorism and nationalist, ethnic, religious, and tribal conflict is far clearer. Out of 100 militants believing with equal intensity in the justice of their cause, only a very few will actually engage in terrorist actions. Out of this small minority, even fewer will be willing to sacrifice their lives as suicide bombers. Imponderable factors might be involved for making such a choice: indoctrination but also psychological motives fed, for instance, by accumulated frustrations.

Sageman (2004) observes that in general Jihadists come from religiously moderate middle-class families (see also Zartman and Khan, 2010). Many of them are married and have children. They have reached some level of education, but regarding their qualification, they are most often underemployed. Although rather "normal" by other criteria, they have been socially alienated and frustrated. They also appear to have become noticeably more religious before joining militant groups. In many cases, pre-recruitment personal crises appear to have been a radicalizing factor. However, still according to Sageman, social, political, and religious grievances can be considered as necessary, but not sufficient for them to join the jihad. The decisive factors are social bonds and networks such as those of friendship and kinship. There is no or little organizational intervention from above in the recruitment process. The drive comes rather from below. Sympathizers of the global jihad approach militant milieus and express their will to join instead of the other way round. Another feature of adhering to the Jihad is that new members join in groups rather than as individuals, and this factor contributes significantly to the growth of the movement. Mosques are the most frequent points of entry into milieus of radical Islam.

Horgan (2009) argues that there is no single root cause behind involvement in terrorist actions. It is a complex psychological process and, with the data we currently have, it seems impossible to establish profiles of terrorists. Thus, it is still a challenge to develop adequate counter-terrorist strategies. However, there are predisposing risk factors for involvement in terrorism such as the temporary emotional state, the dissatisfaction with the current activity, the desire to "do something," the identification with the "victims," the belief that violence is not immoral, and finally social ties existing with people already involved. Terrorists are not a homogeneous population and Hogan contends that social profiling is much more useful and realistic.

Nevertheless, some case studies have been made that help to understand something about how people go from legal to illegal activities, from involvement to engagement. Nesser (2009) uses a typology providing interesting conclusions for future prevention. Through interviews, he isolates four categories of terrorists: the leader, the adventurer, the born again, and the mother martyr. Analyzing the 2005 London suicide attacks, the same author concludes that several functions are performed, such as the "entrepreneur," a leading figure with an idealistic mind penetrated by a strong sense of injustice concerning all Muslims of the world. He receives guidance from a religious figure. The second figure is the "protégé," an activist-minded assistant, educated and skilled. The third type is the misfit, someone with personal problems that he tries to solve by joining the Jihad. He has little education and violent tendencies. The last figure is the drifter, who acts according to circumstances or contacts and is not fully or permanently involved (2006). Converted radical Islamists have also been very recently investigated. They are described as fragile individuals, coming from poor backgrounds, broken families, most vulnerable to influence and looking for a way out of their problems (Pargeter, 2009).

Modernity has also impacted terrorist groups with the benefits of communication technology, the training they receive from some rogue states and the experience they have accumulated through practice (Dolnik and Fitzgerald, 2007). Several attributes give these groups their specificity. They are elusive, of a rationale that is extremely difficult to capture, dangerous and resolute. They are elusive because they are difficult to identify, they are weakly structured, fluid, extremely mobile, volatile, de-territorialized and develop a transnational action. Their rationality is hard to understand because it mixes a system of beliefs, a representation of the world, a demonization of the adversaries, and somewhat opaque goals. They are dangerous in the way they resort to important means of action, they do not mind engaging in an extensive practice of massacres or targeting civilians and innocent people. They are resolute because they believe in the rightness of their cause and do not fear death. In addition, to the contrary of a well spread idea, they are educated and know well how to use most sophisticated technologies and highly performing financial instruments.

When considering the ideologies that drive terrorists' organizational structures and possibly their life cycle trajectories, three major perspectives emerge, although the examples cited will quickly show that the groups do not easily stay within the boundaries of a single category (Hoffman, 1989; Post *et al.*, 2002; Victoroff, 2005; Crenshaw, 1988). Basically, we find the nationalist separatist groups, the social revolutionists, and the religious fundamentalist terrorists.

The *nationalist separatist* groups seek to establish a geographically separate political state based on either ethnic or political criteria, for example the Provisional Irish Republican Army (PIRA), Kurdistan Workers' Party (PKK), Liberation Tigers of Tamil Eelam (LTTE], Euskadi Ta Askatasuna (ETA), Popular Front for the Liberation of Palestine (PFLP), Al-Aqsa Martyrs' Brigades (an offshoot of the Fatah, the Palestinian nationalist movement, which is itself a faction of the Palestine Liberation Organization), a secular terrorist group in the Muslim world. Such groups often include criminal activity besides their fight as separatists. They are trained and have gained considerable experience in military strategy and tactics. The ideology itself is generally an extreme and distorted version of the beliefs of their social group (Silke, 2003). However, a clear rationale for military-style action, violence is carefully and cold-bloodedly planned.

The *social revolutionist* uses terrorism as a way of drawing attention and applying pressure on the authorities to promise changes in social or economic order, for example the Italian Red Brigades, Hezbollah. These terrorists necessarily possess a degree of interdependence with the authorities because their goals focus on fighting for improvement or change in a system of which they are already part. By threatening to kill hostages as a bargaining tool, these terrorists expect to force authorities to compromise or make concessions in support of their cause. Since one of their aims is to gain support for the "revolution," they are likely to tactically avoid levels of aggression that would lessen the public's sympathy, although this condition is not always met (Wilson, 2000).

Radically different from the two secular groups is *religious fundamentalist* terrorism, which is viewed as a "sacramental act" carried out in fulfillment of a theological order (Hoffman, 1989). While the focus of secular terrorists is on using terrorism to change some aspect of the current political or social order, the religious terrorist seeks to directly damage the society, for example al-Qaeda; the Salafist Group for Preaching and Combat in Algeria recently reformed as Al-Qaida in the Islamic Maghreb; Aum Shinrikyo, a Japanese religious sect; Lord's Resistance Army, a Christian/pagan terrorist group in northern Uganda. Their role is one of a martyr figure who, in making a most honorable sacrifice, would expect to receive both social recognition here below and rewards in the after-life (Silke, 2003). This set of goals means that religious terrorists have a clear out-group mentality and are likely to show little interdependence with authorities or hostages. They consider themselves as being at "total war" and their great use of violence is not only morally justified but viewed as a necessary expedient for the attainment of their goals (Hoffman, 1989).

The Abu Sayyaf group, an Islamic organization operating in the southern part of the Philippines who frequently indulges in criminal actions such as kidnapping, is a blend of the three ideal types defined above in the Weberian sense. They practice terrorism on a religious basis, have separatist claims, and aim to change the social structure of the local society.

Over a decade and a half, there has been a radical shift from a technomorphous type of organization to a biomorphous type, which makes countermeasures most difficult to conceive and implement. The technomorphous period was prevailing until the end of the Cold War. Terrorist groups, guerrilla movements were most often financed, controlled, trained and monitored by states that had a strategy whose rationality was, if not shared, at least well understood. The biomorphous stage corresponds to the birth of entities proliferating in a quasi-biological way, uncontrollable by states, most difficult to identify and even more to infiltrate, such as the numerous al-Qaeda networks (Laqueur, 1999; Ganor, 2006).

Whether religious groups or political entities, terrorists offer a wide range of profiles that can usefully be grouped into two additional categories, the "absolute" and the "contingent" terrorist (Hayes *et al.*, 2003; Zartman, 2006). *Absolute* terrorists are those whose action is "non-instrumentalist, a self-contained act that is complete when it has occurred and is not a means to obtain some other goal" (Zartman, 2006: 2). Among absolute terrorists are suicide bombers, whose purpose is to punish the others rather than using some of them as an exchange currency. They are beyond negotiation and ready to sacrifice themselves to their cause. They may belong to the category of apocalyptic ideologues whose purpose is to destroy the world in order to save it. They may have developed a strong paranoid dimension, creating such a considerable gap between them and the rest of the world that there is no room for the slightest possibility of getting them to negotiate.

Al-Qaeda can be usually considered as representative of such a category. There is nothing to be negotiated for the time being as they hit and punish. Their purpose is to weaken the Western system, assuming that one day it will collapse as did many historic empires. Religion is viewed as an absolute, above culture, nations and history. Martyrs' death, the ultimate sacrifice, is perceived as a victory. It is apocalyptic symbolism on the individual scale. The organization is not structured in a way that could make an identical implementation of the global policy possible. Al-Qaeda has not adopted the Leninist type of organization but an acentric loose network. Furthermore, it is not concerned with controlling a territory and thus may easily move its base.

Contingent terrorists are those who seek to exchange their victims against something else such as release of prisoners, publicity or ransom. With such a counterpart, although the relation may be quite antagonistic and the process very strenuous, there is room for trade offs. In the case of hostage-taking, the freedom or the life of the hostages may be considered as a common interest between government and terrorists. In case of threat of deadly attack, a bargaining space may be designed in order to avoid the terrorists' implementing the threat or preventing them from escalating the conflict. In the case of a suicide bomber, it may sometimes be possible to convince him that he will better serve his cause by staying alive than dead.

Hezbollah, Hamas, Muslim Brothers, Groupe Islamique Armé (GIA, or al-Jama'a al-Islamiyh al-Musallaha), and the Nepalese Maoists are or were part of this category. They all try to translate their terrorist actions into political outcomes. War and diplomacy are used in parallel. They either want to join in exercising power with those who govern or simply replace them. Another type of situation fairly common with terrorists concerns those who have been arrested. For the authorities, the point is not just to deliver them to the court to stand trial but also to get information about the structure of the network, the channels for financing, who provide the group with weapons, who the heads are, and where they hide. Usually terrorists in case they are captured are trained to abide by three basic principles when interrogated: deny everything, admit nothing, and keep the other side talking to establish how much they know. The point is to bring some substance to the interrogation by finding a way to make the terrorist more talkative. When possible, one must resort to techniques that go beyond the ordinary use of the carrot and stick routine. It is not just a questioning but a true negotiation in the sense that if the terrorist cooperates, he or she will have a lighter punishment or even none. He or she might get freed, to receive a certain amount of money and live somewhere else under a new identity. This has been the case for those who were called the "repentants" in Italy. Sometimes the police or the intelligence service manages to turn a terrorist who then becomes an informer.

As with any typology, the borderline between absolute and contingent terrorists is not always easy to draw. It is subject to mobility through cultural variations, ideology, time, negotiation process, and context modifications. In itself such a topic is so important and complex that it deserves a major interest from any responsible government. Furthermore, the categories are fixed but their inhabitants are not; individuals and groups can in fact move from one category to another, depending on their internal dynamics and on the strategies and tactics of their adversaries. As a result it can be stated forthrightly, and developed below, that the major challenge for states is to move absolute terrorists to the contingent category, and that takes negotiation. Thus, to qualify for the above categorization, one cannot negotiate with absolutes *as long as they are absolutes*.

A most difficult challenge: terrorists as negotiation counterparts

Negotiation is sometimes viewed as the art of compromise, so that bargaining with terrorists may be understood as compromising with the devil. One of the most consistent themes in the literature is that there should be no negotiation with terrorists. Thus, for most nations, the standard policy is "no concessions." This position has always been strongly advocated by the law enforcement community, primarily because bargaining invites repeated attacks (Elliott and Gibson, 1978). Another common recommendation, often made by criminologists, is that terrorism should be processed by the criminal justice system the same way as other crimes (Crelinsten *et al.*, 1978)

Negotiation with terrorist hostage-takers raises several types of problems: recognizing terrorists as acceptable counterparts; setting up precedents, encouraging terrorists to persist in their methods; becoming trapped in a relationship that may elicit more concessions than necessary. The issue of recognition of the counterpart as a consequence of the negotiation itself comes always to the fore. This is especially a delicate, embarrassing and thorny point for a government. Formally, no government can recognize a terrorist group, an extortionist, or a hostage-taker as a legitimate counterpart. The cost may far exceed the benefits, for it would grant a terrorist group status and credibility that it does not deserve and that it could misuse. Another line of argument points out that there is nothing to negotiate about as terrorist's demands are unachievable or unfathomable. If there is no ZOPA (Zone of Potential Agreement), some would contend that there is no point to negotiate. In addition, there is a widely acknowledged principle that one does not negotiate under threat. One may thus jeopardize reputation or effectiveness, especially if the party in charge is a government.

Ordinary wisdom holds that it is never good to negotiate with terrorists or to concede to their demands, at least while they are still engaging in violence. The United States and many of its allies are officially committed to a policy of "no negotiation" with terrorists. The US policy on American citizens abducted abroad specifically indicates that "to pay ransom ... and make other concessions to terrorists in exchange for the release of hostages ..." is excluded, under the assumption that such practices only increase the danger that others will be taken hostage. At the same time, the United States claims it will "make every effort" including contacting the representatives of the captors to secure the release of hostages. Formally, authorities are just supposed to talk to terrorists in order to convince them that they are wrong and that they should simply release their hostages. In fact, arguments demonstrating that the demands made are impossible to meet and threats issued are meant to help. Nonetheless, rewards or compensations are not supposed to be used, which would leave very few means of action for convincing the terrorists.

Nevertheless, often this policy is simply not followed and operates much more as rhetoric than as reality. The record shows that states negotiate much more with terrorist groups than they would acknowledge (Faure, 2003). As the point is to save lives, if principles are clear, one should not introduce insurmountable prerequisites. The moral duty of intervening has been formalized by a UN resolution (1987), which not only condemns all hostage-takings whatever the motivations may be, but also asks governments to take all necessary measures to put an immediate end to the confinements. Some analysts are quite affirmative on the issue of negotiation on the grounds that through communication there is a way to exert influence (Fisher et al., 1991).

Negotiation is seen as a mechanism for influencing other parties' perceptions and goals. Given the circumstances, negotiation may be the best if not the only way of avoiding an undesirable outcome. One needs to make it clear that a decision to negotiate does not mean acceptance of the other side's behavior or values. What one does accept is the humanity underneath as deserving of due process. In reality, most often governments do intervene, directly or through a third party. Officially, if discussions are carried out, no concessions are made and the content of the agreement is not fully made public. The reason behind is that often the country involved has to make decisions that, if known, would create problems with other countries or with her own public opinion (Faure, 1988).

Terrorism does not accept current laws and rules, whereas governments are bound by them. Laqueur (1999) points out that "In the terrorist conception of warfare there is no room for the Red Cross." The key role in asymmetric warfare should be played by intelligence and security services but may also be complemented by some military forces. If the issue at stake is a certain territory or a demand for autonomy, a compromise through negotiations might be achievable.

But dialogue is extremely difficult to establish, for instance, with Islamist radical movements such as the Salafists. Their demands are often far beyond what is conceivable to offer, even with the best will. This is the case with al-Qaeda's demand for the establishment of a new Khalifate, the removal of all Western forces from Muslim lands, including the abolition of the state of Israel, and the restoration of formerly Muslim territories, including parts of Spain. On the terrorist side, it may appear as paradoxical for Islamic groups to take hostages and trade them. This is especially true for radical Islamist movements because their faith does not normally admit buying or selling human beings. As a matter of fact, some still do so with the purpose of trading them against some benefits.

Dealing with terrorists may raise the issue of sovereignty for a government who wants to take effective and quick action. Rather than abiding by international laws, often governments tend to consider that the end justifies the means and just do what they want or what their public demands. In the same way, the French government secretly tried to negotiate with the FARC of Colombia, and allegedly paid a heavy ransom for the return of its journalist in Iraq. In Iraq, when foreigners are taken as hostages, their governments directly discuss with terrorist groups and finally pay a ransom to obtain the freedom of their nationals, knowing that it is an involuntary financial support to those who want to dominate through terror.

Hostage-taking

Historically, there are two different types of hostages: voluntary hostages, which were a widespread tradition in ancient times when high-ranking individuals handed themselves over to benevolent jailers as guarantors for the proper execution of treaties or promises; and involuntary hostages, real captives whose seizure has been a rather common practice in extremely violent contexts. (For another typology, see the later chapter by David Pinder.) In ancient Egypt, hostages were used as guarantee of the loyalty of vassal kingdoms. Greeks and Romans also widely used this procedure to stabilize a situation. The European Middle Ages provide a lot of cases showing that it was still customary. These practices perfectly illustrated the origin of the word "hostage," derived from the Latin *hospes*, which means "hospitality."

However, this tradition did not perpetuate itself for ever. Since the end of the eighteenth century a radical shift in practices led to having only involuntary hostages. It probably started during the French Revolution with the *Loi des ôtages* (*an* VII). The government decided to take by force nobles and parents of émigrés as hostages in order to prevent uprisings. During World War II and the occupation of France, the German army set a "hostages code" for taking systematically fifty hostages in each city to guarantee the safety of its troops. Later on the number was raised to 100 hostages to be executed for each German killed.

Hostages can be terribly mistreated, as they represent a paradox. They have no intrinsic value to their abductors but they have (and have been selected for that reason) a real extrinsic value. Terrorists tend to consider them so low as being dehumanized while the outside world may highly price their life as human beings and sometimes as symbols. In other words, the hostage's value is a double value that may, on occasion, lead terrorists to kill their victims. But there is a limitation because killing them would be destroying the possibility of gains which was the very purpose of the hostage-taking.

Normally, in all situations the hostages should be kept in a decent shape, as they are to be used as exchangeable goods. However, terrorists can put pressure on the authorities by threatening to kill, or simply start killing, some of the hostages to show their determination. Still, they should not go as far as destroying the positive-sum game potential of the situation unless they frame it in a much longer time perspective. The biggest hostage-taking operation ever conducted was in Beslan, Russia (see the chapter by Dolnik). The case broke many records, such as the largest number of people taken hostage, the bloodiest rescue, the largest number of people (here children) killed, and the most extraordinary equipment used to storm the place where the hostages were held, with not only guns but bombs, bazookas, tanks, and flamethrowers.

Nowadays, a single hostage may become the focus of incredible attention and mobilize the public opinion. Such was the case of Senator Betancourt, a Colombian-French citizen abducted by the FARC, which led to the creation of hundreds of support committees and international campaigns until she was freed by the Colombian military. Such too was the case of Corporal Shalit, captured by Hamas in Gaza and used many times over to buy concessions from Israel. In some cases, the degree of innocence of the victim, the age, the origin, the vulnerability dramatically emphasizes the stake. Among the media, a sense of injustice may work as a strong motivator. People may identify themselves with the victims or with their relatives. The prospect of being (or on the way to becoming) a martyr adds a most dramatic touch to the tragedy. On the terrorists' side, this added value coming on top of the already important value given to the individual in Western society contributes to serve their interest and make hostage-taking a most rewarding activity with an inexhaustible pool of potential hostages.

Two basic types of situation prevail in hostage-taking: barricade hostage actions and kidnappings. In a *barricade* situation hostage-takers are surrounded by legal authorities and have to face a siege. Freedom of movement is extremely narrow and they are always exposed to the risk of an assault. Their resources depend on those who besiege them. The Moscow theater case (2002) is an example of such a situation.

In *kidnapping* situations, the place where hostages are confined is unknown unless the action takes place in a "rogue state" or a state that has no more control on its territory. There is much more room for maneuvering and the risk of having the place discovered and stormed is very small. There is not as much sense of urgency as there is in the first case. The FARC of Colombia has kept some of its captives for more than ten years. Usually the most important, if not unique risk for the abductors is when the authorities and the kidnappers establish a link for the handing over of the ransom. Most of the kidnappings occur in two parts of the world, the Middle East with Iraq and Latin America with Mexico and

Colombia. For instance, in the half-decade after 2003, more than 250 foreigners have been abducted in Iraq.

A third type of hostage-taking is a combination of the two basic models, *skyjacking*. Theoretically, for the terrorist, it combines the advantages of both formulas. Many hostages kept in a very limited space, easy to control, such as the cabin of an airplane, and the ability to move to a friendlier environment, thus, lowering the risk of an assault. The Entebbe case (1976) illustrates that type of practice. Militants from the People's Front for the Liberation of Palestine (PFLP) hi-jacked a plane to Benghazi, Libya, then Entebbe, Uganda, where they were supposed to get active support from the then head of the state, Idi Amin Dada. Another case of a similar rationale occurred in Teheran in 1979 when the staff of the US embassy were taken as hostage by so-called "students." Without having to resort to such a risky business as hi-jacking, the Iranian government managed to reap the benefits of the situation.

The Stockholm syndrome applies not only to hostages but sometimes also to hostage-takers. This is why terrorists do not usually accept any communication with their victims, keeping them blindfolded or themselves wearing a balaclava, at least entailing dramatic psychological consequences for the hostages. Even negotiators may be subject to such a phenomenon and a way to prevent negative consequences is to classically divide the negotiation structure into two circles. The inner circle made of negotiators in direct contact with the terrorists and the outer circle made of the real decision-makers (see the chapter by Combalbert).

How much trust can negotiators place in their terrorist counterparts? Robbers and gangsters are said to still have a code of honor. What about hostage-takers? Once a painful negotiation has finally led to some kind of agreement, it is crucial that the agreement be properly implemented. There are many cases where a ransom was handed over and the hostages were indeed returned but dead. Sometimes terrorist groups such as the FARC have gone as far as trying to trade with the legal government people they did not even detain.

Four strategic options may be considered when facing terrorist hostage-taking: no negotiation, secret negotiation, regular negotiation, and negotiation in order to prepare for an assault. The *no negotiation* policy aims to deter terrorists from replicating that type of action. This is, for instance, the official Israeli policy with regard to the Palestinians. This option will have the most painful consequences on the hostage situation although it may save many potential victims in the longer term. The *secret negotiation* strategy is more frequently used. One of the major advantages of this option is to protect negotiators from external pressures such as those exerted by the public opinion and the media. This was eventually the strategy chosen by the US government after the seizure of the US embassy in Teheran and earlier in dealing with the Lebanese hostages, as examined in Karen Feste's chapter. The *regular negotiation* option is used when there is no way to keep the hostage-taking unknown from public audiences. This was the case with the French journalists in Iraq. It is still supposed to be a discreet form of negotiation but in that case even the amount of money paid as ransom became publicly notorious. *Negotiation in order to prepare for an assault* is an ultimate way of resorting to the discussion process but with another purpose than reaching an outcome. The point is to collect information about the terrorists, such as the number of terrorists, their position in the place, details on their equipments, the weapons they have, and their state of mind. Negotiations may create opportunities for direct observations through bringing food or water or introducing a doctor. Listening and observing devices may be introduced surreptitiously. Discussing endlessly with the hostage-takers is also a means of exhausting them or altering their vigilance level before launching an attack. This strategy is conceivable if the environment is well controlled by the legal authorities. The storming of the residence of the Japanese ambassador in Lima, Peru, is a typical illustration of such a strategy.

These four situations relate to different negotiation paradigms (Faure, 2008). The "no negotiation" rationale is an anticipated "chicken game." There is no option for cooperation. The outcome can only be at best win–lose and at worst lose–lose. The "negotiation in order to prepare for an assault" option excludes any negotiated outcome. It turns the negotiation into a way of reaching a different objective. At some point, the negotiation only sets the stage for the surrender – or the death – of the terrorists. The life of the hostages is also put at risk. The "secret negotiation" and "regular negotiation" options correspond to the "prisoner's dilemma" paradigm. It is a true search for a negotiated outcome that includes competition, but also a potential kind of cooperation by which the two parties can meet, at least partly, their goals.

The negotiation process

Negotiating over freeing hostages pertains to the domain of negotiation analysis but represents a specific and extreme case. As pointed out by Faure (2002), the political/ideological hostage-taking situation consists of very specific attributes: dramatic stakes to manage: namely human lives; positions on both sides of an abyssal gap reflecting the extremely conflicting values of the parties; the impossibility of officially recognizing the hostage-taker as a legitimate counterpart; trust as a mechanism that normally has very little place in such a setting and is seldom well established and implemented during the negotiation process; the issue of the safety of the negotiators themselves when they must work within a hostile context; the importance of third-party intervention such as from the media, the families of the hostages, outside groups supporting the terrorists.

Religious fundamentalists belong to the category with which discussing is the most challenging task, even if the issue is about hostages. The negotiation unfolds at two different levels that never meet because whereas negotiators receive their instructions from their government or from legal authorities, terrorists consider that they receive their orders directly from God or indirectly through their spiritual or tactical leader. Such an imbalanced situation, especially when taking into account the sources on which they base their legitimacy, makes the interaction most complex.

In some situations the point is not to start an impossible negotiation when there is, for instance, no ZOPA (Zone of Potential Agreement) or no real will to discuss, but first to create conditions for in due course negotiating. The Bojinka plot in Manila in 1995, where Bin Laden emissaries began to build tiny nitroglycerine bombs to be put on to eleven American airliners which were to be blown up simultaneously in mid-air, did not leave much room for negotiation. September 11 did not offer more opportunity but the six years in between might have been employed to work on how to prevent any more "Bojinka" ("loud bang" in Serb-Croat language) by considering negotiating, even with the devil, as a serious option.

Hostage-taking might appear as an easier type of situation to deal with compared with other deeds by terrorists because a hostage is a currency for exchange, which means that by definition terrorists accept the idea of negotiating. In fact, there is still a long way to go. Terrorists tend to begin their negotiations by delivering an ultimatum in place of an opening offer. Some situations such as hostage-taking offer obvious possibilities for trade-offs such as hostages against money, prisoners, access to media, or safe conduct. If this is not the case, the point is either to create some "negotiables" or to prepare for an assault. Dealing with terrorists implies working to transform the problem and perceptions. Paradoxically, this is the activity that requires the longest time but has to be performed the fastest because of the context and attached risk.

In other words, reaching the negotiation stage with absolute terrorists, the type most reluctant to accept the idea of negotiating implies meeting two new conditions: create something to be negotiated and convince the terrorists that it is in their own interest to negotiate. The first condition is technical and consists in changing something in the structure of the game: create a ZOPA, introduce new terms of trade, new issues to be discussed. The second condition is of a psychological nature. The point is no less than to turn a decision already made by the terrorists implying destruction and self-sacrifice – in other words a credible ultimatum – into another decision, that of discussing and negotiating from new bases. For example, the task will be to convince the terrorists that they will get more by negotiating than by fulfilling their first intention; that by doing so they will better serve their cause than if dead; that in discussing instead of killing they will promote a more positive public image of their group.

The terms of trade

The essence of negotiation is to set a convergence in positions and this is done most often through an exchange of concessions. To this purpose, what is needed is some "negotiation," something to offer on both sides. Thus, a bargaining space or ZOPA may be built. The basic deal in this type of negotiation is human lives against meeting the demands from the terrorists. However, hostages are not necessarily human beings. Currencies for exchange have sometimes been animals such as pet dogs, as it has been the case in Italy, or famous paintings in Venezuela and Britain. Thus, Cezanne, Van Gogh, Picasso, Gauguin, and

Rubens have played their role in hostage situations. A racehorse was once kidnapped in Ireland (supposedly by the IRA) to be traded for a ransom of £5 million. In China, human remains have been dug from graves to extort money from families.

Still, whether terrorists are ideologues or criminals, one of the most common currencies for exchange is money. The FARC from Colombia, through bank information and taxes statements, have established a database about the potential hostages to make sure they are worth being detained and the level of the ransom that could be obtained. However, a number of other resources may be traded off. In 1985 and 1986, the United States exchanged arms for hostages, in an unexpected deal with Iran, as developed in Karen Feste's fascinating chapter. France pardoned and expelled Anis Naccache, a Lebanese terrorist serving a life sentence for the killing of a bystander in Paris, in a failed attempt to assassinate an Iranian opposition leader (1980). The release of Naccache figured prominently in the demands of Iran and the Lebanese hostage-holders. France got back her last hostage in 1988. Mickolus *et al.* (2000), analyzing cases from 1968 to 1991, observed that negotiation was attempted in over half of the cases of terrorist events involving hostage-taking. Cases where diplomacy worked with terrorists include: ending the OPEC hostage crisis at Vienna in 1975; arranging a prisoner exchange with Lebanese hi-jackers in 1984; catching Carlos, the most wanted terrorist of his time, in 1994; getting the IRA to agree to a laying down of arms in 1998.

Usually, the concessions made to terrorists do not exactly coincide with their demands. They fall into two categories, the first one referring to original demands, for which the hostage-takers seek an exchange for their hostages and which are at the roots of their action: payment of ransom; obtaining weapons, food, equipment, technology, or information; release of imprisoned terrorists; release of imprisoned supporters or sympathizers of terrorism; access to the news media to publicize their cause; withdrawal of troops from a particular territory. The other category refers to the new issues introduced during the negotiation process: provision of transport to another location inside the country or abroad; provision of political asylum or amnesty within a host country; the promise of a fair trial.

The formula for terms of trade – money for hostages – in turn opens the detail question of how much money for which hostages (told with suspense in Pepper, 1977). As a rule, states are very discreet about the amount they had to spend to get back their nationals. Concerning Iraq, France, Italy, and Germany while officially denying any deal, spent a fair amount of money, $45 million, to just free nine hostages (*The Times*, May 22, 2006). According to documents held by Iraqi security officials who played a crucial role in the negotiation, sums from $2 million, $5 million to $10 million were paid per hostage. An average of thirty people a day have been abducted in Baghdad in recent years. Mostly, these kidnappings have been perpetrated by criminal gangs. When the hostages are foreigners, they may be sold to political groups who add more issues than money to the negotiation to come. One of the typical issues added to the potential package is the withdrawal of military troops operating on a given territory. This is the reason why, for instance, the Filipino government and the Japanese government have withdrawn their soldiers from Iraq.

In hostage-barricade negotiations the carrot and stick principle applies but in an adapted way, as time is short and tension extreme. As one is meant to strengthen the other, incentives and threats are used. The major task for negotiators is to have the hostage-takers lowering their level of expectation. Hope and limits have to be sold at the negotiation table. Ideally, every negotiator would love to end up with what is called a "Bangkok solution." It refers to the following incident. Four Black September militants took over the Israeli embassy in the capital of Thailand (December, 1972), demanding the release of Arab guerrillas imprisoned in Israel. After eighteen hours of negotiation, the Thai authorities and the Egyptian ambassador, intervening as a mediator, persuaded the terrorists to drop their demand and release their twelve hostages in exchange for safe passage out of the country (Bass et al., 2005). Subsequently this negotiation profile has been used as a reference and a model for similar situations.

A three-stage process

The three-phase model of Zartman can be applied with much relevance to this type of negotiation: pre-negotiation–formula–details. The *pre-negotiation* consists in scouting and then accepting the idea of negotiating between both parties. It is the basic assumption on which the hostage-taker strategy is devised. Several conditions have to be met to consider that negotiation can take place. Terrorists must have the desire to live; an assault could be an option; demands are presented by the captors for releasing the hostages; the location must be contained; and there must be reliable means of communication with the terrorists (McMains and Mullins, 2001).

Then, an *agreement formula* has to be devised. To keep the process moving, the negotiators have to resort to the carrot and stick routine, showing that they can be helpful and trusted but also that they can punish and strike if necessary, as discussed in the following chapter by Combalbert. This is a most challenging task because of the instability of the situation, the very small amount of time available, the often outrageous demands from the terrorists, the legal and political constraints. Both sides act under heavy threats of hostages being killed by terrorists and the terrorists of being stormed by the legal authorities. The point for the authorities is to modify the objectives of the terrorists and to lower their level of expectation by using tactics such as harassment, attrition, and information manipulation.

In a hostage-barricade situation, time usually works to the advantage of the negotiators. To counter such an obstacle terrorists try to impose their own tempo to the discussions by issuing imperative deadlines. At some point, time pressure turns on the negotiators as public opinion expects results, empathizes with the hostages and may accuse the authorities of being incapable of resolving the situation.

Once an agreeable formula has been elaborated, the discussion moves to the *detail phase*. A way out is in view but still tensions can reach a climax because of the zero-sum rationale of that stage. Whatever is offered to the other party is lost for the one who concedes. Tough techniques can be used such as the salami tactic. Anything given to the terrorists during the siege – even water, food, and other commodities such as power or air conditioning – must call for compensation. The trade-off may be a hostage if there are many of them. Everyone fears tricks from the other side and wonders if the implementation of the coming agreement will be seriously considered. Exhaustion and trust – even as little as it can be – play their part. A sense of the right moment to conclude is necessary. Unexpected initiatives such as reading verses of the Koran have been helpful to trigger that psychological moment (Miller, 1980: 22). Then, if agreement has been reached, the negotiation may get to the final stage, the implementation.

At the *implementation stage*, the hostages have to be released and the trade-offs made. This is again a thorny stage tainted with uncertainties. As this is time for direct contacts, risks are obvious and no one knows how far the other side will go with the execution of the agreement. Its non-implementation by the terrorists may happen, resulting in the murder of the hostage, as it was the case with Aldo Moro, a former Italian Prime Minister, by the Red Brigades. Kidnapping cases offer a number of murders at the end or during the detention. One reason is that the hostage-takers aim to suppress an essential source of information for the authorities to trace them. Sometimes, another consideration may come to play such as long-term perspectives. For instance, al-Qaeda's policy is to keep its word and free the hostages in order to insure in the future the credibility of the organization. Sometimes, the states find it appropriate to fool the terrorists in trying to free the hostages and capture or kill the hostage-takers at the very time of the exchange.

The old solution: the tactical option

As the "Bangkok solution" is most often an unattainable dream, the negotiators have to come to more modest expectations and give away more than they would really like. Sometimes, especially if blood starts to be spilled, if the life of the hostages is clearly in danger, or because there seems to be no way to get any acceptable agreement from the terrorists, one has to think about other options than keeping the negotiation going. In such a case, negotiation is no longer used as a means to reach some kind of agreement but may be used as a tool for solving the situation by use of force. The authorities may finally resort to what is usually called the "tactical solution," the assault. In that new design, the negotiation is only a means of serving this ultimate objective, as discussed by Combalbert in the following chapter. The point is to collect enough information on the hostage-takers, their weapons, their degree of preparation, their attitudes, the particulars of the place of confinement, and their possible external allies. Authorities maintain continuous communication with the terrorists, thus depriving them of sleep and exhausting them in order to reduce their ability to analyze new events occurring and lower their level of vigilance, and then launch an assault. This can be done effectively when the hostage-taking context is favorable to the authorities. In that case conceived as a warlike action, hostage-taking entails a response of a similar nature.

Terrorists often feel that they are totally in control and somewhat omnipotent. Some may be persuaded that they have a mandate of a supernatural force making them invincible. They may also consider that they are so well organized and that their action is so well planned that nobody can defeat them. Strongly dedicated to their cause, they operate from a "win or die" mentality. For them negotiating is not an obvious option. Authorities may then consider that the "tactical approach" is the best choice. Nowadays a number of countries have created highly specialized anti-terrorist units trained to negotiate but also to storm places and kill terrorists. The British 22nd Strategic Air Service, the German GSG-9, the French GIGN, the Israeli Yamam and Saveret Matkal are among the most renowned SWAT (Special Weapons And Tactics) teams.

The "tactical option" has not always led to a dazzling result and some of them have even met extremely dramatic outcomes such as the Munich tragedy (1972). The Beslan school hostage-taking (2004) discussed in the Dolnik chapter, the Moscow theatre hostage-taking (2002), both in Russia, ended up in a terrible bloodbath, with hundreds of victims among the hostages. On the other hand, remarkable operations such as the successful hostages rescue in Entebbe by the Israeli Sayeret Matkal, the French GIGN in Marseilles, or the German GSG-9 rescue in Mogadishu, illustrate the fact that tactical operations may work. In any case, whether tactical response operations fail or work, death is often a by-product.

When the hostage-taking is carried out by a small number of abductors, assault is a quite frequent solution. Based on the surprise effect, tiredness, and lack of vigilance from the terrorists, the rescue team neutralizes them or shoots them down. Such an action not only puts an end to the hostage situation but also may deter other potential candidates from doing the same as the distance between life and death in these circumstances may be extremely short. Among the hostage-barricade situations unlocked by military intervention, a remarkable case was the storming of the residence of the Japanese ambassador in Lima, Peru (1996) occupied by a revolutionary group during more than four months. Fourteen rebels from the Tupac Amaru Revolutionary Movement took 700 hostages during a traditional celebration. They kept seventy-four of them during the whole duration of the detention. The government rejected their demands for the release of 300 prisoners, a change in government economic policy, and a ransom ("war tax"). During the storming of the residence, all the terrorists were killed and one hostage lost his life.

Another typical case was the hi-jacking of the Air France flight at the Algiers airport in 1994 by four members of the Armed Islamic Group (GIA). Three passengers were successively shot and their bodies dumped on the runway. Then the GIA stated that they were going to kill one passenger every half-hour until the plane was allowed to fly to Paris. During the intense standoff, the authorities learned that the aircraft was laden with more than twenty sticks of dynamite and understood that the final purpose of the GIA was to fly the plane into the Eiffel Tower. Air traffic controllers managed to convince the terrorists that they did not have enough fuel to reach Paris. When they landed to refuel at Marseilles airport, the French GIGN successfully stormed the plane.

Hostage-takers are getting more and more trained and more "expert"

Today, terrorists are no longer amateurs just equipped with their beliefs and determination. They are also technicians in hostage-taking. They learn through the experience of their organization, through cases they came to know, through manuals written by specialists for local authorities to deal with hostage situations. They receive training in camps. They have been taught to make the best use of most recent technology. They are no more isolated and bound to make decisions by themselves as they can still communicate with external members of their group. They use techniques to penetrate the operational environment of the hostage-taking site with false journalists, false passers-by, or a hostage who is in fact an accomplice. They resort to listening devices to eavesdrop on communication channels of SWAT teams or local authorities. With the internet they can send messages to the whole world. They elaborate their own manuals. In other words, they are highly professional.

The al-Qaeda training manual is a typical example of what is taught to future hostage-takers. This document has been found by the police in Manchester, England, during a search of an al-Qaeda member's home. It was found in a computer file titled "The military series" and related to the "Declaration of Jihad." It provides basic advice for handling effectively a negotiation with local authorities. Here follow some excerpts of this document (US Department of Justice web site).

> In the name of Allah, the merciful and compassionate:
> The enemy uses the best negotiator he has, who is normally very sly, and knowledgeable in human psychology. He is capable of planting fear in the abductors' hearts, in addition to discouraging them. Kidnappers must remain calm at all times, as the enemy negotiator will resort to stalling, in order to give the security forces time to come up with a plan to storm the hostages location. The duration of the detention should be minimized to reduce the tension on the abducting team.
> The longer the detention is, the weaker the willpower of the team is, and the more difficult the control over the hostages is. In case of any stalling, starting to execute hostages is necessary. The authorities must realize the seriousness of the kidnappers, and their dedicated resolve and credibility in future operations.
>
> **Hostage exchange process:**
> If the enemy submits to the demands, and the purpose of the operation is to release our imprisoned brothers, it is essential to make sure that the brothers are in good and healthy condition. If the purpose of the kidnapping is to obtain money, you have to ensure that all the money is there, that it is not fake, nor traceable. You must be sure there are no listening or homing devices planting with the money.

The brothers must be constantly on alert for possible ambushes. Our Jihadi operations have proven that security forces are not capable of completely seizing control inside the cities. Therefore, the brothers should find ways to transport their liberated brothers even under tight security measures.

Hostage release:
The brothers should be careful to not release any hostage until they have received their own people. It is essential for the brothers to abide by our religion and keep their word, as it is not allowed for them to kill any hostage after our demands and conditions have been met.

For the withdrawal, some hostages – preferably the most important – must be detained until the brothers have safely withdrawn. Detention must not be prolonged. In case of stalling, hostages must be gradually executed, so that the enemy knows we are serious. When releasing hostages such as women and children, be careful, as they may transfer information that might be helpful to the enemy. You must verify that the food transported to the hostages and kidnappers is safe. This is done by making the delivery person and the hostages taste the food before you. It is preferable that an elderly person or a child brings in the food, as food delivery could be done by a covert special forces' person.

Beware of the negotiator. Stalling by the enemy indicates their intention to storm the location. Beware of sudden attacks as they may be trying to create a diversion which could allow them to seize control of the situation. Combating teams will use two attacks: a secondary one just to attract attention, and a main attack elsewhere. In case your demands have been met, releasing the hostages should be made only in a place that is safe to the hostage-takers. Watch out for the ventilation or other openings as they could be used to plant surveillance devices through which the number of kidnappers could be counted and gases could be used. Do not be emotionally affected by the distress of your captives. Avoid looking at women.

How to deal with hostages in kidnapping:
Separate the young people from the old, the women and the children. The young people have more strength; hence their ability to resist is high. The security forces must be killed instantly. This prevents others from showing resistance. Do not approach the hostages. In case you must, you need to have protection, and keep a minimum distance of one and a half meters from them. Speak in a language or dialect other than your own, in order to prevent revealing your identity. Cover the hostage's eyes so that he cannot identify you or any other brothers. Wire the perimeter of the hostage location to deny access to the enemy.

Stages of secret kidnapping:
Look for listening or homing devices that VIPs often carry on their watches or with their money. VIPs could have an earpiece microphone that keeps

him in touch with his protection detail. Use an appropriate cover to transport the hostage to and from the location. It is imperative to not allow the hostage to know where he is. In this case, it is preferable to give him an anaesthetizing shot or knock him unconscious.

A new context: the IT and media

People act according to what they perceive. Negotiators decide upon a strategy and tactics in accordance, among other things, with the counterpart's presumed personality, goals, strategy, and degree of commitment. As a consequence, communication, images and representations play an important role in the potential interaction. A media, such as television, may turn the hostage-taker from a mediocre unknown person, to an anonymous individual among the crowd, into a star in the limelight whose words and motions are repeated all over the world. A quasi-symbiotic relation may thus be established between the media and terrorists, each one providing something essential to the other.

Media consumers may feel involved in the drama related by journalists. Public opinion may thus play a non-negligible role in the strategy adopted by the negotiators. In the case of the skyjacking of the Air France airplane to Entebbe (1976), the Israeli opinion was opposed to a military solution until the terrorists raised their demands, bringing a doubt on the real possibility of reaching any negotiated agreement. Only from this new situation were the Israeli authorities able to implement their usual policy of firmness. They sent two airplanes of paratroopers who managed to kill all the captors, and release all the hostages.

Journalists may play a direct role in hostage-taking situations by meddling imprudently among the protagonists. Thus, in New York, in a case in which the negotiation had led to an agreement including the release of the hostages and the surrender of the captor, a journalist almost derailed the whole operation. He managed to reach the hostage-taker by telephone and interviewed him on the reasons justifying his action. This unfortunate initiative reactivated the grievances of the latter, who started reconsidering the agreement (Miller, 1980).

As a basic principle, authorities normally in charge of the hostages' problem try their utmost to keep at least the media away from the negotiation scene. This strategy is not easy to maintain as hostage families and captors tend to do the opposite to get more leverage on the negotiation process. Another strategy is to manage a smart and productive relation with the media in order to limit the reactions of the hostage-takers. The case of the Church of the Nativity in 2002 provides a good example of an effective synergy between both (Cristal, 2006). A group of armed Palestinians kept 160 people secluded in this most important place for Christians in Bethlehem. During the thirty-nine days of the siege, the Israeli Crisis Negotiation Unit not only carried out thorny negotiations with the hostage-takers, the families of the hostages and the religious authorities involved. They managed to develop a synergistic relation with the international media that became quite influential in the design of the final outcome. One of the major goals attained was to prevent Palestinians from launching a massive attack against the Israeli army that would have led to an obvious bloodbath. Finally a peaceful solution was found and properly implemented.

The new measure: effectiveness

Evaluating the result of such a type of negotiation is a most difficult challenge. One obvious criterion to apply is the survival of the hostages, and their freedom. However, another question cannot be avoided: at what price? Terrorists released, money given, media exposure provided? Would the "tactical solution" not have been less costly, more effective? If we consider, for example, the situation in Iraq since the beginning of the US-led occupation in 2003, over 250 foreigners have been abducted. At least forty-four have been killed, 135 were released, six escaped, six were rescued and the fate of the others remains unknown. Should one consider that negotiations have been rather successful or that the rate of 54 percent of hostages released is insufficient, especially if one takes into account the forty-four hostages who were killed, which means 17 percent of them. Now, if one considers the price paid by governments, $5 million to $10 million per hostage (*The Times*, May 24, 2006), should one still consider the outcome of these negotiations as a success? Is really the "Bangkok solution" the ideal solution? It leaves the terrorists unpunished, which means not deterred at all from doing it again. However, if the hostage-takers are ready to die, if the authorities do not want to submit to their demand, which is in fact an ultimatum, nothing can stop them except, possibly, the tactical solution. There is no easy way to handle a situation including so much uncertainty on so many variables.

Even, if no blood is spilled, wounds can be of a psychological nature. Hostages can never resume their life as if nothing had happened. They carry with them the stigma of their terrible experience until their last days. Being confined in subhuman conditions, terrorized in the worst way, having perhaps to endure the simulation of their own execution, and sometimes getting back to freedom in most violent conditions, leave ineffaceable traces in the personality (Ochberg, 1980).

Most of the time, for the government there is a political gain from saving the lives of the hostages and getting them free. Mediating countries may also get concrete benefits on top of a reputation in doing so. However, the question of the price paid and that of the design of the operation come quickly to the headlines of the media, with the risk of darkening the brilliant image of the success. It has been for instance the case with the arms-for-hostages deal (1984), ending the Iran–Contra affair during the mandate of US President Reagan, and the preceding case of President Carter and the case of the Iran hostages..

Another issue much discussed is that when abiding by some of the conditions laid by the terrorists, authorities may have sold off the long-term interests for short-term results. It is important not only to free the hostages but also to deter other groups from repeating the same operation. Such a consideration may prompt to resort to the "tactical solution." It paid off in the Entebbe, Marseilles, and Lima cases. However, some people may think that this is a way to do rough justice, which is unacceptable in a democracy. A radical position to play long-term is simply to reject any idea of negotiation with the terrorists. This is the attitude adopted officially by the Colombian and the Filipino governments. Nevertheless, hostage-taking has not ceased in these countries. A government who makes the decision to never negotiate and thus abandons the hostages to their fate, faces a moral and political dilemma.

What can also be observed is a change in the culture and goals of the authorities and of the rescue teams operating. There are far more efforts spent trying to find an agreement instead of deciding from the very start to choose the "tactical option," the assault. That concern became quite important in Europe first and then migrated to America. For the intervening squads, there is pride in capturing the hostage-takers without firing a single shot, which means without putting the lives of the hostages at risk. It is a far more difficult task than having a sniper putting a bullet between the eyes of the terrorists. To capture the terrorists and free the hostages appears as the perfect solution. Such an ideal is more and more shared because this is the way to make justice prevail while punishing the culprits as well as putting human rights first by saving lives.

In a number of negotiations with terrorists, there is a potential for mutual gains but still negotiation fails. One of the obstacles to effective negotiation between states and terrorists is the perceived inability of terrorists to engage in credible commitments (Walter, 1997; Kydd and Walter, 2002). A key barrier is that governments usually distrust militants, consider them as criminals, and assume that they are totally unreliable. No enforcement mechanism exists to punish terrorists if they do not abide by their commitments. If terrorists face no costs for breaking agreements, states have no reason to believe that terrorists will stick to their promises (Lake and Rothchild, 1998; Leeds, 1999). Terrorists' actions are often analyzed from the position of the autonomous actor. The terrorists are supposed to operate free from any institutional constraints. This assumption is strongly challenged by facts. If terrorists want to be credible, they must find some way to convince states that defection is not without cost for them. For instance, they have to convince their counterparts that they care about their reputation (Lapan and Sandler, 1988). Nonetheless, terrorist organizations seldom consider that they have to submit themselves to rules enacted by their foes.

Escaping from the dilemma, negotiation versus tactical option

Negotiating has a cost, often difficult to accept, storming the place entails a risk, that of the death of the hostages. However, there is a third way to handle the situation which consists in manipulating the terrorists in order to remove the hostages from their keepers. A 2008 case illustrates such a strategy with the liberation of a number of FARC's hostages by the Colombian forces.

The rescue plan – Operation Jaque – was organized by the Colombian military intelligence with the purpose of tricking the FARC. The hostages were held in three separate locations. The Colombian intelligence had infiltrated one of the FARC fronts holding the hostages as well as the FARC secretariat. They told the front commander that the hostages were being transferred on the orders of the FARC top commander. After gathering the hostages in one location the FARC unit was met by a helicopter, ostensibly from an NGO. Soldiers posing as members of this fictitious non-government organization were supposed to fly the captives to a camp to meet a rebel leader. To prepare, the soldiers had taken acting classes and they played their role accordingly. Then, the hostages were loaded on to the helicopter with the FARC commander and his deputy, who were then subdued in the air by soldiers wearing Che Guevara T-shirts. The fifteen hostages were rescued without firing a shot.

There are many implications to this tremendous success. It shows that Colombian intelligence was mostly relying on information it had gathered from the FARC's internal communications. The FARC are spread out in Colombia's vast hinterland. The hostage rescue operation capitalized on this weakness. Fragmentation requires more communications and thus exposes more information to eavesdropping. However, such a smart ruse may only work with a particularly scattered organization. Nor can it work again and again; it has diminishing returns. Another crucial point was that Colombian intelligence had managed to place a couple of moles within the FARC itself. This can only be achieved on a long-term time span and requires very specific skills. Meanwhile, it shows how much hostage-takers are also hostages of the group of their captives, here Colombia in all its expressions: society, government, and army.

The new questions: when, how, and why?

The aim of the project is to examine and explain when, how, and why negotiations are and can be conducted with terrorists, especially in political hostage-taking situations. We seek to discover patterns and regularities in government–terrorist relations in various types of terrorist situations, including the possibilities of creating preconditions necessary for effective negotiation. The purpose is to find out when negotiations are possible, and when not, and how to conduct them when decided. In some cases (with absolute terrorists, including suicide bombers), negotiations are apparently impossible and irrelevant; in others (with contingent terrorists including insurgents and hostage-takers), negotiation is sought by terrorists but on unacceptable terms. Given the fact that negotiations do take place in many of these cases, this project seeks to explain the process by which such negotiations have been made doable.

One of the fundamental questions to which any negotiator is confronted consists in devising the possible shift from absolute to contingent terrorist. Under which circumstances, according to which modalities, can one consider a possible move of the terrorists' reference points. In other words, how to create a bargaining zone and how to modify some of the priorities of terrorists and governments?

To negotiate with terrorists is anything but ordinary practice. Dramatic stakes are at play, especially human lives within a most violent context. The management of the process itself bears on sensitive variables such as trust, stress, respect of the other, conflicting values, extreme positional antagonism, and high level of risk. Societies are now facing a new bread of terrorists, motivated by ideology, religion with a mindset extremely different from the one of simple criminals trapped in a bank in a failed hold up or kidnappers looking for the booty of their life time. They are very well prepared, educated, more lethal, ready to sacrifice themselves, prompt to dehumanize their hostages and to go much beyond what is usually conceived as acceptable in these types of situations. In the modern world, people respond to fear, not risk. For instance, after September 11, air travel fell in such a dramatic way that, even two years later, it had not yet regained its former level. Risk can be statistically calculated, but not fear. This is why terrorism is such a powerful tool and still will be in the future.

On the methodological aspect, we know how much the label "terrorist" is value-laden, with an extremely negative connotation. However, we kept this label as such for practical reasons of communication to avoid any misunderstanding on the subject. Still, we do not handle the concept of "terrorist" from a moral perspective but simply from a knowledge perspective. Although, as people we care about moral values, our point here is to understand, explain, suggest, not to judge. This book does not necessarily advocate negotiation with terrorists but does not reject the idea. In such a complex causal web, we leave to the practitioners to decide if this is worth giving a try. What we simply draw are recommendations for action, once the decision to negotiate has been made, in order to optimize chances to reach an effective outcome.

This book focuses on terrorists as political hostage-takers. While there has been literature on hostage-taking, much of it bypasses the current form of the problem, which is the combination of the mechanics of hostage negotiation with the wider issue of political terrorism. Thus, this book builds on practical experience on terrorist negotiations with recent in-depth material. In the introduction, Guy Olivier Faure, Sorbonne, Paris, and I. William Zartman, Johns Hopkins University, Washington, DC, tie together the field of negotiation and the subject of terrorist actions while taking stock of what has been done in research since terrorists' hostage-taking has developed into a mass activity. Part I deals with the various aspects of negotiating with terrorists. Laurent Combalbert, himself a hostage negotiator, points out the very specifics of hostage negotiation and provides the reader with a method to handle this type of situation with a reasonable amount of chances for a positive outcome. Alex Schmid, University of St Andrews, Scotland, and Peter Flemming, ITERATE project, analyze the fluctuations of hostage-taking during the last four decades, then draw lessons on "best practice" in the field of tactical negotiation with the "new terrorists." David Pinter, University of Bradford, England, draws a distinction between terrorist and insurgent in order to reveal the differences in "negotiables."

Part II presents detailed studies with much new data, using the previous material as guidelines. Thus, Karin Feste, University of Denver, CO, offers a review of the hostage negotiations in Lebanon and deeper in the Middle East, including mass suicide bombing and arms payments. She draws lessons on terrorists' strategies and their negotiation techniques. Adam Dolnik, University of Wollongong, Australia, sheds light on one of the most dramatic cases in recent history, with a special focus on the concept of "negotiability" and provides an assessment on the effectiveness of the negotiation. Victor Kremenyuk, Russian Academy of Sciences, discusses the rationality of the hostage-taker, insisting on the double nature of the terrorists' agenda and the complexity to handle the negotiation process when it opens on much broader political considerations. P. Sahadevan, Jawaharlal Nehru University, New Delhi, investigates an extremely dangerous and complex skyjacking situation in Kandahar, combining two profiles of terrorists, the nationalist separatists and the religious fundamentalists. Drawing from the cases and the analytical presentations, Guy Olivier Faure and I. William Zartman, in their conclusion, return to the dual theme, underscoring a number of dilemmas still facing both practitioners and analysts. Finally, they offer a three step approach to deal with what is by far the most challenging type of exercise in the domain of negotiation.

Part I
How to negotiate
Kidnapping the kidnappers

Terrorism has multiple faces and if its central figure remains often opaque; its various expressions come to light in action. Kidnappings, hostage-takings, blackmail, suicide bombers are concrete means for terrorist groups to get media attraction and to generate enough fear to consider that they can seriously impact a much wider situation such as the political-strategic domain.

Confronted with terrorists, negotiators share some common attributes with firefighters, for they both have to contain the incident and limit its consequences, and may be burned in the process. What are the immediate measures to take in the case of hostage taking? Which strategy to choose contingent to the counterpart and to the surrounding circumstances? Should negotiation or assault be considered as the most effective option? There are a large number of cases for which there is *a priori* no ZOPA (Zone of Potential Agreement). The point thus is to build one, then to reach an optimal within it. How far can one go in terms of persuasion, which means in modifying the subjective utilities of the terrorists, their goals, at least, those of the present time?

Negotiation is an activity that can be unfolded through three different resolution rationales: concession, compensation, and conversion (or construction). At which of these levels should one operate when facing hostage-takers? Is there any preferable sequential order? What should be the fundamentals of an effective intervention?

The tactical goals of an operation can be understood as elements of a more global strategy, following the example of Clausewitz, distinguishing the engagement from the battle itself or the battle from the war. If negotiation starts, one enters the universe of Machiavelli, made up of many tactics aiming to move toward a predefined goal. Taking into account the counterpart, the carrot and stick system must be especially well thought out and borrow from a much wider register than the usual range of negotiation tactics.

Hostage-takings are situations in which terrorists have selected the context and organized some of its modalities. Regarding this advantage for the abductors, negotiators must intervene in an emergency and face risks of various natures and of some importance. In addition, to save lives is in most cases a priority, but not the only one. To correctly assess the related stakes and risks, the stress management linked to that type of intervention, the behaviors that may have to be devised on the spot, the apparent irrationality of the arguments displayed, implies the implementation of a method borrowing from experience learnt through years of practice of this type of negotiation. This is what Laurent Combalbert, former negotiator from the French RAID, offers.

Kidnapping and hostage-taking logically invite negotiation but imply such a variety of situations that it is quite essential at first to establish distinct categories of hostage-takers, the sequence of steps to be taken by the authorities, the various tasks to be performed by the negotiation team, the ideal profile (if any) of the negotiator and the different phases encountered in hostage situations. Best practice drawn from the experience of law enforcement agencies is displayed regarding verbal tactics. Finally, predictors for anticipating the outcome based on verbal cues from terrorists are reviewed in the chapter by Alex Schmid, St Andrews University, and Peter Flemming, of the ITERATE project at St Andrews.

Knowing the "enemy" is an essential requirement to put as many chances as possible on the side of the negotiator. David Pinter, Department of Peace Studies, University of Bradford, offers a further and quite functional distinction between terrorist and insurgent, for both types of counterparts have different long-term perspectives, different representations of the situation and different strategic choices to carry out their action. As a consequence, different negotiation approaches have to be used for dealing with them. Both categories still have in common something that they also share with the governments, their extreme reluctance to be seen as "supping with the devil," whichever side of the negotiation table is considered. Caught in a trap both strategic and tactical, state and terrorist are each other's hostage, seeking collaboration yet refusing the other's price and even the occasion to discuss price. These three chapters lead us inside the process of how it is done.

1 Guidelines for negotiating with terrorists

Laurent Combalbert

From interpersonal conflict to the management of high risk situations, from daily behavior in personal relations to the resolution of serious social and commercial crisis, each manager spends a good deal of his time in negotiating. However, many do it in the style of M. Jourdain, who spoke prose without knowing it, without any real method to grasp and tame the risks involved. Finding agreements on sensitive subjects, stabilizing a difficult or demanding client, settling a dispute between collaborators, leading a commercial negotiation with high stakes – these are some of the situations that a manager must resolve by constantly balancing firmness and flexibility. Firmness because each problem must find a solution as rapidly as possible for the proper functioning of the enterprise. Flexibility because the resolution of conflict in an authoritarian manner settles nothing about the underlying problem and instead leads to the resurgence of the phenomenon. Few negotiators today are prepared to conduct negotiations in which power relations are unbalanced to the extreme, time becomes an insurmountable constraint, and physical and psychological threats are an unacceptable means of pressure.

Today many are the internal and external conflicts and undertakings where the notion of risk is unavoidable. Here is the risk associated with business, the risk that can come from threats to capital that puts in danger the survival of an activity or a service, or a physical or psychological risk (in any case perceived as such) or violence in interpersonal relations or threats weighing such relations. Risk is an element that can no longer be avoided in the analytical phase of the context, the preparation of the strategy and the constitution of a negotiating team. This is true in the general business of negotiations; it is above all true in the matter of negotiating over hostages or over wild political demands.

Crisis negotiation

Crisis negotiation developed out of a need of police forces and intervention groups to deal with situations of terrorism and hostage-taking; and it has developed over time to extend to the business world and even official or private diplomacy. The methods and techniques that came out of hostage and terrorist negotiations can be adapted for business enterprises or political undertakings as modified by the perception of managers or negotiators in situations of urgency and risk, of high stakes, of power struggles, of team functioning, of the management of stress and the communication of influence. By enabling the creation of reasoned and durable solutions to complex situations, crisis negotiation adds another tool in the kit of diplomats and businessmen.

It is possible to adapt to the business world the typology of situations where police negotiators intervene. Even if the actions involved are different and only loosely comparable, they often develop according to the same logic. The following categorization of typical terrorist situations is used in police action: the psychotic (individual acting alone), the hostage-takers (one or more individuals holding one or more captives), and the "Tehran embassy" (a collective action).

The situation of the psychotic involves an action of self-isolation. This isolation can be physical (for example, the case of a person who closes himself up in his silence, in a refusal to communicate with others) or psychological (the person who hides behind his ideological certainty or his vision of a problem and refuses to enter into discussions with others). The origins of these situations are multiple: a difficult personality who is misunderstood or badly handled, an emotional crisis due to successive losses, or personal and/or professional difficulties, a millenarian belief, are antisocial reactions of desperation and millennialism.

The hostage situation involves an action of capturing others. In police situations, the objective is to impose a power relationship at a particular moment in

Table 1.1 Terrorist types

	Psychotic	*Hostage-taker*	*Collective occupation*
Description of the main action	Psychological or physical retreat	Sequestration or holding of one or several persons or goods	Collective action of retreat in a specific location
Associated actions	Mutism Threats against third parties Suicide threats	Threats of violence toward persons or destruction of goods	Threats to pursue retreat Threats to the environment/surroundings
Origins of the crisis	Difficult personality Psychological distress Psychopathology Emotional	Social action Psycholoical distress Psychopathology Desperation Millennialism	Social action Collective distress
Motivation	Need to be listened to Call for help	Need for publicity or payment Impose a demand	Publicity Demand
Examples	Repeated interpersonal conflicts Isolated and reclusive collaborator Aggressive client for no reason	Physical occupation of site with capture of leaders Halt of production Hostage-taking	Invasion of store Occupation of plant Occupation of technical offices Lock out

order to get a deal or even just to be listened to. This is particularly the case in certain social situations where the threat to hold up production, to disrupt normal activities, or to occupy buildings is brandished or sometimes put into effect.

The "Tehran embassy" situation involves a collective occupation. In this case a group of people occupy the buildings or a particular site and refuse to leave before having obtained publicity for their cause, public attention about their action, or a response to their demands. The number of these types of actions is continually increasing in recent years.

It would be difficult to draw up an exhaustive list of situations for which crisis negotiation is necessary, since negotiation can be useful in business and politics whenever it opens the way to peaceful solutions in potentially risky situations. In the end negotiation is a communications technique placed within the frame of technical and psychological preparation and teamwork.

The consideration of risk in negotiation

To the question whether negotiation is risky, the answer is clearly yes. It is one of the principal means of putting an end to particularly dangerous situations, whether within the context of international conflict resolution, of degenerating social crisis, or of interpersonal differences. But it carries with it great risk and so it is important to examine the way negotiators regard the inherent risks involved (Avenhaus and Sjöstedt, 2009). Some are filled with confidence, often to excess, in dangerous situations, while others are deep into stress and pressure in situations that are relatively simple and clear, at least at first sight. It is important to examine the perception and apprehension of each party, particularly in the context of team negotiations. It would be best to choose a negotiator who is able to identify risk to its proper extent and who can therefore show a behavior appropriately adapted to the situation.

In the framework of crisis negotiation, there are four principal factors of risk perception on the part of negotiators: urgency, stakes, constraints, and instability.

Urgency. Marshal Lyautey used to say, "You can do it or not do it, but if you do it, do it well." It would be important to add "particularly under the pressure of time." In fact it is surprising to see the extent to which many negotiators impose devastating time pressure on themselves, often setting ultimatums for themselves where there are none. As a result, the situation is perceived as risky because it seems necessary to make urgent decisions, and the distance which separates urgency from precipitation is not very great.

Stakes. The police negotiator has a clear stake in his work: save lives. From that moment on, all other stakes can appear less constraining, but it is not so: the notion of stakes is highly dependent on the perception of each party and it is often not rare to see negotiators in commercial discussions with high interests involved perceiving their stakes as so exorbitant that they are troubled, in fact inhibited, in their pursuit of their negotiations.

Constraints. Again it is surprising to see that many diplomats, businessmen or managers are not prepared to carry out negotiations within the constraints of the situation. Constraints can result from physical pressures; conducting discussions with terrorists or hostage-takers under the threat of sequestration or recourse to violence adds an extra dimension to the negotiation. The pressure can also be psychological; a narrow margin of error can indeed often rapidly destabilize even an experienced negotiator.

Instability. There are many factors of instability, but five stand out:

1 The unpredictability of behaviors, which can be the result of the emotional state of the parties, their psychological profiles, or group dynamics.
2 The irrationality of arguments or of tactics, over which control is difficult because of the absence of a rational basis.
3 The bad faith of parties who refuse to recognize eventual errors and thus by their reactions reinforce their feelings of injustice at the hands of the others.
4 The context that gives a volatile character to the negotiations, for example a conflict over salaries before a group of clients, or a social demonstration in a sensitive location.
5 The issues in the conflict: a negotiation over a political goal is always more unstable than the discussion about the use of the Christmas tree.

When two or more of these factors come together, the situation takes on a character which should lead the mediator trying to bring a solution to step back a bit and make sure s/he has taken into account the potentially unstable character of the event. The perception of risk in a negotiation and more particularly in a complex crisis situation is equally linked to the state of stress and emotion of the conflicting parties. To deny that risk factors are conducive to a particular state of emotion, capable of modifying the perception of each party, would be counterproductive and disqualifying. Learning to recognize and overcome one's own stress is a much more professional and effective an attitude and shows a willingness to prepare properly for a successful negotiation.

The management of risk: the PACIFICA method

The PACIFICA method has been developed out of years of practice in crisis negotiation by the police and developed to be applied as well to situations of private diplomacy in businesses. Its object is to furnish negotiators, whatever their type of activity, with a clear and pragmatic process of preparation and behavior for conflict situations. Its steps are: Possession, Analysis, Characterization, Identification, Formation, Influence, Closure, Assessment. Each step of the method is a precondition for the next, none of which should be neglected even if all do not require the same amount of time of preparation and application.

1 Possession

The first step in the process of crisis negotiation, capital but often neglected despite its importance, is to take possession of the situation. When a crisis negotiator has been called on, there is a potential conflict of authority, present or prospective. Acting as a fireman, the negotiator should take possession of the situation without however denigrating or weakening those who either are at the origin of the conflict or have initially tried but have been unsuccessful in managing it.

The mediator can take possession of the situation by imposing or by associating himself. By imposing himself personally, the negotiator claims his expertise is required by the situation but runs the risk of cutting himself off from previous interveners. It is easy to alienate those who have tried initially to limit the conflict by thanking them for what they have done and asking them to leave the work to professionals. By acting this way and disqualifying them, the negotiator turns off those who could be a source of information and assistance. It is a counterproductive attitude. The negotiator can also impose himself through a rule or procedure that requires a new level of management for a conflict judged to have reached a higher level of seriousness. This is often the case when a stalemate threatens to damage the diplomatic, commercial or social relationship and regulations require recourse to a mediator. This means of taking over can rapidly degenerate into take-over by imposition while relying on the law.

Using association is the best means of imposing one's style of negotiation on a team or a situation. It is useless to make internal enemies since the conflict itself will be the source of pressure and tension. The idea is to explain the mission of the negotiator clearly to the initial interveners and to remind them that they will be involved in understanding the context and eventually in the pursuit of the negotiation as part of a team.

2 Analysis

The objective of analysis in a crisis negotiation is to understand the general environment that needs to be managed up to a peaceful resolution. A number of questions need to be asked in order to understand the context (Figure 1.1).

What is the real nature of the conflict? What are the main factors of risk: urgency, instability, stakes, etc. (Fisher and Ury, 1982). Often it will appear that there is no real conflict but simply hidden and unexpressed rancor to which a more classic means of settlement could be applied. It is notably the case of "boxers" who seek a confrontation for pure show rather than to obtain satisfaction to their demands.

What is the relationship between the protagonists? The history, environment, and quality of the relationship between protagonists are important factors for analysis. If the parties to the conflict know each other and have had frequent incidents and problems in their relationship, the conflict will not be the same as in a passing relationship that has no reason to last beyond the settlement of an immediate problem and within which the protagonists have no prior contacts. In fact, many conflicts, notably between colleagues, do not begin with the incident at hand but rather grow out of a mutual animosity or dislike which emerges whenever an occasion is given. Normally, in hostage conflicts, the hostages are personally anonymous to the hostage-taker, but the status of the hostages or the

36 L. Combalbert

relationships that may have developed during the period of the conflict – including the Stockholm syndrome, where the hostages develop friendly and understanding relations with their hostage-taker – can be of use in the negotiations.

What are their objectives? The question allows the negotiator to analyze the conflict as a clash between goals and thus to look for win–win solutions. Antagonism between the objectives of the negotiator and the other party make initial contacts more difficult and give both sides the impression that the situation cannot be settled peacefully.

Conflict reality
Established conflict — Ongoing conflict — Fully fledged conflict — Not very realistic conflict — Sparring display

Relationship between the actors
Open quarrel — A priori negative — Neutrality — A priori positive — Cooperation

Objectives
Opposing objectives — Different objectives — Similar objectives — Shared objectives

Power relationship
Established conflict — Ongoing conflict — Fully fledged conflict — Not very realistic conflict — Sparring display

Negotiability of the situation
Useless negotiation — Pseudo-negotiation — Possible negotiation — Requested negotiation

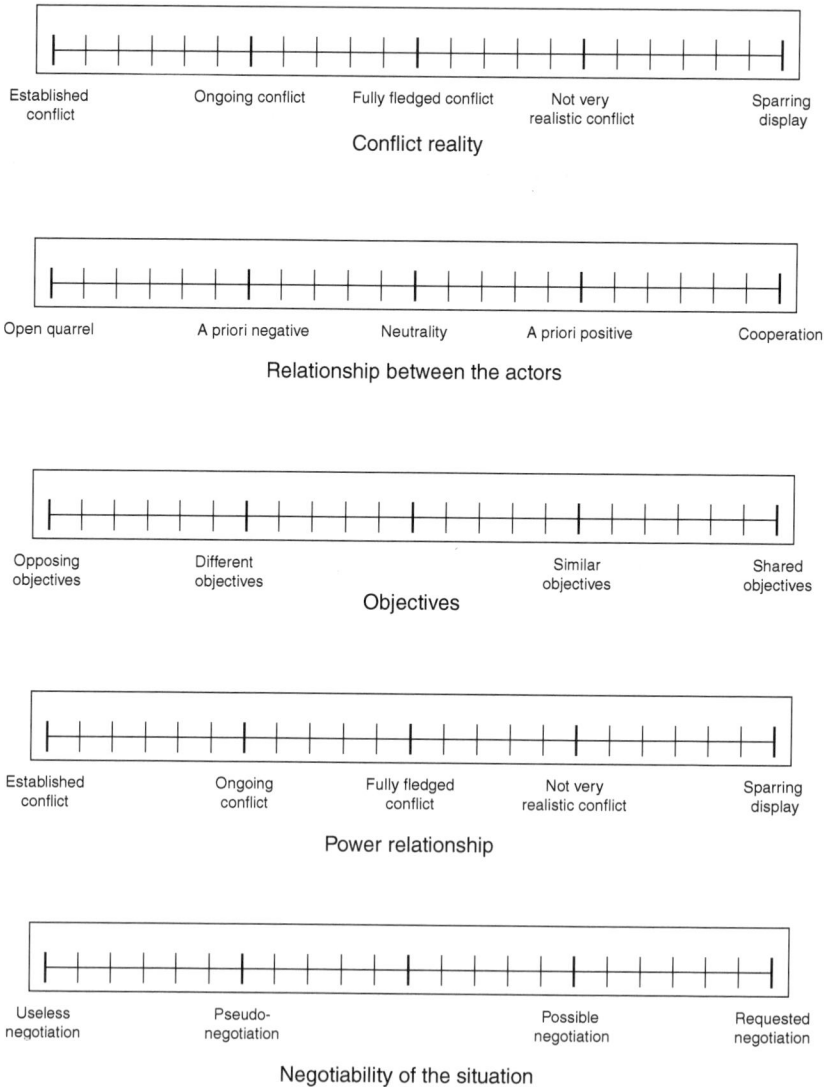

Figure 1.1 Analysis of the context indicators.

What is the power relationship? The rapid determination of a symmetrical or asymmetrical relationship brings out the initial elements that a crisis negotiator needs to maneuver in a situation (Zartman and Rubin, 2000). Too great asymmetry with a constrained negotiator unable to defend his or her point of view can push the negotiation into a strategy of confrontation and make more difficult the re-establishment of a balance of forces.

How negotiable is the situation? The question of negotiability focuses on the capacity of settling the problem by negotiation (Dupont, 2006). There are situations where it is extremely difficult to obtain a negotiated resolution, particularly when so much violence has been used that the recourse to military intervention is likely to be required. Also, in certain situations dialogue is only pseudo-negotiation because the only possibility open to resolution lies in winning time or information. However, it is important to keep alive the idea that the crisis negotiation is a true specialty which when carried out by professionals or by well trained managers can bring a critical situation to a successful conclusion that on first glance might not appear possible.

3 Characterization

The negotiators need to develop a precise understanding of those with whom they will have to deal. Characteristics involve a certain number of factors: what are the ties between the protagonists, what are their conflicts of interests, do they act in their own names or are they proxies for others, etc. Other questions include the identification of psychological bases of the protagonists, by observing their profiles or their conditions at the moment when they enter into negotiation. There are a number of methods to establish the profile of a personality but it is important to establish the difference between personality, attitude and condition of the parties.

Personality. For L. A. Pervin (1984), "personality corresponds to the characteristics which explain the habitual frameworks for the behavior of a person." The advantage of using habitual behaviors as the basis of identification of a personality is that they are directly observable by the negotiator and thus are useful elements in the determination of frameworks for action. Personality as described by Pervin assumes a constant nature but is always susceptible of evolving with time; it undergoes modification through experience and confrontations with others.

The examination of personality is complex because it takes time. Basing one's actions on the habitual behaviors of an opponent requires continuous observation over a long enough time to develop an effective analysis. Generally, it is difficult to enter very deeply into the examination of a personality in a negotiation or a settlement of conflict and therefore one is reduced to an analysis of the attitude and the condition of the interlocutor.

Attitude. The attitude of the opponent concerns his ways of action at the moment where one enters into contact with him. Directly observable, the behaviors that inform attitude will allow the negotiator to identify adaptive or protective courses of action in order to avoid serious risks, notably in the case of aggressive attitudes.

There are a number of components to attitude, including expression and relationships. The party can have an expressive attitude that is calm and deliberate, as is usual in the case of a person who presents a problem rationally. But s/he could also have aggressive attitudes, from physical expression of scorn to verbal aggression and insult. Such expressions give the negotiator an indication of the opponent's agitation and his emotional capacity to receive a message. When confronted with an aggressive attitude, the negotiator should first work to establish a more peaceful basis for communication before continuing.

The parties can have an attitude favorable to a relationship, showing an open, extroverted indication that they seek contact. This is not a necessarily friendly attitude, for an aggressive client who goes to meet his interlocutor can adopt an outward behavior that seeks a relationship but one that does not benefit the other party. In this case, the contact is a means of fighting a resolution to the conflict. The opponent can also be unfavorable to any relationship, closing himself off from the outside world or refusing to express himself clearly. In this case, the negotiator needs first to create a relationship and act so as to establish communication before he can go any further.

Condition. During a crisis situation of instability and stress, a person can move outside the classical frame of his usual personality. Thus, the definition of Salvador Maddi (1989) complements the approach of Pervin: "Personality is an ensemble of characteristics and tendencies which determine points of difference and commonality of the psychological behavior of people, behaviors which present continuity in time and cannot be easily attributed only to the social and biological pressures of the moment." The condition of the party in a conflict is thus as important as his personality and attitude. In fact, a person can have a personality that is well adapted to a relationship to the other party but can be in a state of anger such that the personality cannot express itself any longer and is overridden by the emotional state that will dictate the attitudes of expression and relationship. Or, on the other hand, a difficult or pathological person can be very calm so that nothing negative appears. Thus the negotiator has to be attentive not only to the personality of the interlocutor, but also to his emotional state or other condition at the moment of initial contact.

4 Identification

The negotiator needs to know about his or her team members and their association with conflicting organizations. They can be internal negotiators chosen for their crisis experience or the management of conflicts at risk, or members chosen primarily as consultants. This stage is primordial for the formation of a negotiating team and it is not the easiest, for there is no typical or ideal team profile. Certain fundamental qualities are necessary, such as verbal competence, ability to listen, and self control, but anyone can be a negotiator and any person can become a crisis negotiator. Sometimes, like M. Jourdain, some people negotiate without knowing it. Naturally empathetic persons, mediators by temperament, sometimes handle conflictual situations without really applying any strategy but still being successful. In police situations, certain notable policemen, largely because of their charismatic personalities and their indisputable aura before the criminal population, have played the role of negotiator for years, often with success. However, today one sees that negotiation necessitates the use of particular techniques and is an affair of specialists who are prepared, trained, and engaged in developing a formula for an agreeable outcome. A certain number of rules have also been developed for a successful negotiation.

One such rule is absolute and accepted by all crisis negotiators of the planet: the chief does not negotiate and the negotiator does not have the power to make decisions. Negotiations with a hostage-taker, troublemaker or demanding group often need to open an even more difficult pre-negotiation: to make the chief understand that it is not up to him to negotiate. All the decision-makers who have been engaged in situations of crisis testify to the difficulty in undertaking both the function of crisis chief and crisis negotiator. The place of the decision-maker is not to conduct negotiations but to decide. In fact, to decide is to make strategic choices on the objective of negotiation and on the strategies of crisis resolution. It is difficult to hope to decide objectively if one keeps one's nose on the handlebars in the negotiations. The other risk is to see the chief involved in contacts with the opponent, particularly if that happens in the first moments. The chief has the ultimate power of decision, and if he has the possibility of turning attention immediately to the demands of the crisis party, how can he avoid making his choice known? That is why the negotiator, who does not have the ultimate decision power, must use the necessary techniques to develop an empathetic relation and impose himself as a positive interlocutor, accepted by the two sides as the best qualified to find a solution to the situation.

If the decision-maker steps in too early, he runs two strong risks for relations with the opponent in the crisis. The first is a danger of narcissistic inflation on the part of his opponent. The opponent will see his position as so important that he has been asked to directly address the decision-maker, and after that it can be very difficult for the negotiator to bring him into a more rational frame of mind and make him come down to earth. Then, second, if the decision-maker steps in on the first contact, it will be impossible to impose a lower-level negotiator later on without the conflicting party's considering the change to be a depreciation of the relationship. It may be that at a particular moment the decision-maker will have to enter into the negotiation to validate and guarantee the engagements taken by the negotiator. Nonetheless, it will be necessary to avoid any precipitation and to give time to arrive at that phase of closure.

The negotiator's first mission is to analyze in all objectivity the situation in which he and his team will be engaged and thus be disengaged of the responsibility of strategic decision. He is not the strategic decision-maker: He does not decide the management of the conflict. He should have sufficient margin of maneuver to be able to take the necessary tactical and organizational decisions for the good pursuit of his mission, but not to authorize the final deal.

Imposing oneself in a relationship where one is not the decision-maker is not always easy, particularly if the antagonists do not want to negotiate. That is often the first difficulty to overcome: to be accepted as a legitimate and useful representative in the relationship. It is there that the techniques of communication and influence come into play: the negotiator uses them to create a link and develop an empathetic and efficient relationship. Although not the decision-maker, he will be considered to be the one who is really in search for a solution to the problem.

To do this the negotiator must demonstrate his legitimacy in leading the discussions and the relationship with his protagonists. This legitimacy can result from his status, from his function or from his designation by the decision-maker. He should also explain his involvement in the final decision, presenting himself as the one who will finally try to convince the decision-maker, for he turns to negotiate with the decision-maker once has negotiated with the opponent. Finally, he will utilize all the active listening techniques to develop empathy and to make himself accepted as the efficient interlocutor by the other party.

5 Formation

It is the crisis situation that will decide the choice of members of the negotiation team, and more specifically of the lead negotiator. One will have to look at the available profiles, identified during a preceding phase, in order to choose the one who will be best adapted to initiate the dialogue. It could for example be a woman when the circumstances demand it, or a person with a particular status. This choice of the principal negotiator justifies the need for various profiles, and the identification from the beginning of those personalities and competences that are available. Not all groups and organizations have necessarily a multitude of personnel who can be trained and employed as crisis negotiators. Early identification of the individuals and disposable resources is an incontestable factor of efficiency.

One element in the choice of the negotiator is indispensable, and that is his determination. Determination and a will to settle the problem are in effect primordial: the negotiator who will have to take the initiative to contact the crisis parties should be willing to do it. It is very difficult to show efficacy simply by fulfilling a mission against one's wish. Sensitivity in difficult situations, a good training in negotiation, preparation in the techniques of communication and influence all favor the capacity of the members of the team to launch themselves into complex contacts.

Negotiation, and even more so private diplomacy, are definitively jobs for team work, covering a number of indispensable functions. The mission must be led by one person so that the assignment of tasks to the negotiating team can be adapted to the situation. Alongside the decision-making authority, there are five functions to be filled within a team of negotiators: contact negotiator, back-up negotiator, referee, intelligence manager, and coordinator.

The *contact negotiator* is the principal spokesman, the one who will direct the discussions and bear the responsibility for direct contact. S/He is assisted in the task by a *back-up negotiator* who listens to the content of the discussion without intervening but remains ready at any time to enter into the game to assist or replace the first negotiator. S/He functions like an understudy in an opera or the

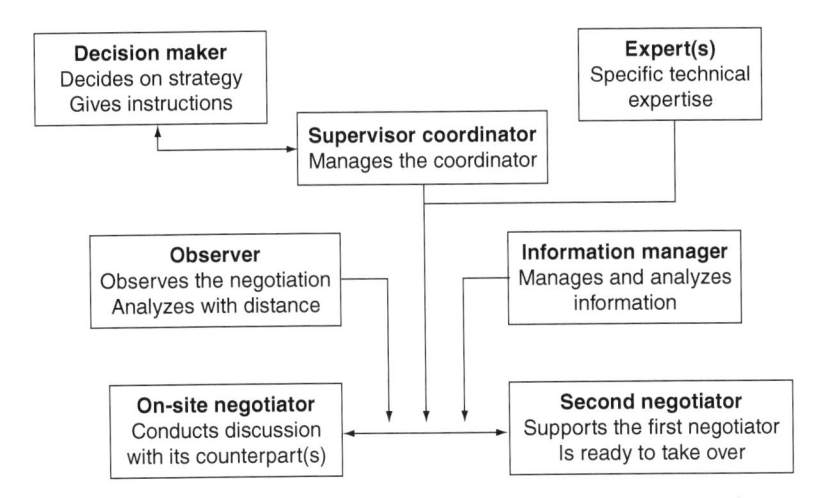

Guidelines for negotiating with terrorists 41

```
┌─────────────────────────┐              ┌─────────────────────────┐
│    Decision maker       │              │       Expert(s)         │
│  Decides on strategy    │              │   Specific technical    │
│   Gives instructions    │              │       expertise         │
└─────────────────────────┘              └─────────────────────────┘
            ▲         ┌──────────────────────────────┐
            │         │   Supervisor coordinator     │
            └─────────│   Manages the coordinator    │
                      └──────────────────────────────┘

┌─────────────────────────┐              ┌─────────────────────────┐
│       Observer          │              │   Information manager   │
│ Observes the negotiation│──────        │ Manages and analyzes    │
│  Analyzes with distance │              │      information        │
└─────────────────────────┘              └─────────────────────────┘

┌─────────────────────────┐              ┌─────────────────────────┐
│   On-site negotiator    │              │   Second negotiator     │
│   Conducts discussion   │◄────────────►│ Supports the first negotiator│
│   with its counterpart(s)│             │   Is ready to take over │
└─────────────────────────┘              └─────────────────────────┘
```

Figure 1.2 The organization of a negotiating team.

member of a football team, at the edge of the field, dressed, ready to play and psychologically prepared to enter the action at any moment. The replacement of the negotiator can occur for various reasons, but the two principal ones are rejection and strategy. Rejection can occur when the contact between the first negotiator and the crisis party does not work: mood incompatibility, systematic rejection, incapacity of the negotiator to click for all kinds of reasons. Replacement for a strategic reason applies the well known strategy of "good cop–bad cop." In this scenario the contact negotiator will deliberately adopt an attitude of confrontation used in function of the attitude of his opponent in order not to get into a spiral of escalation. The objective of this strategy is to let the source of the conflict spill out his emotions, getting it off his chest and clearing the air so that productive negotiations can then begin. In the meantime, the backup listens to the discussion, preparing alternatives to the demands of the crisis party and entering into contact after a more or less long time in order to take up the relationship himself and profit from an effect of contrast.

The role of the *observer* is important in teamwork, particularly in the management of stress and emotions. His or her first mission is to follow the negotiation without at all entering into the discussion. While staying in the background, s/he will observe the form and content of the relationship in order to bring support to the contact negotiator. S/He will also try to decode the ways of operations or attitudes which are not necessarily perceived by the negotiators, who are too engaged in the relationship to be able to grasp all the subtleties. The observer will also observe the emotional engagement of the negotiator towards his or her opponent. While seeking to create an empathetic relationship, the negotiator can find himself caught instead in an emotional relationship that s/he does not control and which will unconsciously make him loose part of his objectivity. By standing in the background of the negotiation, the observer will be able to detect this dysfunction and inform the contact negotiator. By acting in this way s/he performs the role of a facilitator in the relationship and preserves the effectiveness of the discussion and of the teamwork.:

The collection of information about the situation and its centralization and treatment have a basic role in a difficult negotiation. Analyzing the relations of strength, studying the profiles of the antagonists, preparing a strategy and defining the margins of negotiation all require much information coming from diverse sources. The *intelligence officer* is charged with managing this resource; s/he must find the pertinent information for the task of negotiation and filter the many sources of intelligence which will come to the team in order to separate useful information from the noise. In addition to collection and centralization, the intelligence officer will put the information into a form that can be used by the negotiator. Another mission of the intelligence officer is to keep a log which contains the essential elements of the negotiation, both in form and its content. This can be equally useful because negotiations can last a long time with many contacts that will need to be put into the context of preceding discussions.

The function of the *supervisor* is to ensure the proper functioning of the team. S/He will make sure that each party fills his or her mission and that all the negotiators are well coordinated. S/He is in a sense the conductor of orchestra of the negotiations.

The *experts* are not officially members of the team of crisis negotiators but are often indispensable to the conduct of the discussion. When specialist opinion is necessary to understand the demands of the opponent; technical experts, political officers, commercial agents, psychiatrists, and translators may be needed. When an expert is called upon, s/he needs to be well briefed about the contents of his mission and the expectations of the rest of the team so that s/he stays within the bounds of the job, rather than entering into the negotiation itself.

6 Influence

The purpose of the negotiations is to convince the antagonist by means of influence through communications. This step involves a number of practices, such as neurolinguistic programming, transactional analysis, active listening, among others, with the aim of rapidly creating an empathetic contact with the antagonist, a contact that must have credibility within the relationship and truthfulness in the communications with the negotiator.

Credibility. When credibility is absent or called into question during the discussions, it can destroy the impact of other elements in the search for a win–win solution with the opponent. To be considered credible, the negotiator must make sure that his words are believable within the frame of reference of his opponents. S/He can be completely discredited while speaking the truth; if his language, even if completely true, is considered to be false or doubtful it can discredit the whole negotiation. It is the frame of reference of the opponents which will determine the credibility of the discussion. As Gilles Amado and André Guittet (2005) indicate, "contrary to legitimacy, which is a matter of status, credibility can be questioned, and so it needs to be demonstrated, argued, persuaded." Failing credibility can destroy legitimacy that was believed to be beyond questioning.

Truthfulness. Lying is completely forbidden in crisis negotiations. First of all, a negotiator who has to use this strategy shows weakness and failure in his approach. A lie always ends up being turned against the person who uses it, because it always ends up being recognized by the opponent. When it is brought to light, it is the end of the confidence relationship between the parties. Still, a negotiator does not have to say everything in his discussions with his opponent. Holding back his key arguments and privileged information in order to save them for opportune moments is not lying, but rather managing the timing of revelations.

One of the important elements of influence in private diplomacy is the creation of empathetic relations. There is no point in having a well established strategy for arguments if there is no relationship with the other party and the other party is not listening: the negotiator listens to himself talk, but has no impact on the opponent. The basis of an empathetic relationship has been laid down by Carl Rogers, the American psychologist and psychotherapist who was the initiator of numerous reflections on non-directive communication. His research emphasized the necessity, particularly in a helping relationship, to abstain from any pressure on the other party to orient his responses or his choices, whatever the form. This type of non-directive listening has the purpose of developing empathy, the capacity to put oneself in the place of the Other, to perceive the referenced framework of the other party, his emotions, his feelings, his unconscious and dissimulated objectives, his problem frames. Empathy aims at realizing an authentic comprehension of the Other.

In the creation of efficient and influential relations, the crisis negotiator should display the highest degree of neutrality toward the other party. This neutrality is the basis of a primordial technique in all effective interpersonal relationships: active listening. Active listening is a method for developing empathetic ties by using simple techniques applicable by everybody in interpersonal relationships. The method has been taught since the 1990s, notably in a course of crisis negotiation at the FBI academy, and it permits the stabilization of an aggressive individual or one who refuses relationships.

7 *Closure*

Particularly when it is difficult, a negotiation should not last indefinitely. One must know how to end it. However, time is a parameter which generally works against the negotiators. Nobody has control of time but one must accept the fact that it is part of the game, as also noted in the following chapter by Fleming and Schmidt. Therefore, the negotiator has to know how to get out from under the pressure of time and to make of it a strategic advantage in the negotiation.

The perception of urgency in a conflict is a constant, but one which generally has a disastrous effect on negotiators who are not prepared. It leads to the desire to go too fast and to act immediately without real reflection. Decision-making under urgency is a way of counteracting a feeling of discomfort, of ill ease and of anguish that many people feel in a situation of stress. Indeed stress is a powerful incentive to action and often pushes those who are its victims to confuse urgency and precipitation. Time can exert considerable pressure on the decision-maker by giving the impression that if a strategy is not chosen immediately, it will no longer be possible to limit the conflict. This pressure, linked to the false necessity of making a rapid decision, can put a strain on the negotiators who will have to manage their hierarchical authority in order to permit a calmer negotiation.

In private diplomacy, time is not a constraint; it is an advantage for the negotiator. It allows the negotiator to bring out a number of parameters of the relationship that constitute elements of efficiency in negotiation. Among other things, time permits the construction of a relationship: as time passes, the effective crisis negotiator will be able to develop an empathetic relationship susceptible of stabilizing or reabsorbing the conflict. Time permits the ventilation of destabilizing emotions: speaking, the other party frees himself of his emotions and his stress. He can even let his anger burst out in order to come back to a more stable mode of functioning. Time favors the identification of deep motivations and real objectives. And finally it allows the elaboration of alternative solutions: with time the negotiator's team can identify acceptable alternatives to the demands of the other party and can propose them to the contact negotiator. Crisis negotiators adopt the culture of "time advantage" by integrating this parameter in their strategy of efficient communication.

A negotiation can be temporarily interrupted from time to time. Temporary interruptions can be more or less long beneficial to the conduct of negotiations. They permit the parties to talk among themselves, to examine the state of progress toward a solution, and to provide a respite when the relationship is strained. Interruptions can be unilateral or consensual. Unilateral interruptions are breaks in contact called by a single interlocutor. They are generally an explosion of anger on the part of the other party; a crisis negotiation team that is well prepared avoids this kind of rupture on its own, except if it makes some sense in the framework of the strategy, as during the change of negotiators for example. This could be the case when one wants to mark a strong disagreement with the methods or the vocabulary that do not correspond to the rules of negotiations that have been established at the beginning of the contact. Unilateral breaks should be as short as possible; if they are the result of an important disagreement, one must not leave the other party ruminate on what they have seen as a difficulty or a misunderstanding. The negotiator should reestablish the relationship as soon as possible, even if that leads to a second interruption that must be agreed to by all the parties.

Consensual interruptions are unilateral ones that are agreed to by the parties. They should not last too long either, particularly because of physical and psychological fatigue that could lead to a tense relationship. One must therefore know how to make breaks and accept demands initiated by one party for the benefit of the whole negotiation. This is particularly the case if the team feels the need to lower pressure and manage the emotions of the contact negotiator. Breaks can also be initiated by the opponent if it has to consult its decision-makers. This provides a good occasion to do the same thing for the crisis negotiator.

Requests for interruption on the part of a single interlocutor are often the mark of physical or psychological fatigue. They can also be a sign that the other party needs a moment of reflection and introspection, which is a favorable element for a reasoned resolution. In the case of consensual breaks it is important to maintain the continuity of contact and to propose a time or date for reviving the negotiations that will be accepted by all. Whatever happens, the relation should pick up at that moment, unless the other party would like to revive it earlier.

Definitive interruption of the negotiations is the end of a complex and often unstable process. It is either the result of an agreement accepted by all or the realization that no solution has been identified and that the resolution of the conflict has to be achieved by other means. But when an agreement is finalized and is approved by all the parties, the crisis negotiator closes the contact and assures himself that all the conditions are fulfilled for the implementation of the elaborated solution. This definitive interruption rests on a mutual confidence established among the protagonists during the negotiations, confidence which will guarantee that each party will fulfill its engagement until the definitive resolution of the situation.

8 Assessment

A difficult negotiation cannot be complete if one does not go back to learn what worked and what did not work. Progress is change from error. Debriefing is a fundamental act of an effective negotiation team who knows how to capitalize on its practices and learns from its errors. Debriefing can take the form of a linear chronology, tracing day by day and hour by hour the whole collection of events which occurred during the negotiation. Once this work has been done, one can then establish linear chronologies by themes, laid out in parallel: information obtained, contacts undertaken, arguments laid out, threats and ultimatums issued, acceptations granted, etc....This breakdown permits the analysis of all the actions and facts phase by phase and particularly the detection of gaps in coordination or strategic coherence. At the end of this analysis, factors for improvement can be identified in order to permit the negotiators to increase their efficiency, preparation, collection of information, strategy, communication, influence, etc.... Every debriefing should be followed by an updating of the modus operandi no matter how small.

Crisis negotiation: a useful tool in the formation of managers and directors

Crisis negotiation is the tool of specialists, intervention units, or special force units but also of private mediators and business managers. The practice demonstrates its extraordinary capacity to regulate conflicts in complex situations in the diplomatic, social and business worlds, is now taught in policy and business schools and in management and diplomatic seminars, showing that humility, preparation, technical skills, and management of human factors are the keys to perform in a complex situation. If one element is key, as this presentation of tactics and approaches has emphasized, it is "relationships." The negotiator rides on the construction of a personal relationship with his or her opponent as s/he constructs a formula agreeable to all for an agreement to be then proposed to the decision-maker. Behind both parties hover the other method of solution – the "tactical alternative" or the use of force, so both sides operate in a situation of risk and threat. The terrorist also operates between two outcomes: compromise and surrender. Unlike peace treaty or cooperative economic negotiations, the outcome is not a split-the-difference solution that accommodates the demands of the opponent in a balanced fashion. It is a means of getting the terrorist, kidnapper, hostage-taker or social revolutionary to give up. Yet it is negotiation, like any other, because it is an exercise in giving something to get something, the very definition of negotiation.

2 Quantitative and qualitative aspects of kidnapping and hostage negotiation

Alex P. Schmid and P. Flemming

Terrorist events are usually broken down in single-phase incidents (e.g. shootings, assaults, and bombings) and dual-phase incidents (hi-jackings – aerial, terrestrial or maritime – kidnappings and barricade hostage attacks). Here we discuss dual-phase incidents, including hi-jackings which are, in a way, a combination of kidnapping and hostage situations. Table 2.1 gives an idea about the relative frequency of dual-phase incidents. It should be noted that in this and subsequent tables, only incidents of international terrorism are covered, not the much more frequent domestic incidents which involve no foreign perpetrators or victims. Two-thirds of these incidents are in the form of kidnapping, with the remainder involving barricade and hostage seizure, aerial hi-jacking and hi-jacking of other non-aerial means of transportation.

We will, on the one hand, look at kidnapping and hostage situations from a quantitative point of view – using data from ITERATE (Mickolus 2006) for the period 1968 (in some cases 1978) until 2005. These data (Figure 2.1) allow us to see, for instance, the considerable fluctuations in the level of hostage-taking in the four decades. They show that both 1999 (eighty-eight) and 2004 (eighty-six) had relatively high numbers of these events.

On the other hand, we will, in this chapter, also look at some "best practices" and "lessons learned" in the field of tactical negotiations. Most of the lessons are not new; rather, it is a summary of some conventional wisdom, mainly obtained from crisis management situations. That wisdom might be in need of updating in the face of the "new terrorism"[1] in some aspects but it offers, in our view, a

Table 2.1 Type of international hostage incidents, 1968–2005

Type of incident	Frequency	%
Kidnapping	1,302	68.4
Barricade and hostage seizure	180	9.5
Aerial hi-jacking	363	19.1
Takeover of non-aerial means of transportation	59	3.1
Total	1,904	100.0

Sources: ITERATE; Mickolus (2006).

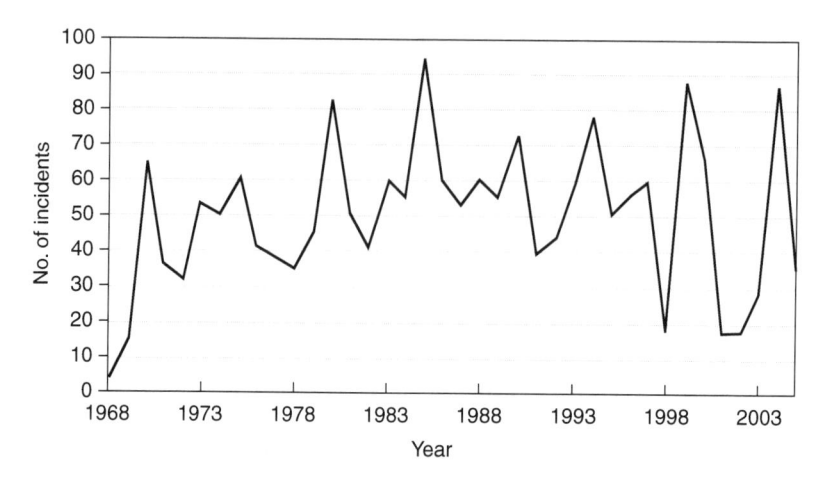

Figure 2.1 Hostage incidents, 1968–2005 (source: ITERATE; Mickolus 2006).

fairly solid basis for discussion and further exploration. This qualitative part is mainly based on secondary literature, but also includes references to some grey literature from the Netherlands and from international organizations. We will not address strategic truce/peace negotiations for a political solution to conflicts involving the use of terrorism that restricts our focus to tactical crisis management negotiations linked to kidnappings and acts of hostage-taking.

It is useful, at this point, to define our understanding of the two key terms – Terrorism and Negotiation. In our understanding, terrorism is:

> ...an anxiety-inspiring method of repeated violent action, employed by (semi-) clandestine individual, group or state actors, for idiosyncratic, criminal or political reasons, whereby – in contrast to assassination – the direct targets of violence are not the main targets. The immediate human victims of violence are generally chosen randomly (targets of opportunity) or selectively (representative or symbolic targets) from a target population, and serve as message generators. Threat- and violence-based communication processes between terrorist (organization), (imperiled) victims, and main targets are used to manipulate the main target (audience(s)), turning it into a target of terror, a target of demands, or a target of attention, depending on whether intimidation, coercion, or propaganda is primarily sought.
>
> (Schmid 1988, p. 28)

Negotiation we perceive as:

> A bilateral or multilateral interactive communication technique to manage conflicting interests through direct dialogue between representatives of the parties to a dispute or conflict. Negotiation is a standard diplomatic technique

used by states in peacetime to harmonize their interests, or to live with their differences by taking into account respective needs and power potentials. While some observers view negotiations as an alternative or substitute for (armed) conflict, in reality (secret) negotiations often precede, accompany or follow other, more violent forms of interaction.

(Schmid 2000, p. 55)

While we often tend to see negotiations as a process of essentially rational bargaining, negotiations in terrorist contexts, especially during a hi-jacking or in a siege-barricade hostage situation, are often highly emotional. Contrary to kidnapping situations where the kidnappers' lives are not in direct danger, in hostage-barricade situations the outcome of the negotiations, or of the breakdown of them, it often a matter of life and death for the terrorists, and often even more so, for the hostages. While that should enhance rationality because the stakes are so high, it very often does not.

For the terrorists involved in a hostage situation, success in negotiations can mean obtaining some of the things they want, e.g. the release of imprisoned comrades and a free retreat to a safe haven, with or without (some of the) hostages. For the hostages it can mean regaining their freedom. Yet what does it mean for a government confronted with terrorist demands? It is often a situation of "Damned if you do and damned if you don't."

- If a government gives in to save lives, it demonstrates that it cannot protect society from terrorist blackmail.
- If it refuses to make a deal with the terrorists and the victims are harmed, it is accused of failing to protect citizens from terrorists.
- If it attempts to rescue the hostages by force, it risks killing some of them in the attempt and appears incompetent. (Kennedy 1997, p. 100)

There is, on the side of governments, considerable hesitation to negotiate with terrorists. However, this book's distinction between "tactical–practical" negotiations as in a case of hi-jacking, kidnapping or terrestrial hostage-taking, and "strategic-political negotiations" involving some more permanent settlement between a terrorist group and a government is important. While the tactical types of negotiations (or the semblance thereof) are rarely completely avoided, the opposite is true for strategic negotiations. Here the gut reaction is: "One does not shake hands with murderers," "One does not do a deal with people who threaten or take innocent lives" – to quote some of the standard arguments used to justify a policy of "no negotiation." Negotiating with terrorists amounts, from this perspective, to rewarding terrorism and gives them some status or even respectability. It could also, as it is often argued, encourage further acts of terrorism.[2] Therefore, the declaratory policy of states is generally one of "no negotiations, no concessions" with and to terrorists. That applies to strategic negotiations but is sometimes extended to tactical negotiations as well.

The official or "declaratory" policy of a country is often not exactly what happens in reality. Many – not all – governments have made deals with terrorists after negotiating with terrorists or one of their front organizations or more respectable representatives of political parties that share an overlapping constituency with the terrorists. Often this is done indirectly and under deep cover and with safeguards that allow what, in intelligence parlance, is called "plausible denial." From time to time the fact that governments make deals with terrorists surfaces, as in the case of the Irangate scandal in 1986 that showed that US President Reagan secretly supplied arms to Iran to get back American hostages held by Hezbollah in Lebanon, as discussed in the later chapter by Feste (Jajanpour 1992, pp. 34–35). The results were disappointing: only three Americans gained their freedom through this deal. In the end more Western hostages were in the hands of kidnappers in Lebanon than at the beginning of the secret negotiations. This would imply that negotiations for hostages encourage further acts of hostage-taking. Yet the opposite is not necessarily true. In fact, there appears to be some evidence suggesting that states with a "no concessions" policy – such as the United States, United Kingdom, and Israel – face as many attacks as states that negotiate.

Let us now explore what happens on the ground in cases of kidnappings and hostage-taking during siege-barricade situations

Kidnapping and hostage crisis negotiations

While we know not enough about contemporary secret political negotiations with terrorists, we know much more about crisis management – negotiations where hostages and kidnapped people are involved. However, much of that knowledge comes from purely criminal rather than terrorist hostage situations. As pointed out earlier, terrorist incidents come in two sorts: single-phase incidents and dual-phase incidents.

Single-phase incidents usually have already occurred when first responders come to the scene: the shots were fired, the bomb has exploded or is about to explode. You cannot negotiate with someone who announces in a call that a bomb has been placed at Heathrow Airport and is about to go off. The person who does the calling and who might use a code word that allows the police to distinguish a hoax call from a genuine call from a known terrorist organization like the IRA is likely to be a different person from the one who is near the site to trigger the bomb to begin with. Terrorists would not directly call up the police. They call up a radio station or a hospital that, in turn, informs the police. You cannot negotiate when there is on one side only a messenger and, on the other, only a switchboard operator while the bomb might already be ticking.

Where negotiations at the law enforcement level come into the picture are the so-called "dual-phase incidents." Common to both kidnappings and hostage-taking is that targets of opportunity or specially selected persons are seized and kept in a location while demands are made on third parties in return for the lives and freedom of those kept. Dual-phase incidents consist of an initial criminal act, usually followed by a negotiation process and/or a denouement.

Table 2.2 Definitions of kidnapping and hostage-taking, with examples

Definition	Example
Kidnapping Abduction of a person (sometimes several) and confinement at a secret location, for coercive bargaining about a ransom or another asset	The case of the Italian five-times Prime Minister Aldo Moro, who was seized by the Red Brigades on March 16 1978 and found dead on May 9, 1978
Hostage-taking Seizure of a group of persons and holding them, usually at a known location, in involuntary captivity, often as a bargaining tool to secure compliance with demands of adversary	The seizure of a school in Beslan, Russia, on September 1, 2004, where 331 people (out of more than 1,200 hostages), including 172 schoolchildren, died after a shoot-out on September 3, 2004

In a hostage incident, the scene of the crime is known. These are the kinds of incident where negotiating with terrorists usually takes place. The ideal outcome is a negotiated surrender without bloodshed. A less desirable outcome is to allow them to escape – to let the hostage-takers depart to a place of their choosing in exchange for the freeing of the hostages. This is sometimes called the "Bangkok solution" after a hi-jacking incident that took place in Thailand in the 1970s. It is sometimes granted when the hostage-takers have not yet used lethal violence. Yet other outcomes are the suicide of the hostage-takers together with the murder of their hostages. Then there are the rescue attempts by armed force like the Entebbe raid by Israeli commandos. Unfortunately, according to one, now dated, study (Vasey 1985), statistically more hostages, rescuers, and terrorists have been killed by rescue operations by the authorities than have been killed by hostage-takers themselves. In some cases, the hostage-takers manage to negotiate the release of imprisoned comrades. For instance, some 300 Shiite prisoners were released by Israel after a hi-jacking of a TWA jetliner on June 14 1985 with 153 passengers and crew, among them many Americans. President Reagan had publicly stated that he would never negotiate with the terrorists but put pressure on Israel to release Shiite prisoners for the American hostages. They were freed on June 30 1984 (Bapat 2006).

Kidnapping incident negotiations

Kidnapping offers a number of advantages to the perpetrators, as the whereabouts of the abducted victims is generally not known. Nor is the location of the involved terrorists known. This gives kidnappers a much better bargaining position than the perpetrators of barricade-hostage incidents that are usually quickly surrounded by the armed forces of the opponent in a place like an embassy and must constantly fear a surprise attack. They have often been successful, as the list from the early days of political kidnappings in Table 2.3 makes clear.

Table 2.3 Some diplomatic kidnappings of the 1960s and 1970s

June 1969	The Brazilian government released forty prisoners in exchange for the US consul-general in Porto Allegre
September 1969	The Brazilian government released fifteen prisoners to secure the release of a kidnapped US ambassador
March 1970	The Brazilian government released five prisoners in exchange for the Japanese consul-general in São Paulo
March 1970	Guatemalan rebels kidnapped German ambassador Count von Spreti, demanding the release of seventeen prisoners with $700,000. Despite pressure from the German government, the demand was refused and von Spreti was murdered on April 4, 1970
January 1971	The Brazilian government released seventy prisoners in exchange for the Swiss ambassador

Source: adapted from CSTPV St Andrews database.

In addition to diplomats, many other government officials, military (both from the host nation and foreign states) and non-governmental parties have been the victims of hostage-taking. As governments have become increasingly aware of the risks associated with sending personnel abroad, they have enhanced protective services for these individuals in an effort to deter hostage-takings. In this situation, corporate officials and civilians who are not as well protected as their government counterparts have become the favored victims of hostage-takers. This has been particularly apparent during the last two decades where civilian victims have been targeted as often as 82.4 percent of the time in 2001, compared to 76.5 percent in 1998 and 75.9 percent in 1994. The frequency of victim type is illustrated in Table 2.4.

Kidnappings can last for extended periods of time. One British kidnapping victim, Terry Waite, was held for nearly five long years before he was released. Statistics of international terrorist incidents from 1978 to 2005 indicate that over 20 percent of hostage incidents lasted at least one week while another 10 percent lasted in excess of one year.

Table 2.4 Types of immediate victims of international hostage incidents, 1968–2005

Type of immediate victim	Frequency	%
Host-government officials	33	1.7
Foreign diplomats or official non-military	295	15.5
Host-government military	14	0.7
Foreign military	75	3.9
Corporation officials	400	21.0
Prominent opinion leaders	88	4.6
Private parties	960	50.4
Suspected terrorists	12	0.6
Indeterminate	27	1.4
Total	1,904	100.0

Sources: ITERATE; Mickolus (2006).

Table 2.5 Duration of incidents, 1978–2005

Duration of incident	%
Less than one week	20.2
One week to one month	13.3
One month to one year	10.5
Greater than one year	10.8
Irrelevant	23.3
Unknown	21.8
Total	100.0

Sources: ITERATE; Mickolus (2006).

Hostage-takings are usually of shorter duration than kidnappings, although there are exceptions. The longest recent diplomatic hostage situation lasted 444 days and involved initially more than sixty US diplomats (November 4 1979–20 January 1981) (Kushner 2003, p. 175). The hostage-takers released the hostages minutes after the inauguration of Ronald Reagan as US President. The official price the United States paid was the unfreezing of $8 billion in Iranian assets and immunity from prosecution for the Iran government. What made that particular incident so long-lasting was the fact that the hostages became objects of a power struggle within the Iranian revolutionary regime and the incident could not be resolved any time sooner because the US government was in reality for a long time only a third party in that power struggle. Sometimes a kidnapping is performed by criminals who subsequently sell the victim to a terrorist group. Criminal kidnappings for ransom are often easier to handle than political kidnappings, provided the ransom can be paid. Otherwise, they often have fewer scruples to kill and bury the victim. About 20 percent of kidnapping victims are killed (Kennedy 1997, p. 110)

Kidnapping is a widespread and often lucrative business. A conservative estimate of the United Nations puts the annual number at more than 10,000 (UNODC 2006, p. iii). While Colombia was, in the late 1990s, the scene of thousands of kidnappings, after 2003 Iraq stood out. According to one police report, about thirty people were abducted every day in Baghdad alone in 2006. More than 250 foreigners were kidnapped following the US invasion of Iraq: 135 of them were released, forty-four were killed, three escaped and six were rescued, while the fate of the others is not known. The money made is considerable (Table 2.6). France, Germany, and Italy paid, in 2004 and 2005, despite public denials, almost $45 million for seven citizens taken hostage in Iraq (*The Times* [London] 2006).

From 1978 through 2005 there were hundreds of international hostage-taking incidents where a monetary ransom was demanded. Some of these demands linked hostage releases to ransom payments in excess of $1 million. Perhaps even more problematic than the vast sums of money that have changed hands is the fact that hostage-taker demands are also tied to unrealistic deadlines, or replaced

Table 2.6 Ransoms reportedly paid for Western hostages in Iraq

Demand	Country and case
	France
$25 million	Florence Aubenas, held for 157 days, freed June 2005
$10 million	Christian Chesnot and Georges Malbrunot, freed December 2004. Ransom $15 million
	Italy
$11 million	Giuliana Segrena, taken February 2005, freed March 2005
$6 million	Simona Pari and Simona Toretta, taken September 2004, freed twenty days later. Ransom: $5 million
	Germany
$8 million	Susanne Ostloff: taken November 25, 2005, freed three weeks later
$3 million	Rene Braunlich and Thomas Nitzschke, taken January 24, 2006, freed on May 2, 2006. Ransom: $5 million
	Britain
None paid	Kenneth Begley, taken September 16, 2004, seen being beheaded on video made public on November 16
None paid	Margaret Hassan, abducted October 19, 2004, murdered on November 16

Source: adapted from various issues of *The Times* (London), 2006.

with an escalating set of new demands that seem to defy logic. There are a plethora of reasons why terrorist hostage-takers choose to structure their demands in the manner in which they do (Table 2.7). These range from the idiosyncrasies of terrorist leaders to strategies designed to maximize terrorist propaganda. As a consequence, demands have been increased or decreased without clearly identifiable patterns of hostage-taker behavior and corresponding deadlines. With respect to deadlines, ITERATE data indicate that sometimes deadlines were allowed to pass without negative consequences for the hostages (Table 2.8). In other cases, threats linked to deadlines were carried out (Table 2.9).

From a humanitarian perspective, the well-being of the hostages is generally the focal point of negotiations. The more hostages held, the greater the opportunity for hostage-takers to demonstrate their resolve to act through the selective use of violence against their victims. A strategy of this nature provides both the players and the setting for one of the ultimate life-and-death morality plays. Hostage-takers enjoy enhanced powers of manipulation and can show themselves as either tyrannical or benevolent in negotiations. For example, hostage-takers can manipulate negotiations through the execution of sacrificial victims, demonstrating that they bargain from a position of strength. Conversely, they can resort to sequential release of their hostages as a sign of "goodwill." In that case, they are often able to attach a certain degree of humanity and hence legitimacy to their cause.

How do authorities respond to the terrorists playing with the lives of people? An analysis of responses on the part of the authorities indicates that compromise is not high on governmental agendas (Table 2.10). As is typical for political terrorism, hostage-taker demands are often not simply of a monetary nature, but rather are shaped to fulfill terrorist tactical or strategic-political objectives. For instance, the release of hostages is sometimes also tied to demands for media coverage (Table 2.11). It is a demand often granted, because it seems to be of no major consequence. Other demands focus on political change. Some demands

Table 2.7 Hostage-taker behavior, 1978–2005

Behavior of hostage-takers	Frequency	%
Lessened one or more demands without increasing any	111	7.9
No changes in demands	262	18.6
Replaced demands with others	9	0.6
Increased one or more demands without decreasing any	27	1.9
Mixed behavior	18	1.3
Irrelevant, negotiations were not conducted	564	40.0
Unknown	419	29.6
Total	1,410	100.0

Source: Mickolus (2006).

Table 2.8 Deadlines allowed to pass, 1978–2005

No. of deadlines allowed to pass	Frequency	%
None	137	9.7
One	28	2.0
Two	6	0.4
Three	2	0.1
Four	1	0.1
Five	1	0.1
Concession	2	0.1
Unknown	51	3.6
Irrelevant	1,182	83.8
Total	1,410	100.0

Sources: ITERATE; Mickolus (2006).

Table 2.9 Deadlines where threats were carried out, 1978–2005

No. of deadlines allowed to pass	Frequency	%	Cumulative %
None	225	16.0	16.0
One	18	1.3	17.2
Three	3	0.2	17.4
Seven	3	0.2	17.7
Unknown, but at least one threat carried out	12	0.9	18.5
Irrelevant	1,149	81.5	100.0
Total	1,410	100.0	

Sources: ITERATE; Mickolus (2006).

are made on the state in which the incident occurs, and other demands are made on the state of which the hostage is a citizen. Still other demands are made against multinational corporations or the families of the victims taken hostage. Yet other demands focus on the release of political prisoners. Such demands are illustrated in Tables 2.12–13.

In addition to the above demands, some terrorists will also ask for safe passage out of the location of the incident, or even request safe haven in a more

Table 2.10 Types of government response, 1978–2005

Type of response	Frequency	%
Capitulation	53	3.8
Stalling, with compromise on demands	109	7.7
Bangkok solution	9	0.6
No compromise, no shoot-out with the perpetrators	190	13.5
Shoot-out with the terrorists	122	8.7
Government double-cross	3	0.2
Massive nationwide search, with no compromise	28	2.0
Irrelevant, negotiations were not established	533	37.8
Unknown, indeterminate	363	25.7
Total	1,410	100.0

Sources: ITERATE; Mickolus (2006).

Table 2.11 Demands for media coverage, 1978–2005

Demand for media coverage	Frequency	%
Terrorists did not demand media coverage	1,154	81.8
Newspaper statement	17	1.2
Radio statement	11	0.8
Television statement	5	0.4
Circulate propaganda statement, medium unspecified	9	0.6
Unknown as to exact type of medium	22	1.6
Mix of above	6	0.4
Not known	186	13.2
Total	1,410	100.0

Sources: ITERATE; Mickolus (2006).

Table 2.12 Demands for political change, 1978–2005

Demand for political change	Frequency	%
Yes	160	11.3
No	1.059	75.1
Not known	191	13.5
Total	1.410	100.0

Source: ITERATE; Mickolus (2006).

Table 2.13 Prisoner release demands, 1978–2005

No. of prisoners' release demanded	Frequency	%
None	1,064	89.7
One	27	2.3
Two	16	1.1
Three	9	1
Four	3	0.3
Five	6	0.5
More than ten	61	5.1
Total	1,186	100.0

Sources: ITERATE; Mickolus (2006).

friendly state. This is but one of the more problematic dilemmas negotiators and their political authorities are confronted with. In essence, the trade-off for securing the safe release of hostages is allowing the hostage-takers to escape and possibly perpetrate more acts of terrorism at a later date. At the same time, and of equal concern, is the appearance that states willing to agree to safe haven demands are somehow in collusion with the terrorists. This is especially true if there are no restrictive conditions (e.g. house arrest) attached to the demands. As Tables 2.14–15 make clear, safe haven and safe passage demands occur in about equal numbers.

While the prime consideration for hostage negotiators is the safe release of all hostages, additional concerns include minimizing material damage, monetary ransoms and, in particular, denying terrorists the opportunity to use the incident

Table 2.14 Safe haven demands, 1978–2005

Demand safe haven?	Frequency	%
Yes, demand was made	119	8.4
No, demand was not made	1,099	77.9
Unknown	192	13.6
Total	1,410	100.0

Sources: ITERATE; Mickolus (2006).

Table 2.15 Safe passage demands, 1978–2005

Demand safe passage?	Frequency	%
Yes, demand was made	99	7.0
No, demand was not made	1,124	79.7
Unknown	187	13.3
Total	1,410	100.0

Sources: ITERATE; Mickolus (2006).

as an effective propaganda tool or avenue to future activity. Thus, the hostage-taking environment continually creates pressures to pursue multiple, sometimes conflicting, goals simultaneously.

Concomitantly, the outcomes of hostage-taking incidents are also varied in nature (Table 2.16). These outcomes are, in turn, tied to the success or failure of negotiations. Contrary to widely held beliefs, hostage-takers are not very successful negotiators, as Table 2.17 indicates. This low success rate of hostage-takers is partly due to the superior negotiation tactics (backed up by the threat of force) of hostage negotiators. However, in kidnapping situations, the balance of power is often on the side of the perpetrators.

Best negotiation practices in kidnapping and hostage situations

Since the 1970s, a number of manuals have been written on negotiations with criminals in general, and with terrorists in particular. In this section, we will look at some "best practices" highlighted by them.

One of the most recent guidelines is the UN Counter-kidnapping Manual. It elaborates that there are three main negotiation strategies in kidnapping situations (Table 2.18). The first point refers to buying time. It allows the authorities to get a chance to establish the location of the victim. In case demands are unrealistic, e.g. when the ransom is too high, "delay and keep communicating" offer a chance to reach agreement later when the kidnappers might be willing to settle

Table 2.16 Hostages' fate, 1978–2005

Fate of hostages	Frequency	%
No damage or casualties, hostages released, no capitulation	531	37.7
No damage or casualties, hostages released, capitulation or compromise	161	11.4
Victims killed, no target capitulation	102	7.2
Victims killed, capitulation or compromise by targets	1	0.1
Damaged material, no target capitulation	1	0.1
Victim killed while attempting escape after initial capture	2	0.1
Victim successfully avoided capture	27	1.9
Victim successfully avoided capture after incident began	39	2.8
Hostages killed in shoot-out	20	1.4
Hostages killed, no provocation, during negotiations	21	1.5
Hostages killed during negotiations, deadline had passed	5	0.4
Hostages rescued by authorities	124	8.8
Incident forestalled by authorities before initiation	25	1.8
Victim escaped after initial capture	1	0.1
Irrelevant	6	0.4
Unknown, indeterminate	344	24.4
Total	1,410	100.0

Sources: ITERATE; Mickolus (2006).

Table 2.17 Hostage-taker negotiation success, 1978–2005

Hostage-taker negotiation success	Frequency	%
Received some of their demands	174	12.3
Received all of their demands	43	3.0
Received none of their demands	248	17.6
Irrelevant, no demands made	545	38.7
Unknown	400	28.4
Total	1,409	100.0

Sources: ITERATE; Mickolus (2006).

Table 2.18 Three main negotiation tactics in kidnapping situations

1 Delay to allow other options to be considered
2 Direct exchange of ransom for victim
3 Release after ransom payment

Source: adapted from UNODC (2006): 32.

for less. The second tactic is usually chosen when the appearance can be upheld that the police are not involved in the negotiations so that a "private" deal can be done. This is a risky strategy; the kidnappers might be arrested during the exchange if the police are informed; a sniper from either side might come into the picture if things go wrong. The third option, "Release after ransom payment," is also risky as the kidnappers might not want or be able to release the victim after obtaining the ransom (e.g. because the victim had been killed) or those who collect the ransom might not be the real kidnappers.

The public version of the UN Counter-kidnapping Manual lists a number of negotiation tactics and good practice, including those listed in Table 2.19. Given the range of responses that negotiators can choose from, it is not surprising that there have also been a wide variety of outcomes to kidnap – and hostage-taking incidents. These have ranged from the outright release of hostages with no ransom to capitulation on the part of the blackmailed party. There have, on the other hand, also been cases where hostages were killed with no provocation from the authorities. Hostages have also been rescued and, occasionally, managed to escape without outside help.

When negotiations with terrorists take place, it does not mean that the incident will be resolved without the use of force. In some cases, the negotiation might just take place to win time and to bring the SWAT (Special Weapons and Techniques) assault team into place. A triangular situation can be found: two armed groups, a "man without a gun" as negotiator – and the helpless hostages in the middle (Picco 1999). That makes it difficult for the negotiator to establish credibility and achieve results. Yet, contrary to expectations, results have been surprisingly good. Four decades of experience in crisis negotiation procedures for managing barricade hostage situations have led to a success rate of almost 95

60 A. P. Schmid and P. Flemming

Table 2.19 Kidnapping negotiation tactics and good practice (UNODC)

1 Prepare a written note containing prompting phrases for the person communicating with the offenders, in order to focus their conversation
2 Avoid "police speak," or the use of police jargon, in all dealings with the person communicating with the offenders
3 Avoid making promises that cannot be kept and be realistic about demands that are unachievable
4 Refer to the victim by name and ask to see a photograph or picture of the victim and to speak to him or her
5 Seek to keep the negotiations ongoing but be realistic about delays in meeting the demands of the offenders

Source: adapted from UNODC (2006).

percent for US negotiators in mainly criminal hostage incidents (McMains and Mullins 2001, p. 33). For political incidents, the outcome is probably less favorable for the negotiators, but they are still more favorable than those of the terrorist side. Some of the basic principles were summarized in a document elaborated by a G-7 working group in 1999 (G-8 1999).

Let us look at some best practice and principles of successful crises negotiations (Table 2.20). These are rather general and abstract principles and a hostage negotiator will find that his hands are tied if he is taking the third point ("To oppose concessions to hostage-takers") too literally. However, the hostage negotiator's hands might not be the only ones who are tied. One of the things that are important for him to find out is whether or not the terrorist spokesman at the other end of the phone is his own man or whether he is answerable to someone else. Often terrorist hostage-takers have been given very strict instructions with little flexibility for negotiation and compromise. The hostage-takers are often not in contact with their leaders. To control the communication of the terrorist to his outside supporters is something that counter-terrorist units will try to do as soon as possible, for instance by cordoning off the site of a siege or by cutting telephone links. However, today, with mobile telephones and means to access the internet, it is no longer easy to isolate the hostage-takers.

Let us look at a typical hostage situation. The first thing hostage negotiators have to do is to establish what type of terrorist they are dealing with. Is he a risk avoider or is he suicidal? Is he on drugs or is he sober? Does he have a common language with the negotiator or is interpretation necessary? Is there a deadline or is there no ultimatum? Has the terrorist issued a set of demands or not? Does the terrorist group primarily want publicity? Or does the group want the liberation of imprisoned comrades? There are important differences between a kidnapping and a hostage situation. The release of a kidnapped victim might be negotiated outside the limelight of publicity. A hostage-taking is usually designed to force a confrontation with the government and will attract and hold media attention (USG 2003, pp. 36–37).

Table 2.20 International "best practice" in dealing with hostage-taking situations: key objectives

- To uphold the rule of law while seeking a peaceful, negotiated resolution of the case
- To preserve human life, without endangering others in the process or afterwards
- To oppose concessions to hostage-takers, to deter similar crimes
- To seek to ensure that the host government fulfils its responsibilities and consults appropriately before acting
- In cases where several nationalities are victims, to ensure that all victims are given equal priority, and that an agreed, consistent message reaches:
    - the host government
    - the perpetrators
    - the victims' families
    - the media

Source: adapted from G-8 (1999).

Critical for any successful negotiation outcome is to know your opponent. Regarding the terrorist personality, Irvin Goldaber identified nine categories of hostage-takers whose typical behavior/reaction he outlined in each case (Table 2.21). Part of the information for identifying which type of hostage-taker is on the other side might come from an intelligence background check of the perpetrator (if he has a criminal record) or it might come from information obtained from escaped hostages. The answer co-determines strategy and tactics. After this has been established, a number of others steps need to be taken (Table 2.22).

Earlier we pointed to the fact that there are very different types of hostage-taker. That might also determine the choice of negotiator. Richard Clutterbuck (1978, p. 115) has noted in his book *Kidnap and Ransom*, "The choice of the principal negotiator is probably the most important single decision of the crisis management team." The choice of the authorities for the position of the negotiator is often not what the terrorist has in mind. He might want a high-level official, while the authorities might wish to see a lower-level trained police officer conduct the negotiations (Bailey 1995, p. 374). What profile should the negotiator have?[3] In the 1970s, the Dutch government, following a spate of hostage-takings, developed the ideal-type profile in Table 2.23, which still holds true.

Table 2.21 Typology of hostage-takers

Type	Motive
Suicidal person	Wants someone else to fulfill his death wish
Vengeance seeker	Wants to gain revenge
Disturbed individual	Wants to achieve mastery and solve his problem
Cornered perpetrator	Wants to effect escape
Aggrieved inmate	Wants to obtain freedom or bring about situational change
Felonious extortionist	Wants to obtain money
Social protestor	Wants to bring about social change or obtain social justice
Ideological zealot	Wants to redress a grievance
Terrorist extremist	Wants to obtain political change

Source: adapted from Goldaber (1979).

Table 2.22 Tasks of the negotiation team

Gather intelligence about the incident, the hostage-taker, the hostages, etc.
Develop tactics that will defuse the incident, influence the hostage-taker, and reduce the risk of loss of life
Establish communication with the hostage-taker
Record relevant intelligence information
Keep a record of negotiations, including demands and promises
Maintain equipment
Co-ordinate and communicate with field commander and tactical team

Source: adapted from McMains and Mullins (1996): 240.

Table 2.23 Profile of a (Dutch) negotiator

He has to be intelligent, inventive and subtle; he needs to gain quickly insight into the personality of the perpetrators, their mutual relationships and the situation in the hostage location
He ought not to be or get emotional
He has to be aware of his specific position: he is a go-between between the lawful authorities and the perpetrators ... he should not play an independent role
He has to have a certain psychological preponderance
He should never have the authority to take decisions on his own; he must always come back to the lawful authority and the government ...
He should never be a member of the lawful authority

Source: adapted from v. d. Feltz (n.d.).

Crucial is point 3. Here the Dutch instructions elaborate and stress that:

> He has to follow the lines of authority yet nevertheless he has to keep a certain autonomy within this framework. On the one hand he has to be loyal vis-à-vis the lawful authorities and has to act in the framework of the government. Yet on the other hand he has to win the confidence of the perpetrators and has to be able to see the situation from their perspective. He has to be motivated to act within the framework of the lawful authorities but has to be able to maintain his own judgment and present his insights to the lawful authorities of which he is an advisor.

Regarding point 5, the Dutch guidelines elaborate by saying that "The advantage of this is that no forced decisions are taken under psychological pressure and that he can keep his relationship with the perpetrators detached from favorable or unfavorable decisions in response to the demands."

As a negotiator in hostage situations one must, first of all, aim to slow down and calm down events. He should be able to take abuse and cope with stress and avoid being caught up in other people's emotions. He needs, without question, good listening and interviewing skills. Above all, he has to be credible, honest and straightforward. Lying should, in almost all circumstances, be avoided because credibility is too important an asset to squander. He (it is usually a he, not a she, since terrorism is by and large still a predominantly male business) needs to have practical intelligence – what is also called "being streetwise." He has to be able to cope with uncertainty. The good negotiator should be committed to a peaceful outcome of the negotiation process but should also, if things do not go in the right direction, have to play a role in the psychological preparation of the assault (McMains and Mullins 2001, p. 242).

The situation of the negotiator is characterized by a big dilemma. As a representative of a democratic government he has to keep in mind the public, which on the one hand does not want to see hostages die and on the other does not want the government to give in to terrorist demands. How can he meet such contradictory demands? What does negotiation mean in this situation?

In a normal situation, when no bomb is ticking and no ultimatum to the lives of the hostages has been set, negotiations are an attempt to reduce destructive behavior between antagonists by getting a situation that got out of control back under control. The two parties attempt to solve a conflict or dispute through some form of joint problem-solving, with the goal of reaching a mutually acceptable solution. In terms of process, negotiations can be seen as explorations of the strengths, positions and perceptions of each side and then reconcile these in a bargaining process. Yet a hostage situation is not a normal negotiation situation. Time is playing a larger role. The threat of violence looms large. Lives are at stake. The media are watching.

Hostage situations usually go through three phases (Table 2.24), where the first and the last are the most critical (The problem, however, is that you are never quite sure which phase you are in.) And all this happens against a background of shocked hostages and very nervous hostage-takers (Schmid 2004, pp. 338–339).

Over the years, a number of "best practices" have emerged in hostage situations. Many of them were codified in the United States, based on the experience of the FBI. After the WACO incident of 1993,[4] where negotiation failure was obvious, a number of "lessons learned" have been formulated (Table 2.25).

Table 2.24 The three phases of a hostage situation

1	*The initial (containment) phase.* In this phase the only correct form of action is to freeze the situation; yet there should be contact between authorities and perpetrators ... the perpetrators are in this phase very nervous, anxious, aggressive and alert
2	*Middle phase.* After the initial phase there is a period of a certain and increasing calmness during which negotiations can take place
3	*End phase.* The third phase, in which a solution, either a non-violent surrender or a surprise attack, is the goal

Source: adapted from v. d. Feltz (n.d.).

Table 2.25 Basic principles for dealing with hostage situations

Save lives – those of the hostages, the hostage-takers, the crisis team
Exercise patience to build up a relationship
Negotiators should build trust with the hostage-takers
Negotiators should avoid escalating stress
Exercise genuineness in communications
Meet legitimate interests of both parties
Establish reliable communications (language)
Take into account the personality factors of the hostage-takers
Provide assurance of the safety and security of the persons in the crisis
Conduct negotiations without challenging the hostage-takers' sense of control
Negotiators should not set deadlines for incident resolution
Avoid making decisions based on fatigue
Resist pressure from tactical teams to resolve the conflict with an assault
Communication between components (i.e. the command team, the negotiating team and the tactical team) of the crisis response team is imperative
CS gas is unreliable and dangerous, and should be used only under very specific circumstances
Assault should be backed by emergency medical services personnel and the fire department

Source: adapted from Wright (1999). A more recent study (Docherty 2001) came up with an additional, and partly different, set of lessons.

The challenge of establishing a negotiation relationship between parties with not only opposite interests but also divergent world views is a formidable one. The bridge across the gap has to be built with appropriate language. In kidnapping and hostage situations, language is usually the primary and often only tool as communication usually takes place by phone. The hostage-taker will make demands and often set deadlines. What are "typical demands" (Table 2.26) depends whether it is a criminal or political hostage-taking. Yet some of the demands are overlapping. Such demands are generally accompanied by explicit or implicit threats like shooting one hostage every hour, or, in the end game, to blow up all hostages. The hostage-takers might wish to find out whether there are any especially "valuable" hostages in their possession who can be utilized to generate extra pressure. One tactic is to make one young female hostage plead for her life on the phone. ("If you don't withdraw the SWAT team he will kill me!") Both hostages and hostage-takers are excited and very tense.

What sort of language should negotiators use in such situations? Obviously, they are not going to ask "What is your deadline?" or "Which hostage are you going to shoot next?" In general, the negotiator also should never say "no." Some examples of appropriate language are listed in Table 2.27. In order to assess how the negotiations are going, the negotiator, or a psychologist next to

Table 2.26 Typical terrorist demands

Change of politics of a country
Publication of political demands or statement of grievances
Freedom for imprisoned colleagues
Free departure with liberated prisoners to country of terrorist's choice
Presence of a certain person (as mediator) at the negotiations
Get-away transportation (e.g. helicopter)
Money
Additional weapons (in exchange for hostages)
Alcohol, cigarettes, drugs (if the terrorist is a drug addict), medicines to keep the hostage-takers awake
Water, electricity, food, blankets and even guns

---

him, will look for verbal cues. If things go well, he is likely to get signs like those shown in Table 2.28. If things do not go well, some of the signs that can be picked up are shown in Table 2.29.

Language matters a great deal and words can literally tip the decision between life and death for terrorists and hostages. The ideal outcome in a hostage situation is a bloodless resolution where hostages walk away unharmed and terrorists are apprehended thanks to skilful negotiations. How to achieve this? On the level of the work floor, where the negotiators have to do their persuasive talking, a certain consensus has evolved about the dos and don'ts of negotiation practices. Some of the "common wisdoms," based on the consensus of at least forty out of fifty hostage negotiators who all "agreed" or "strongly agreed" with them, are listed in Table 2.30.

Some conclusions

How important are hostage negotiations? What stands out without a doubt is that they have saved many lives.[5] One study (Aston 1984) surveying 146 incidents of political hostage-taking in Europe over a twelve-year span found that 94 percent of the hostages were released whether or not demands were met. Yet it also showed that granting demands was no guarantee of the safe release of the hostages. Another study, surveying ninety-one hostage events from 1968 to 1977, found that partial compliance with demands was associated with increased hostage safety in 56 percent of all cases while whole compliance led to 96 percent hostage safety – regardless of the type of event or the nature of terrorist demands (Waugh 1982). Together, such findings indicate how important tactical negotiations can be, if properly conducted. Kidnapping and hostage negotiations have, on the whole, demonstrated that the Homan theorem holds true here as well: "The more the items at stake can be divided into goods valued more by one party than they cost to the other and goods valued more by the other party than they cost to the first, the greater the chances of successful outcomes" (Homans 1961, p. 62).

Since both sides usually want different things, there is room for a negotiated settlement. To rule out negotiations for the lives of kidnapped persons and hostages on principled grounds, arguing that one should not do deals with terrorists and should not reward terrorism and that more terrorist attacks will follow, is inhuman. Contrary to the terrorists, for whom lives are often cheap, those who

Table 2.27 Verbal tactics of hostage negotiators: typical phraseology

"I'd really like to help you"
"I appreciate how you feel"
"Let's work together to be sure everyone is safe"
"Let's see what other solutions are possible"
"I know it's taking a long time, but we are trying"
"I'll need to check with my commander and will have to get back to you"
"Let's see what my boss says about that"
"Let's take this next step real slow so nobody gets hurt"
"Excuse me, I'm writing down what you said so as not to forget it"
"I understand you're getting thirsty, and I want to work with you to satisfy your needs"
"I realize your position and I'm really concerned about you and your people in there"
"I know this is difficult, and I know we can work it out"
"I'll back the tactical team off if you release one of those persons"
"What do you think the tactical team will do if you hurt one of those people?"
"Would you like to release a person now or wait fifteen minutes?"
"Why don't we let this issue lie and come back to it in a few minutes?"
"When you're ready to discuss this we'll work on it and see if we can resolve the issue"
"I'll take all the time necessary to resolve this issue, but you know how SWAT teams are"

Source: adapted from McMains and Mullins (1996): 149, 154–155, 158, 170.

Table 2.28 Predictors of how negotiations are progressing (I) positive signs

There is less violent content in the hostage-taker's conversations
The hostage-taker talks to the negotiator more often and longer
The hostage-taker speaks at a slower rate and his speech pitch and volume are lower
The hostage-taker talks about personal issues
A deadline is talked past and there is no incident
Threats from the hostage-taker decrease
Hostages are released
No one has been killed or injured since the onset of negotiations

Sources: adapted from McMains and Mullins (1996): 152.

Table 2.29 Predictors of how negotiations are not progressing (II) negative signs

The hostage-taker setting a deadline for his own death
The subject insists on face-to-face negotiations (i.e. provoking the police to kill him)
A depressed hostage-taker denying thoughts of suicide (he is lying to the negotiator and setting up "suicide by cop")
The hostage-taker talking about the disposition of his belongings

Source: adapted from McMains and Mullins (1996): 152.

Table 2.30 Common wisdoms on hostage negotiations: percentage of hostage negotiators agreeing or strongly agreeing with statement ($n = 50$)

Common wisdom	%
A key function in hostage negotiations is buying time while attempting to defuse the situation	100
A hostage negotiator must be on the constant lookout for a "suicide ritual" by the hostage-taker	100
The main objective in a hostage situation is the preservation of human life, including that of the hostage-takers	96
The "Stockholm syndrome" applies not only to hostages but also to hostage-takers and hostage negotiators as well	94
The most dangerous time for hostages is the first minutes after being taken hostage	90
In a hostage situation it is important for the negotiator to try to find a face-saving solution for the hostage-taker	88
The key to successful hostage negotiations is flexibility	86
Nothing is owed to the hostage-takers, and if an opportunity becomes available to liberate the hostages safely it should be taken	84

Source: adapted from Vasey (1985): 53–62.

oppose them should demonstrate that each life matters and that, when there is a clash between principles and the affirmation of the value of human lives, dogmatic principles should not automatically have the upper hand.

When it comes to tactical negotiations, this has become the unofficial position of many governments. While the official policy of most states is one of "no concessions" to discourage further hostage-taking, the fact is that in more than half of all hostage takings in a survey covering international terrorist incidents in the period 1968–1991, negotiations were attempted (Mickolus *et al.* 2000; Bapat 2006, p. 214). The argument that negotiations and concessions may encourage future blackmail and extortion is valid. Yet the real possibility of saving the lives of real human beings at the present moment should not without very good reason be sacrificed to the probability of preventing future victimizations. In the words of Martin Hughes (1990, p. 82), "'Never negotiate with terrorists' is a false moral principle."

Notes

1 For "new terrorism" see Adam Dolnik and Keith M. Fitzgerald, *Negotiating Hostage Crises with the New Terrorists*, New York, Praeger, 2007
2 One study surveying a series of hostage-takings found that "Governments that make major substantive concessions under threat experience continuing terrorism and may experience increases in it. Governments that adopt very firm policies during incident management and demonstrate resolve over time and across events will experience reduced terrorism, especially of the types on which they have been firm." (Hayes 2003.)
3 Since most terrorists are male, to have a female negotiator is generally not considered wise. However, governments (e.g. the one of the Netherlands) also train women for this role.
4 On February 28 1993 FBI men from the Hostage Rescue Team of the Bureau of Alcohol, Tobacco and Firearms started a fifty-one-day siege of the Branch Davidian religious cult at Waco. After an initial shootout in which six cult members and four federal agents died, the two parties settled for a long siege in the course of which the FBI thought it was a clever thing to play loud music and shine strong lights on the farm so that the cult members could not sleep and would be weakened when the final assault came. In the end they did not capitulate but committed collective suicide when the federal agents stormed the place on April 19 1993. David Koresh and more than seventy people, including children, died in the fire they themselves had apparently started. However, that was not the end of a badly handled hostage situation. Exactly two years later, on the day of the Waco siege, the Bureau of Alcohol, Tobacco and Firearms in the federal building in Oklahoma City was destroyed by a car bomb, killing more than 160 people and injuring hundreds more. The person convicted for the attack, Timothy McVeigh, was a decorated Gulf War veteran and member of one of the numerous armed militias on the extreme right in the United States. He had apparently identified with the victims of the strong federal state and decided to hit back at "the system," creating the most lethal domestic terrorist bombing on US soil. (Collins 1997, pp. 253–254.)
5 On the other hand, one study found that, out of 1,000 persons killed in various hostage incidents, 780 were killed during rescue operations. (Rand study, quoted in Bolz *et al.* 1990, p. 147.)

3 Supping with the Devil

David Pinder

It can be convincingly argued that there is a need for a variety of definitions of terrorism, depending on the use for which that definition is required. However, there is one important aspect of the debate that is often neglected – the distinction between a terrorist and an insurgent. That neglect is perhaps the more surprising when one considers that the difference has been highlighted long ago, not least by Paul Wilkinson in 2001 (p. 1):

> [I]t is grossly misleading to treat terrorism as a synonym for insurgency, guerrilla warfare or political violence in general. It can be objectively defined as a special method of armed struggle ... which can be used either on its own, or, as is more often the case historically, as part of a wider repertoire of armed struggle. Hence just as it is possible to engage in acts of terrorism without mounting a full-scale insurgency, so it is possible to wage an effective insurgency by relying on a combination of guerrilla and conventional warfare, and eschewing the weapon of terror.

At one level ignoring any distinction between the two is perhaps understandable in terms of the damage they cause by their actions, but if the maxim of 'know your enemy' has any contribution to make in containing or defeating the threat posed, then failure to understand the distinction will severely prejudice the chances of success in both the short and the long term. Notwithstanding what is contained in the above quote most, if not all, insurgents will however employ the use of terror in a variety of ways during the course of their campaign; initially because they are too weak to use other methods, or later, either to continue to apply pressure on those in power and/or to intimidate or coerce the population – or finally, to intimidate or discipline their own members and supporters. The 'pure' or core terrorist, if such terms can be used, may have a general aim concerning the society he/she attacks but will seldom have a coherent strategy for achieving that aim or for constructing an alternative society. This is often termed the nihilist or anarchist approach and in Western Europe can perhaps be best illustrated by groups such as the Angry Brigade and the Baader-Meinhof gang.

A relatively new arrival into this category is the 'single interest' violent activist such as those belonging to the wilder fringes of the animal rights campaign.

Groups such as the Irish Republican Army (IRA) and Euskadi ta Atisuna (ETA), while it suits politicians to refer to them as terrorists in order to reduce any potential sympathy for their cause, are in reality always insurgents – as subsequent events have proved. Organizations such as Brigate Rosse fall somewhere between the two. While possessing many of the characteristics of the former, Brigate Rosse differed from them, at least for a while, in seeking and achieving a broad base of support among the community and had ambitions for political power. It has been said in a variety of ways that all successful revolutionaries (insurgents *et al.*) end up having tea at Buckingham Palace: terrorists do *not* get invited to tea with the Queen! Flippancy aside, the difference between a terrorist and an insurgent is therefore real, and understanding that difference is fundamental for any state hoping to contain or defeat the threat they pose. Before leaving this introductory paragraph some attention should be directed towards the definition of 'negotiation'; shades of meaning will emerge during the course of this chapter but in general terms it will be assumed to mean dialogue in whatever form, from the indirect and covert to what might be termed a full-blown peace process.

Know your enemy

Governments will use the term 'terrorist' to distance such groups and individuals psychologically from the rest of the population and hopefully thereby remove any claim to legitimacy for their aims and actions. In the public arena there is merit in this approach, which is often accompanied by the policy of viewing all associated acts of violence as straightforward criminal acts, rather than giving them the status of 'political violence'. Having adopted this approach, it is entirely consistent that a government will declare that there can be no negotiating with the terrorist. In regard to the 'pure' or absolute terrorist, such a declaration may be the truth, with the exception of what may be termed 'incident-specific negotiation' (ISN), to be discussed below. However, with regard to the terrorist/insurgent (T/I) the reality will almost always be very different.

Whether terrorist or insurgent, the state attacked will want to know more about the organization and individuals concerned. The appropriate agencies will be tasked to gather information at a variety of levels and by a variety of methods; these will vary depending on the organization, nature and culture of the state. Depending upon the size and immediacy of the threat assessment, the resources allocated for this task will also vary but the process of information-gathering will begin immediately. This process will include contact with other agencies, both within the state and without – although may not extend as far as intelligence sharing at this stage. It will also include the tasking of existing sources and informants by both the police and other more clandestine security agencies. If the level of threat remains low (or acceptable!) – as assessed by the state, not necessarily by the general public – then these activities may not rise much above the routine, care-and-maintenance level.

However, a higher threat assessment will generate higher levels of activity. These will include more active attempts to identify individuals through both informants and by surveillance; perhaps even with a view to detain and question suspects, whether activists or supporters. It is also at this stage that thought will be given to attempting to begin penetration of the organization, once sufficient is known about its personalities and activities to render this feasible. Some of these insertions will be intended to be long-term, with the potential to rise within the organization, others will have the more immediate intention of finding out more about the organization, its methodology and any operations being currently planned. The questioning of suspects, whatever the reason given for detention, will have the ancillary (or in some cases the primary) aim of learning more about the organization and its members; nor should it be forgotten that the occasional 'arrest' of sources allows them to be briefed and debriefed in secure conditions and may also help their credibility. Depending upon the security awareness of the organization and the detained suspect (which in itself may indicate training in anti-questioning techniques), such questioning may yield much information which, when collated with that of other sources and other agencies begins to build up firm intelligence on the targeted organization.

It is important to distinguish between information and intelligence. The aim of gathering information is to match it to what is already known, or suspected, from other sources; only when the quality of both the information and the source of it have been evaluated against other information does it become intelligence. Among the best information will be that gained from members of the organization itself. It is here that the state begins a further stage in the intelligence process. Whilst inserting its own agents into the targeted organization is sometimes a viable option, it is a difficult one and one always fraught with risk; where the organization is one based on a particular national and/or ethnic group it may be impossible in the short term. Accordingly, the state's security agencies will be assessing detained suspects for their potential to be 'turned'; such a process normally requires lengthy discussions to discover the individual's personal circumstances, motivation and values. In some cases it may be possible to genuinely change the person's adherence, in others the reason may be more venal; in yet others, controversially, the approach may be close to pressure which might be described as 'blackmail'. This type of pressure can of course backfire, as the British found in Northern Ireland (NI) (Ganor 2005, p. 186):

> ... attempts were also made by British security forces to obtain intelligence information on the IRA by arresting young Irishmen, putting pressure on them to give up information in exchange for their release and dropping charges against them. Sometimes, in particularly grave cases, suspects were threatened that if they refused to give information, rumours would be spread that they were collaborating with the British – rumours that were liable to jeopardise their lives. The use of intelligence of this kind compromised the government's legitimacy, and in effect, aided the IRA.

In the case of 'pure' or absolute terrorist groups there may not be much that can be reliably achieved by any of these approaches; however, in the case of T/Is, notwithstanding the above quotation, the prospects of success are higher; the British did succeed in recruiting some insiders. In former counter-insurgency campaigns such attempts were common and seen as essential, often yielding spectacular results – including the raising of entire units of 'turned' T/Is who operated with lethal success against their former comrades. General Sir Frank Kitson (1971, 1977), the near-forgotten master of counter-insurgency and counter-terrorism campaigns, makes it plain in both his classic works, *Low-intensity Operations: Subversion, Insurgency and Peacekeeping* and *Bunch of Five*, how valuable such units were, not only in directly countering the insurgents but also in affecting them psychologically. In the more recent past, in Vietnam and some parts of Latin America, the United States has also experimented with similar schemes. However, this process is only now being cautiously rediscovered in Iraq and Afghanistan; the failure to utilize this approach earlier has undoubtedly been due, in part at least, to the stance taken publicly by politicians that there can be no dealings with terrorists. Having tied themselves into this hard-line position, and having branded all such groups as terrorists, it is understandable, particularly in today's world of twenty-four-hour media, that they have difficulty in acknowledging that there are circumstances where dialogue is both productive and essential.

By its very nature much of the above activity will be secret and may not even be shared between the state's own agencies, much less with those of other countries. In a concurrent process it may be that third parties will be approached, either for information and assistance or to provide non-attributable avenues of communication with the targeted organization. Both by the questioning of known or suspected members and supporters and by the approach to non-attributable third parties the state has entered into dialogue with an illegal organization, no matter what its publicly stated position may be. Study of the United Kingdom's campaign against both the IRA and, beginning later in the late 1960s, the Provisional IRA (PIRA), shows an almost textbook example of concealed dialogue with T/Is and only now is the full extent of that process coming to light. It is not the purpose here to fully examine the whole process but in addition to the crude attempts to subvert possible adherents outlined above, communication channels were established, including allowing PIRA to use certain agreed code words to authenticate bomb warnings. The secret use of a well known Londonderry businessman to provide indirect – and later direct – discussions and meetings with senior members of PIRA; the earlier-mentioned 'plants' who in time rose to senior positions in the movement; and, although not yet fully admitted, contacting states and individuals outside the United Kingdom, such as the Republic of Ireland, Libya and the United States, to make use of their channels of communication with PIRA to achieve indirect dialogue. The fact that the IRA's political 'wing' had a separate and legal existence as Sinn Fein also undoubtedly helped this two-way flow.

It is important to remember that during most of this time the UK government was resolutely committed to defeating the IRA and equally resolute in denying that it would have any communication with terrorists; nor, apart from occasional self-declared cease-fires, did the IRA stop killing British soldiers and civilians. Clandestine dialogue, and later open dialogue, were only possible, however, because the IRA, whatever the nature of its component parts and individuals, had identifiable aims and was embarked on a progression towards some form of acknowledged legitimacy for its cause. It equally understood the need for secrecy over these 'negotiations'. Martin McGuiness, one of PIRA's most formidable commanders, after one such high-level meeting on British soil, is alleged to have acknowledged laconically the similarity between his position and that of Michael Collins (one of the principal architects of the earlier struggle for Irish independence, who was afterwards killed in a gun battle with his erstwhile comrades in the bitter civil war which followed the Free State's independence from British rule). There was never at any stage any guarantee, from either side, that these discussions and negotiations, whether indirect or direct, would lead to a mutually agreeable resolution of the conflict but they nevertheless took place on a regular basis. Undoubtedly study of similar campaigns around the world will reveal other examples of such lines of communication being established and maintained, even in the face of extreme and continuing hostility. However, the case can be made that these lines of communication are only possible because the illegal organisation is more insurgent than terrorist and therefore has identifiable, if disagreeable, aims and a need to strive for some form of acceptance no matter how much it despises the government against which it is engaged.

Nothing new?

These covert lines of communication are of course not a new development in any form of conflict – rather they are a nuance in a long tradition. Pre-twenty-first-century warfare never precluded diplomatic activity, whether direct or indirect, and while irregulars or partisans might be dealt with severely when caught at the wrong time they would nevertheless often be accorded some sort of *de facto* status. More recently, the hackneyed phrase 'One man's terrorist is another man's freedom fighter' might have more meaning if modified to read 'One state's terrorist is another state's freedom fighter'. Arguably this concept reached its zenith during the Cold War as the White House and the Kremlin waged their proxy war around the planet. The Iran–Contra affair, examined in Karen Feste's chapter, and US support for Afghan resistance to the Soviet occupation provide excellent examples of the flexible morality of Western states towards 'terrorists' during this period; and Soviet, Cuban, and Chinese support for various 'liberation' struggles demonstrate equal hypocrisy when compared to their attitude to liberation struggles closer to home.

In what used to be termed 'small wars', a term first used formally by C. E. Callwell (1986), insurgents had been countered by a mixture of conventional and unconventional tactics alongside a mixture of war and negotiation. Each of the major powers had developed its own doctrines and strategies, which generally reflected the culture of the armed forces involved, coupled with the nature of the opposition they faced and the environment in which the campaign took place. Even if not clearly defined, a need for knowledge of the enemy, plus sound and developing intelligence, was seen as essential. Terror was employed by both sides in such conflicts. As the so-called colonial wars continued, more coherent methods were developed and incorporated into doctrine. The American experience follows a slightly different path, from being T/Is themselves in their battle to free themselves from British rule, through the Indian wars and their own civil war, in which both sides employed irregulars to wage terror campaigns against civilians alongside their battles with regular forces, to their operations in the Philippines against the Katipunan leader Emiliano Aguinaldo and later after World War II against the Hukbalapaps.

In addition to understanding the need for sound and timely intelligence as a basis for both combat and negotiation, increasing emphasis began to be placed on the need for military success to be accompanied by political and civil activity. All of this implied considerable contact and dialogue with both insurgent movements and local populations, nor was negotiation to be seen as something to be avoided at all costs; although equally, it must be allowed that dialogue and negotiations were sometimes regarded more as a tactic than as sincere attempts to resolve a situation. The progression of this experience and doctrinal development finds fulfilment in the works of experts such as Colonel David Galula (1964), Sir Robert Thompson (1966) and the aforementioned General Sir Frank Kitson. While the first two emphasize political primacy, sound information and the need to secure the support of the local population, Kitson, whilst agreeing, places greater stress on the need for excellent intelligence and the use of 'turned' insurgents against their former colleagues – a tactic which the British used to great effect in Malaya, Kenya and Dhofar. Dialogue was not seen as incompatible or at variance with rigorous military activity to end the insurgency and it is against this background that the earlier comment concerning Buckingham Palace was made.

While throughout most of the above history the words 'terror' and 'terrorist' are sometimes used, they are not used to describe a particular individual or organization. Indeed, it was only in Malaya during the so-called Emergency when the British military began to refer to the insurgents as CTs (Communist Terrorists) that the term assumes its modern usage. It may be that with the growth of modern communications and commensurate expansion in size and influence of the media, modern governments have found themselves trapped into a situation where, by using the term 'terrorist' to produce a sense of revulsion and alienation amongst their own populations they have limited their options for dialogue with T/Is. The impact of modern media conditions will be explored later in this article.

Modern terrorists/insurgents

The reason for covering the past at such length is to show that we are dealing with a continuum rather than a totally new phenomenon. However, admittedly the middle of the twentieth century saw the advent of several new factors. The first is the emergence of a new breed of disaffected and violently disposed groups. Predominantly urban, educated and middle-class, this new variant has the destruction of the Establishment as its goal. They are not interested in participating in the political process, nor even in gaining popular support – indeed, their contempt for the ordinary people whose interests they claim to be representing is often barely concealed. Although a new factor, they do perhaps share some characteristics with the nihilists, anarchists and revolutionaries of the late nineteenth and early twentieth centuries. Dialogue or negotiation in the traditional sense is likely to prove futile, since, to the extent that such a group's demands are coherent at all, they are likely to include the complete destruction of the system itself. It can be fairly argued that any such attempt by the state serves only to enhance the profile and credibility of the group concerned. Accordingly, attempts at dialogue or communication are likely to be limited to ISN. A sub-category of this development is the disaffected solo terrorist such as Theodore Kaczynski, the infamous Unabomber in the United States, and more recently, in the United Kingdom, the case of Neil Lewington, an unemployed electrician, described as a white supremacist and neo-Nazi, who was arrested at a railway station for unrelated reasons and found to have two firebombs in his sack.

Secondly, following the end of the Cold War, the United Nations appeared at first to be about to enjoy a new lease of life – or, perhaps more accurately, seemed to be about to function as its founders had intended. This led to a significant increase in both traditional and new types of peacekeeping missions, some of which were more correctly interventions. As in many of these operations there was actually no peace to keep and often a variety of indigenous groups – some of whom were no more than criminal gangs (such as the West Side Boys in Sierra Leone) – fighting amongst each other, the UN military and civilian staffs found themselves having to negotiate on a daily basis if their mission was to stand any prospect of success. Whether such groups were terrorist, insurgent or purely criminal was incidental in the process of trying to carry out the mission in the short term and this experience has undoubtedly helped to further blur any distinctions between the three. This process and the attempts by the military to carry out this difficult task lie outside the scope of this work but are covered very well by Deborah Goodwin in her book *The Military and Negotiation* (2005).

Confusion arises because, whilst these groups and individuals frequently dominate the headlines through the high-profile incidents they create, the more traditional T/I is still highly active around the world; and there has been considerable cross-fertilization between the two. One by-product of this is the increasing tendency for insurgents to carry the struggle outside the immediate conflict zone by conducting terrorist attacks against the perceived enemy and its supporters wherever they are to be found – and in doing so to include purely civilian targets in their strike list. al-Qaeda may be a further stage in the evolutionary process. Whatever al-Qaeda may or may not be, it does seem to combine the nihilistic desire to destroy with some form of vision for the future and in that sense conforms to the T/I profile more than to that of the 'pure' or absolute terrorist, albeit on a global scale.

Another recent development that is a significant factor in determining the utility of negotiation is the emergence of suicide operations as a deliberate offensive tactic rather than as a weapon of last resort. While the willingness of insurgents to countenance death or even to welcome it and to offer their lives dearly as a consequence of their activities is not new, setting out with the deliberate intention of using one's body as a weapon is new and in all senses of the word is definitely a terror tactic. As Wu Ch'I, an early Chinese military philosopher, said, 'One man willing to throw his life away is enough to terrorize a thousand.'

The classic insurgent, whether utilizing terror tactics or not, offers the possibility of negotiation by all the methods mentioned above. All wars and insurgencies end sometime, and whatever the outcome various forms of dialogue will have played a role throughout, eventually leading to formal and acknowledged negotiations (Ikle 1971). In the early stages such dialogue will have been covert, and both then and later the very fact of dialogue carries potential penalties for the insurgent as well as for the state, as discussed here in the introductory chapter. A less obvious but equally valid reason for denying such contact affects both sides and that is the possibility that the insurgent movement may fracture into mutually antagonistic groups with the consequent difficulty of having to combat a variety of new groups whose structures and identities may be unknown; and whose activities, freed from the control of the more moderate insurgency leaders, may be more brutal and extreme. Fracturing an insurgency movement may seem superficially attractive and in some circumstances may even be productive in that it may create internal stresses for the insurgents but, if the stage of real negotiation has been reached, it is potentially disastrous for the state. In Northern Ireland, once a process of informal/formal negotiation had been reached, it now seems clear that the British government went to some lengths to 'protect' those IRA leaders who had entered into the negotiation process (Marston and Malkasian 2008, p. 184).

One other aim of bringing insurgents into the negotiation process is to introduce them to the realities of administration and to psychologically bring them into a relationship atmosphere – this is sometimes known as the Sarajevo syndrome after the success of the Mixed Military Working Group in Bosnia-Herzegovina in 1992–1994. Those with a mordant sense of humour will no doubt derive some grim satisfaction from watching the difficulties of Hamas since their election success – being responsible for schools and drains is much harder and considerably less fun than firing off rockets!

In summary therefore judicious dialogue with insurgents, whether indirect or direct was (and is) an accepted and necessary part of the process for dealing with such problems. However, those who argue that it is the only way forward need only look to the Israeli–Palestinian conflict to realize that dialogue and negotiation, of themselves, hold no guarantee of success. Perhaps, in such circumstances, it may be said – to misquote Clausewitz – that negotiation is sometimes warfare by other means.

Incident-specific negotiation

Beyond the question of a need for states to have some form of dialogue with insurgents or terrorists as a matter of necessity or principle and, if so, how and why, there is another circumstance in which there will be a need to communicate, whatever the state's intentions and inclinations – and that is with regard to specific incidents. This applies to both insurgent and 'pure' terrorists. The most obvious example is where hostages have been taken, either as a deliberate act or as a consequence of some other operation that has malfunctioned. Whether the incident has occurred on the state's own territory or elsewhere, the state will be expected to act to secure the safety of the hostages. There is, of course, a range of options available depending upon the situation. In recent interventions and counterinsurgencies around the world hostage-taking has become increasingly multi-layered but broadly falling into five categories:

1. Criminal gangs 'snatching' indigenous individuals in the hope of extracting a ransom for their safe return. Figures for this type of activity are difficult to obtain as, in many cases, neither the gang nor the victim's family or firm wish anyone to know about the incident and in most cases the ransom is quietly paid and the victim is returned relatively unharmed (e.g. Pepper 1977).
2. Similar to the first example but the victim(s) is a non-resident, possibly working for a foreign firm or NGO. The initial response may also be similar but secrecy is much less likely to be maintained and official agencies are likely to become involved at some point.
3. A further development of the above two examples is where the criminal gangs conduct the kidnapping and then 'sell on' the hostages to a T/I organization.
4. T/Is conduct their own kidnapping operations and attempt to force concessions or conditions through negotiations for release of the hostages. There may be a willingness to allow these to drag on, as for example in the case of high-profile hostages such as Terry Waite. However, there appears to be a trend with the more extremist groups to seek publicity as much as genuine concessions by such operations. Modern technology allows the terrorist or insurgent to exert great pressure immediately upon the authorities by use of the internet and live broadcasts. This is often promoted by an intent to inspire terror through threatened ill-treatment and even execution. The fact that, in some cases, such executions are often carried out 'on screen' relatively soon after capture suggests that this was the intention from the start, rather than any genuine intention to negotiate.
5. 'Siege operations' where T/Is seize a building, holding hostage all those captured within, in order to negotiate concessions from the state, as in the seizure of Israeli athletes by Black September at the Munich Olympic Games in 1972. Hi-jacking an aircraft or a ship also falls into this category although such operations have been used less frequently by T/Is at the

moment. Such operations are high-profile events from the beginning and place enormous pressure on the state, as will be discussed below. The hostage-takers in earlier operations may have been willing to run the risk of death as consequence of their actions but more recent attempts were mounted with a deliberate suicide element planned from the beginning.

In response to any of these incidents, the state will invariably declare initially that there will be neither discussions nor concessions, against rising pressure from the relatives, a variety of non-government organizations (NGOs) and possibly elements of the media to do so. In the case of categories 1, 2 and initially 3 above, the state will have the option of declining to become involved, although diplomatic pressure may be exerted behind the scenes; however, in the latter cases where there is clearly a political intent behind the seizure that option is not available. If the hostages come from more than one country the situation will be complicated even further since some countries may not be as unwilling to negotiate as others, or may not be directly affected by the demands made by the hostage-takers. If the hostage-takers have taken refuge in a friendly or neutral country that country may also pressure for any demands to be met.

Several states have negotiated in the recent past, openly or otherwise, to secure the release of hostages – Italy in the case of the captured journalist Daniele Mastrogiacomo in 2007. Other countries are extremely robust no matter what the pressure, taking the view that to negotiate is to legitimize the terrorist and that concessions granted to hostage-takers will weaken the state and guarantee that the tactic will be repeated elsewhere:

> The terror group's desire is to enter into negotiations with a sovereign government under the strain of pending death to compromise that state's power and prestige; the state risks much merely in negotiating; to make concessions amounts to a double undermining of legitimate government. Terrorists are delighted even with limited concessions, for they have not only placed themselves on the state's level, but then gained something demonstrable in the negotiations.
>
> (Harmon 2001, p. 239)

However, even here there will probably be some attempt, directly or indirectly, to establish contact with the hostage-takers. This may take the form of contacting another state, NGO or even an individual, perhaps known to be sympathetic, or at least non-hostile, to the group involved. In the case of insurgents, channels may be used to contact insurgent leaders rather than the hostage-takers themselves; and where the incident has taken place in another country there may be agreement that they may contact the hostage-takers, allegedly on their own initiative. Where the act takes place on the state's own territory there may still be recourse to intermediaries. None of this precludes the fact that the state may have already decided to undertake violent action to free the hostages, since appearing to be willing to listen and negotiate buys time to plan and prepare for the assault. It is in fact an almost universally adopted Standing Operating Procedure (SOP) that direct communications will be opened with the hostage-takers – if indeed they have not already done so themselves. Private companies in the 2008–2009 cases of piracy hostage-taking off the coast of Somalia have immediately entered into negotiations, at the same time as official navies have more or less actively carried out prevention and rescue operations. In the case of category 4 hostage-taking, the situation may well be complicated by the fact that the location of the hostages may be unknown and will be changed at frequent and irregular intervals, with the hostage-takers' only communication being through a third party.

The siege negotiation scenario is the most complicated of all. First, it will be under a time constraint imposed by the demands and threats of the hostage-takers; second, there will be immediate public pressure from the media and opposition parties to do something; and third, as opposed to less confrontational discussions, both the state and the hostage-takers will be aware that the other side may not be sincere, a problem discussed in the introduction of this book. In fact, when faced with such a situation, most states will prepare immediately for the eventuality that armed assault will be necessary to end the affair, this will be especially so if the hostage-takers are thought to be intent on suicide or have indicated a willingness to execute hostages as a part of the negotiating process. The negotiators therefore have a double role, as Combalbert has noted in his chapter: they must endeavour to convince a possibly sceptical hostage-taker that they are sincere and that any delays or hitches are genuine while, at the same time, assisting the security forces in their preparation and planning. Unsurprisingly, this dual role is sometimes controversial and where the negotiator is not a member of the security forces there may be reluctance to undertake the latter role. In this case, the negotiator may be kept in the dark in order to ensure that operational security is maintained.

An additional complication in such scenarios today is the range and availability of modern communications. When, during the initial stages of Operation Nimrod, the SAS assault on the Iranian embassy in London, May 1980, television news cameras were actually filming, the coverage was not broadcast live and mobile phones were not able to transmit live pictures to another phone or to the internet; today it would be virtually impossible to prevent accidental, or deliberate, real-time visual warnings being passed to the hostage-takers. To balance this, advances in modern technology also allow police and military to form a much more accurate picture of the target area and positions of the hostages and their kidnappers. However, even with modern technology and the accumulated experience of military forces in such operations, they remain very high-risk situations, and while supporters of such action can point to spectacular successes such as outlined above, there are equally spectacular and catastrophic failures such as the storming by the Russian army of the village of Pervomayskaya on the night of 15 January 1996 or the ill coordinated attack on the school at Beslan in 2004, examined in Dolnik's chapter.

Another case involved the seizure of the Dominican embassy in Bogotá in 1980 by M-19 terrorists (Asencio 1982). During a diplomatic reception the terrorists occupied the building, taking hostage some eighty individuals, including eighteen ambassadors. They demanded the release of more than 300 prisoners in jail in Colombia, including 200 suspected M-19 members, a ransom of $50 million, safe passage out of the country and publication of their manifesto by all countries represented by their hostages. The siege lasted sixty-one days but was ended not by assault but by negotiation in which both sides modified their position. The Colombian government refused to release the prisoners but agreed to set up a panel of ten leading lawyers to process the trial of the suspect M-19 members, with the Inter-American Human Rights Commission of the Organization of American States being brought in to monitor the trials; the hostage-takers received a guaranteed safe passage to Cuba, where Castro had offered them asylum; the government refused to accede to the ransom demand but allowed the business community to pay the hostage-takers $2.5 million. It can be argued that this was a defeat for the government but in view of the likely consequences of an armed assault and the complications of so many hostages from so many different countries it can equally be argued that a much more difficult situation was avoided.

In the end, there can be no infallible blueprint, academic or otherwise, for negotiating with terrorists or insurgents. There may be useful guidelines, case studies of former situations, psychological assistance, predictability charts etc which assist in the process; and in this regard Brian Gongol (2004) has attempted masterfully to reduce the process to a mathematical equation. It would undoubtedly be useful if a similar table of conditions and equation could be produced for insurgents. Such an equation might indicate whether or not it was time to open meaningful channels of communication. However, useful though such aids may be they can only ever be indicators, in the end-analysis success will be due to the human mind and the qualities and abilities of the negotiators in each situation. After all, terrorists and insurgents are not so much outfought as out thought!

So what?

In sum, since negotiations not only take place but do in the many forms discussed, it may be helpful to try to summarise why, when and how?

Why? States need to identify the threat in order to find the appropriate countermeasures. Only by knowing your enemy can you hope to understand his rationale, his methods, his strategy, his likely actions and critically, his weaknesses. To rule out, from the beginning, any way to gain this information is nonsensical. It is particularly important in this process to ascertain whether one is faced with 'pure' absolute terrorists who, whilst dangerous, can be dealt with only as criminals, or whether one is faced with a nascent insurgency in which terror will be only one factor. In the case of the former it is unlikely that those involved will be able to sway any significant proportion of the general population to support them; in the case of the latter, it will be important to identify those grievances which might find resonance amongst some or all of the general public in order see which, if any, can be resolved and thus render the insurgent cause invalid.

When? If one is dealing with 'pure' terrorists, having gained the above initial information, it will often be unnecessary or undesirable to go beyond using limited forms of dialogue to keep oneself informed and hopefully to either penetrate the movement or at least to unbalance the movement psychologically. The exception to this is the ISN situation when it may be necessary to negotiate – even if that negotiation is insincere. In dealing with T/Is, different conditions apply. Having established what the aims and aspirations of the movement are states will have to develop a wide-ranging, strategic and coordinated multi-agency response. There are examples where such early identification of the aims has allowed the state to make concessions and thus to begin a form of negotiation, whether direct or indirect, which the insurgent leaders have also been willing to accede in, successfully preventing further escalation. Soon after World War II, in the north-east Alpine region of Italy of Alto Adige, or Süd Tyrol, terrorism broke out over the status of the German-speaking minority; negotiations between Italy and Austria involving the local populations led to an augmentation of local self-rule and the terrorist violence ended soon afterward (Weinberg 2008).

Admittedly, such bloodless successes are rare and one can find more examples where attempts to negotiate concessions have merely led to demands for more concessions. If the state cannot or will not take such preventative action, the T/I campaign may develop such momentum that, regardless of its chances of success, no government can risk open negotiation. In such cases some time may have to elapse before either side is willing to open real dialogue. However, at some point, indirectly or directly, dialogue will take place. This may be because the T/I movement has, itself, realised that it will not achieve its goals by the gun and bomb alone. At first it is likely that the process will not run smoothly on either side and there may be interruptions and breakdowns before real negotiation can begin – but once the process has started it is unlikely to breakdown completely. It is at this stage that one can begin to speak of a peace process because irrespective of differences, past 'wrongs' and future difficulties, the parties involved have unilaterally come to the conclusion that it is time to talk. However, it should not be assumed that it will be the state which calls the tune when such a stage is reached; there are also times when the peace process is in some ways a euphemism for getting out. Whilst past counter-insurgency operations such as those of the British in Malaya and Dhufar can legitimately be claimed to have been successful, there are many other similar operations such as the British in Aden, the French in Indo-China and Algeria, the Americans in Vietnam and Iraq, where the negotiations were those required for withdrawal.

How? Initially the state should be trying to establish what it is facing. Is it a 'pure' terrorist group or a wider threat that has ambitions and possibly the capacity to escalate into a full-blown insurgency. Unless a hostage-type situation develops the state is unlikely to consider the option to attempt dialogue with the former. However, if dealing with T/Is the state should include consideration of such an option in its strategy from the beginning even if there is no intention to actually begin dialogue at that early stage. Only then will it begin to look across a sufficiently broad spectrum for the correct information and intelligence. Bard O'Neill (1990, p. 17) identifies seven types of insurgency movement: anarchist, egalitarian, traditionalist, pluralist, secessionist, reformist, and preservationist. Each, he believes, has its own characteristics, and understanding these characteristics and the dynamics of the organisation will lead to understanding its strengths and weaknesses. For example, is it likely that some of its members and supporters can be weaned away from the aims of the leadership? Certainly misidentification of the threat has had dire consequences in the past. Had the United States realized that many of the Vietcong and indeed the North Vietnamese government were not part of some global communist movement but merely considered themselves to be nationalists fighting to liberate or recover their own country, American strategy and tactics might have been very different and less costly.

Having established the nature of the threat, the state is then in a position to evaluate counter-measures. Can some acceptable reforms or concessions take the ground away from the insurgent leadership or at least cause internal fractures amongst its members and supporters? Concurrently, is there some non-attributable conduit, either direct or indirect by which to establish contact with the leadership? Are there external backers with whom contact can be established? None of this precludes seeking to hunt down the T/Is, as it is still too early to know whether any form of dialogue may be productive. At some stage, if the insurgency continues long enough, there will emerge the necessity and opportunity for dialogue. The question then is what form should the dialogue take; is a cease-fire likely to be proposed or to be acceptable to both sides? Is the T/I leadership likely to be genuine, or is it a tactic to buy time or respectability? Will the T/Is's leadership be able to deliver even if they are genuine?

For any genuine peace process to develop both sides must be able to demonstrate, even if only covertly, that they are sincere, otherwise any initial concessions will prove counter-productive. There is an old northern English saying, dating from before the Norman Conquest of 1066, that if you pay Danegeld you will never be rid of the Dane! Whatever deal the Pakistani government negotiated with the Taliban in the Swat Valley seems to have confirmed the sentiment and if newspaper reports (Nelson 2009) are correct concerning an alleged peace deal between the Afghan government and the Taliban to buy a temporary truce until after the 2009 elections and the freeing of Malawi Dastigir from a sixteen-year sentence on his promise (already broken) not to attack security forces in the Murghab district, it would appear that there has been a similar lack of success there. Such incidents do not invalidate the argument for dialogue but they do illustrate the problems that occur when states make injudicious concessions for the wrong reasons.

The state should also not neglect opportunities to turn individuals away from violence. It is deeply unfashionable to mention psychological warfare operations (PsyOps) but the T/I volunteers and even relatively highly placed members of the organization are only human; they can tire of the struggle, come under family pressure to leave or become disillusioned with the leadership and thus become susceptible to offers of resettlement and rehabilitation. Leonard Weinberg (2008, p. 164), quoting Cynthia Irvin (1999), speaks of T/I groups having three types of members:

> Ideologues are often the 'hard' men and women of militant ... organisations. They are drawn to action more than to political discussion, and they are committed to the belief that organisational goals can only be obtained as a result of the armed struggle of their military wings. Radicals share the ideologues' commitment to action but sense that violence alone will not be sufficient to achieve the group's goals. They support the use of terrorist violence as a tactic not as a means of personal catharsis. Politicos are far more willing than their more 'militarist' counterparts to acknowledge that acts of political violence, particularly those in which noncombatants are killed, invite both crippling repression and the organisation's alienation from all but the core base.

Sound though the above categories are, the ordinary foot soldiers of the group may not fit any of them. The rank and file may believe in the aims of the organization in a general sense, or be motivated by personal experience, and they may initially believe in the violence or even be drawn by it but their commitment is neither enduring nor unshakeable. Pay, food and quality of life may come to be of more concern than the high-flown aims of their leaders. In such circumstances a clever and well researched PsyOps campaign, accompanied by an offer of some form of amnesty, may well severely damage the insurgent movement and bring in disillusioned members whose debriefing may yield significant intelligence with which to guide further negotiations.

Final thoughts

States may also be subconscious victims of their own inability to distinguish between terrorist and insurgent. When referring to counter-insurgency very infrequently do they give it its correct and full title of 'counter-insurgency warfare', as if shying away from the full term and thus placing it more acceptably in the peacekeeping category; paradoxically, we have a 'war on terror' when it would be more sensible to demote the terrorist to a more criminal status. In warfare, dialogue with the enemy is acceptable, even desirable at certain times. For example, dire though the Taliban may be, they are not al-Qaeda and see themselves as warrior combatants; when the conditions are right negotiation may yield some form of mutually acceptable accommodation.

States do have dialogue with T/Is and it is sensible that they do so, provided that it remains firmly within the overall strategy and unrealistic and naive expectations are not pursued or declared. More difficult for Western democracies and their media to accept is the fact that states are often correct in denying such dealings: what interests the public is not necessarily in the public interest.

Finally, there is one occasion – still in the future – when even the most determined and obdurate state will have to consider negotiation with both the 'pure' or absolute terrorist and the insurgent. The day, long dreaded, will come when some group acquires usable weapons of mass destruction and has the capability and will to use them. On that day negotiation may well be the only alternative. It would be irresponsible not to plan for it now.

Part II
Practical/tactical
Freeing the hostages

The three cases and associated commentary add depth to the preceding operational and conceptual chapters. Terrorists have their patterns of behavior and prove to be skilled at the practice. They drive a hard bargain; it is up to the state negotiators to drive hard too, forcing both to look for possible meeting points. Sometimes these lie outside the normal political expectations, as in Lebanon and Pakistan; sometimes they are not sought, as in Russia. They are generally present for the searching, but only when the parties come to feel that they are better off with an agreement than without.

Hostage negotiations with terrorists go well beyond the police and hostage-taker exchanges that usually come to mind when it becomes a matter of negotiating with hostages taken by a political terrorist organization. The ramifications reach deep into the organization and its allies, and also into the various agencies of the negotiating state. The extraordinary story of hostages taken in Lebanon, analyzed by Karen Feste of the University of Denver, shows the power that outlaw terrorists have over a major state in international relations, and the complicated length to which negotiations for their release need to go. More than a few individuals were held hostage: the victims were the entire US foreign relations system. But the hostage-takers were also hostages, of each other, of US counter-measures, and eventually of world public opinion. Negotiation was carried out at many levels, some of them exceeding the legal limits, but in the end rational, reciprocal behavior was exhibited by the terrorists

Based on decades of experience, negotiation manuals for hostage-taking have been put together by diverse authorities to create the conditions for a possible negotiation and ultimately to resolve the crisis by negotiating with the terrorists. On their side, terrorists also benefit from this type of manual to build up their strategy as well as inputs such as al-Qaeda's online manual, which provides instructions for carrying out barricade hostage operations. Adam Dolnik (Institute of Defence and Strategic Studies, Singapore) takes one of the most dramatic cases in recent history, Beslan, in order to analyze it in the light of existing manuals. The issue of the "negotiability" of the incident is studied and the relevance of authorities' strategy assessed. Again, made hostage by their own tactics and by the refusal of the Russian authorities to bargain with them, the hostage-takers perished along with many of their victims in their own hostage situation. None of the operational insights of seasoned negotiators was employed.

Most of the incidents comprising hostage-taking reveal on the terrorist side two different agendas: one visible and expressed through concrete demands; another invisible referring to much broader issues and goals. The visible agenda concerns the whereabouts of the hostage-taking, whereas the invisible agenda refers to the causes at the origin of the overall struggle. For the authorities, the point is then to manage complexity as both agendas combine and intertwine. Thus, when the negotiators' action is meant to reduce the possible damages of the hostage-taking, its consequences must be thought of in a conflict resolution perspective. It is at the analysis of this strategic duality that Victor Kremenyuk, Russian Academy of Sciences, invites the readers.

Among the various types of hostage-taking, nationalist separatists are probably the most difficult counterpart, if taking into account their resoluteness and spirit of sacrifice. Religious fundamentalists are no less committed on these two dimensions, which then are so heightened by a vision of the world and a reference system that are so peculiar that they make communication extremely uneasy. When these two profiles combine in the same group, one may confront one of the most dangerous situations that can be imagined. This is precisely the case of the Kandahar hostage crisis studied by P. Sahadevan from the Jawaharlal Nehru University, New Delhi.

4 Terrorist negotiation strategy in Lebanon

Karen A. Feste

The history of anti-American terrorism in Lebanon in the mid-1980s is sad and shameful. Following in the wake of the dramatic Tehran hostage-taking incident that marred Jimmy Carter's presidential term, it was shaped by two events in the 1980s with diffusion effects that led to a spiral of declining respect for US power in the Middle East, marking a legacy that has carried forth into the twenty-first century. First came the massive suicide bombing against US Marine barracks in Beirut in October 1983. Alleged to be the largest non-nuclear blast ever detonated until that time, the attack killed 241 soldiers (Hammel 1985, p. 303). President Ronald Reagan, in response to the tragedy, decided to withdraw all of the approximately 3,000 remaining troops a few months later; the last soldier left on March 31, 1984. The second incident involved an illegal (and, most thought, unethical) negotiated solution to free abducted American citizens who were being held captive in Beirut by local terrorist groups: the arms-for-hostages exchange. What eventually became known as the Iran–Contra affair produced high-level political scandal when the secret agreement surfaced in November, 1986.

True to form, terrorism struck the innocent. Fear and frustration followed. Attacks and abductions affected those who had believed a ring of security surrounding their immediate environment would protect them from the violence of Lebanon. The soldiers had been deployed as neutral peacekeepers, not partisan warriors; most were sleeping when the attack hit in the early morning hour on a Sunday. Kidnapped American professionals living in Beirut – nearly all of them academics, writers, or members of the clergy – were grabbed openly in daylight near their home or workplace. Lamenting this sorry state, terrorist expert Bruce Hoffman (1989) noted: "The legacy of one presidency destroyed by its inability to free American diplomats held hostage in Tehran and another tarnished by its futile attempt to trade arms for hostages in Lebanon is a constant reminder of America's failure to loosen terrorism's grip."

How is it possible to loosen the grip? Does it make sense to negotiate with the terrorists? Under what conditions will negotiations succeed? What standards should apply for measuring success? The situation in Lebanon during the final quarter of the twentieth century offers one lens in a laboratory of discovery to help us understand some of the features of modern-day global terrorism and grasp its strategic bargaining complexity. The following analysis, focusing on the grim decade-long American terrorism experience there, is designed to explain why violent acts were directed at US targets and when and how an apparent conflict resolution phase seemed to be achieved as a result of negotiation. One of the important conclusions to emerge from the research suggests that a specific style of negotiating with an enemy who employs terrorism, an interest-based bargaining framework including a fair exchange of goods to produce mutual gains, is an important, perhaps necessary, feature in stopping terrorism. Such agreement will not terminate the full set of conflict issues between antagonists, nor bring about party reconciliation; rather, it remains a stop-gap measure to push aside the use of terrorist tactics and thereby it lessens public fear of randomly generated violence. With resurfaced physical violence in the region in mid-2006, it is unclear whether the temporary halt in attacks was directly linked to a longer-term strategy of struggle and conflict against the West. However, particular evidence, strongly worded verbal assaults directed at the United States by Iranian President Ahmadinejad, and a new fighting phase in the Arab–Israeli dispute initiated by Lebanese Hezbollah, suggests continuity with the past.

Contextual issues

Lebanon's long period of twentieth-century domestic warfare and government instability – from 1975, when civil war began, to the early 1990s – consisted of conventional combat between factional forces and substantial terrorist activity committed by smaller groups of varying allegiance. A number of countries were drawn into the conflict in addition to the United States. Two of Lebanon's neighbors engaged in the fight through direct military intervention: Israel, a US ally, entered the fray in 1978, left, and in 1982, returned with fuller force, remaining almost two decades; and Syria, an ally of Iran, occupier continuously from 1976 (originally invited by Lebanese forces during the civil war), stationed between 30,000 to 40,000 troops in the country until the century's end. Cobban (1999, p. 23) asserts that "of all the shadow contests between these players [Israel and Syria] the confrontation in Lebanon was by far the bloodiest." Iran, an important regional player, provided substantial military training and financial support for Hezbollah, the Islamic Shiite group eager to acquire mass-based power in order to join the country's confessional-based political system. Major Western powers, Britain, Italy, and France (former colonial master of Lebanon) participated in the multinational protection peacekeeping force brought in after the 1982 Israeli invasion. And, between 1982 and 1988, nearly 100 foreign nationals living in Lebanon (among them, British, Italian, French, Russian, German, Swiss, Irish, Italian, Norwegian, and American) were taken hostage and kept in slave-like, tortuous confinement for months, sometimes years, in storage as power levers under operating rules of conflict engagement and bargained exchange.

Kidnapping has deep roots in the Middle East, stemming from desert diplomacy (Alani 2004, p. 5); the objective, then as now, was to apply pressure on the target to meet financial or political demands. Hostages were rarely killed, but it was not unusual to keep them for years. Abduction, kidnapping, and hostage seizure: what are the distinctions between these forms of terrorism? Clutterbuck (1987, p. 4) defines abduction as "forcible and illegal carrying off or detention of a person for any purpose, criminal, political or domestic"; kidnapping refers to abduction of a hostage for the purpose of financial or political gain to an unknown location; hostage seizure means victims are held in a known location, for political concessions. In all cases, terrorism is a tool, a tactic of intimidation directed at one's opponents in order to advance an agenda and achieve a desired end. The anti-American terrorism in Lebanon is best understood as a strategic campaign. Distinguished from a string of isolated attacks, it was an organized, rationally intended effort by one group to demonstrate political power through a central goal: to oust the United States from the region.

The terrorism campaign of hostage-taking was directed, in the main, by Iran. Attacks on American targets in Lebanon expressed the conflict between the United States and Iran. Iran had a grudge against states of the West and sought restitution. The terrorism tactics – bombings, then kidnappings – worked, due in large measure to Iran's particular grievances and the special chaotic situation of Lebanon that allowed them to apply their strategy of violence very creatively to meet intended effects. The American group of hostages abducted in Lebanon consisted of eighteen men; each had been kidnapped separately under different conditions by Iran-sponsored Hezbollah to be held as bargaining chips, swapped as political capital for monetary rewards. Only three, by most accounts, were eventually freed through Iran–Contra negotiated deals. Three others died. Two more escaped. Two were unexpectedly released in April, 1990, apparently, according to public announcement, by the goodwill of their captors. The largest number, following years of incarceration, found freedom with the help of third-party involvement through mediation and negotiation. These men rounded off the barter material in a complex negotiated financial deal concluded at the end of 1991, an agreement crafted from international claims court decisions at The Hague and through the good offices of the UN Secretary General, especially the work of Giandomenico Picco. Various mediators made cameo appearances to move negotiations along – Terry Waite, envoy of the archdiocese of Canterbury, Algerians, and the Swiss – but had little or no impact. None of the kidnappers has ever been arrested and brought to justice (Voss 2004, p. 455); there have been no indictments. Few political issues have distressed Americans more in recent years than the terrorist act of hostage-taking. Although the number of US citizens kidnapped in Lebanon was not large in absolute terms – it pales when set against figures for Iraq (several hundred locals in addition to ample numbers of well publicized abductions of foreigners) or reports for Colombia or Venezuela, where kidnapping is lucrative business – it was the affront to America in the calculated strategy behind the act: the direct assault on common values and principles held by citizens of liberal democracies, and the pressures and threat of lost credibility, that accompanied media exposure of the events. The kidnaps were undertaken for symbolic value, a means of demonstrating the power of terrorists and the impotence of US authorities, in essence, extortion intended to bring about changes in official policy to benefit the terrorist organization and its backers. In weighing alternative responses to these threatening acts, US thinking seemed to run as follows. If the American government did not "do something" in retaliation to punish the terrorists, the public would be outraged. Negotiating a solution might be unwise, for it implied making concessions and that strategy would only demonstrate a sign of weakness. However, in a broader frame, an openly declared stance of "no concessions" might reduce a governments' flexibility and more importantly, would not necessarily ensure safe release of hostages. Faure (2003) has described issues of the continuing debate that surround this problem. Should parties negotiate with kidnappers? Should ransom payments or other political concessions be part of the bargain to secure hostages' freedom? What price concessions?

The act against hostage-taking, defined by international law as:

> Any person who seizes or detains and threatens to kill, to injure, or to continue to detain another person in order to compel a third party, namely a State, an international intergovernmental organization, a natural or juridical person, or a group of person, to do or abstain from doing any acts as an explicit or implicit condition for the release of the hostage

was adopted by International Convention in December, 1979. A decade later, neither Lebanon, Iran, nor Syria had signed it. Since the early 1970s, the United States has publicly espoused a no-negotiations, no-concessions policy in dealing with politically motivated kidnappings (Vetter and Perlstein 1991, p. 141), based on the assumption that terrorists' continued failure to extort ransom will convince them of the futility of their efforts and encourage them to abandon further attempts. "No negotiation" means no direct communication between American authorities and terrorists. The United States has designated the host country responsible for the safety of its diplomats stationed abroad, and expects local governments to negotiate hostage release of kidnapped Americans. Naturally, this is difficult in situations of domestic instability and weak host governments.

When is it in the national interest to negotiate with terrorists rather than refuse to do so? What does it mean to negotiate with terrorists? The word "negotiation" incorporates distinctly different types of processes ranging from distributive bargaining through power-based contests of will to non-adversarial, integrative, interest-based exchange. The process of hostage release negotiations is not usually one of accommodation or conciliation; rather, it is based on force, deception, and even brinkmanship. Yet a focus on interests may be critical in the process of moving complex political hostage-taking situations toward a resolution framework. Both types of negotiation – distributive and integrative – occurred in the Beirut hostage release case.

Does a hard-line policy of "no negotiations" fit in today's times and circumstances? One argument is yes: a "fight fire with fire" policy, adopting counterterrorist measures such as seizing the families and assets of the perpetrators, would probably detract significantly from the glamour and thrill that potential terrorists associate with their daring acts. Cutting off recruitment motivation, if terrorists know beforehand that they have nothing to gain and much to lose, they will never abduct hostages. From another perspective, though, the answer must be no. Circumstances vary from one situation to the next. Who was kidnapped? How many hostages are being held and for what reason? To what extent are the victims' lives at risk? A blanket policy not to negotiate may be an inappropriate, even dangerous guideline to adopt.

Is there a way to have dialog with terrorist groups without necessarily making concessions? Yes. Terrorist groups have what they believe to be legitimate grievances; they want to express their rights, make their case, and get others to listen. No. Terrorists go to the trouble and risk of kidnapping and holding hostages because they want something from the other side; talking to them only legitimizes their acts and leads them to believe violent tactics are an effective way to meet their objectives. Bargaining only invites repeated attacks. Giving in to terrorist demands may change the pattern of violence, but not end the violence.

Terrorists believe their acts of violence constitute the only method of achieving their goals. Targeted, victimized parties find these acts morally abhorrent and totally without value. The relationship between terrorist and targets is one of mutual hate. In considering whether to negotiate or not, the target side has costs and benefits to weigh in this process. What rational choices are best under different conditions? Gongol's (2004) theory suggests the following approach. In advance of any terrorist event occurrence, official policy should be simply "no negotiations ever" with terrorists; after a terrorist event occurs, however, official policy needs to be more complex, keeping in mind one goal: to lower the bargain-chip power of the act. This can be done in several ways: minimizing public attention to the problem (a hard route to follow, in the Media-prominence Age), striking back with brute force (risky, for it often sacrifices individual victims in the process), or responding erratically to terrorists' demands in calculated negotiated moves – either granting them or rejecting them or granting, then immediately reneging on promises to meet them. Victims reap greater benefits by randomly selecting among all the available responses, argues Gongol: the appearance of erratic behavior will disrupt the terrorists' ability to predict victim strategy, and hence reduce their ability to select an appropriate response and to anticipate the value of their bargaining power.

America and Iran had recently sparred over the hostage crisis in Tehran that started when the Shah, the corrupt, wealthy, recently deposed dictator of Iran, was allowed into the United States in October, 1979. A group of Iranians seeking his extradition took more than sixty American officials at the US embassy as potential barter, holding fifty-two of them hostage 444 days. The United States decided to take a non-confrontational, slow-moving approach toward resolving the issue. The proposed exchange did not happen. Never returning to Iran, the Shah left the United States a few months after arriving and died of lymphoma in Cairo in mid-1980. The Algiers Accord of January, 1981, freed the hostages, but did so in a different bartered arrangement: their release was exchanged for Iranian assets under US control that had been originally frozen right after the Embassy barricade.

Roberts Owen, a US government official participating in final negotiations leading to the Algiers Accord, says complex maneuvers by both the US and Iran in their financial dealings – seizure of American properties in Iran and contracts with US companies cancelled, and the executive freeze order on Iranian assets under US control – made it politically impossible for officials of the Iranian government to release hostages without obtaining some commitment from America for a corresponding release of Iran's assets under US control, and simultaneously made it impossible for the United States to release these assets unilaterally, without negotiation, declared "delinkage had become impossible." From the American perspective, release of hostages was the top priority, and were US claimants against Iran abandoned in the context of the hostage crisis it might have been regarded as payment of ransom for their release, a condition the American administration found unacceptable.

Successful negotiation depends not only on communication but also on leverage. "Diplomacy divorced from power is futile. Good faith must be shown in any negotiation; positive incentives have a role as well as negative incentives," states Peter Rodman (1981, p. 10), in his critique of the Carter administration's approach to resolving the Tehran crisis. Two days after the hostages were taken, the United States announced it had ruled out the use of force – no military alert, no movement of troops, no resort to military contingency plans – to avoid hints of provocation, and publicly stated it had virtually no leverage in the situation. America appealed to Iran for its sense of reason, humanitarianism, and compliance with international standards of conduct. Rodman (1981, pp. 15–16) argues that President Carter's strategy showed willingness to compromise in the eagerness to prove goodwill, which to an intransigent opponent made a settlement less likely, stating that "Americans find it congenitally difficult to grasp the possibility that an adversary can be implacably hostile, uninterested in compromise, determined only on doing America harm." By misunderstanding the terrorists' intentions and reacting cautiously, the United States, in relinquishing control over events, prolonged the crisis rather than bringing about a quick and appropriate resolution.

The bitter conflict that developed between the United States and Iran, and the Algiers Accord, in which Iran refused to negotiate directly with the "Great Satan," relying instead on Algerian intercession and mediation, revealed the two countries' widely different views on what constituted terrorism and what would be an appropriate approach to negotiating with an enemy. Neither the negotiation process nor the negotiated end reached in the Algiers Accord was perfectly satisfactory to either side. Loose threads remained, to be settled in the Claims Tribunal established in the agreement and also to resurface in the subsequent hostage-taking and release patterns involving the Beirut abductions.

Terrorism, for the United States, defined in Title 22 of US Code, Section 2656f(d), means "premeditated, politically motivated violence perpetrated against noncombatant targets by subnational groups or clandestine agents, usually intended to influence an audience." By contrast, an Iranian definition (Samii 202, p. 2) states that "terrorism is an act carried out to achieve an inhuman and corrupt objective, and involving threat to security of any kind, and violation of rights acknowledged by religion and mankind." Its meaning does not extend to activities against occupying forces or rejection of dictatorship. The implications are clear: the United States viewed the Iran acts as terrorist; Iran, in turn, viewed the US acts as terrorist; neither saw itself as a perpetrator of terrorism, but rather as a benign participant in the struggle of honorable rights. Thus, each side had asked the question: whether or not to negotiate with terrorists.

Regarding negotiation, cultural differences between the United States and Iran in the manner of dealing with conflict and dissent had a major impact in their process of interchange and reaching agreement. The American approach in foreign policy practice is based on tenets of Alternative Dispute Resolution (ADR), Beeman (2005, p. 5) argues, which comes from the notion that disharmony is seen as something that needs to be controlled, and even in cases of injustice coercive harmony can be used to stifle dissent. The United States considers flexibility to be appropriate to resolve differences. By contrast, Iranians are adverse to compromise, seeing it as weakness and loss of honor; compromise with evil is impossible, even blasphemous. Parties can be estranged for years until third-party mediation brings conflict resolution. UN negotiator Picco (1999, pp. 71, 286) experienced negative effects from both sides in his mediation efforts. Iranian reluctance to change position and even willingness to revisit what seemed to be settled ground compounded difficulties in forming an agreement. He had a bad encounter with US "flexibility" when told, in 1992, a few months after the last American hostage was freed, that there would no longer be any "goodwill to beget goodwill," a complete reversal from America's position in 1989. The magic phrase, key to his negotiation work, had disappeared. Describing the risks of international mediation, Hampson (2006) highlights these issues and others.

Violence in Lebanon

The first civil war in Lebanon in 1958 developed out of a government crisis in the delicate factional political situation that escalated into street violence. In July, the United States intervened, sending 14,000 army troops and Marines, not only to shore up pro-Western Arab regimes in the region but in response to the military *coup* that had just overcome the British-protected monarchy in Iraq. In Jonathan Randal's (1983, p. 161) opinion, "Iraq meant oil, and the United States feared the Iraqi revolution would spread throughout the Arab world, thereby threatening Western oil interests everywhere in the region. Lebanon was a sideshow in American eyes." The US military presence froze the fighting; by the end of the summer, things looked stable. The last units left in October. In the Marine Corps report, Shulimson (1958) states that, over three months of occupation, just four solders died, three of them in accidents. Analyzing the situation afterwards, two contradictory views emerged. One was of "dumb relief that the United States had been able to extricate itself so painlessly from a mess," and the other was that by sending in Marines the United States had blocked the natural and inevitable development of a revolution within Lebanon (Randal 1983, p. 162). In the following years, the American embassy in Beirut, largely reflecting the absence of any concerted policy toward the country, became a backwater. After the Arab–Israeli 1967 war, though, it took on regional responsibilities when major Arab countries broke diplomatic relations with Washington. Lebanon had decided not to follow suit. American interest in Lebanon focused on the Palestinians who lived there, particularly their use of terrorism in aircraft hi-jackings and attacks on Israeli citizens. The United States developed an important intelligence network from its Beirut post, a factor not insignificant to understand the age of the 1980s with the unfolding anti-American terrorist campaign and the negotiated arms-for-hostage response to it.

The second civil war in Lebanon started in 1975. Active fighting led to political realignments. The central government disintegrated, allowing private militias to multiply. By the end of 1981, more than forty armed factions existed. The Lebanese conflict empowered local Shia Muslims, heretofore an insignificant factor in national politics. In 1982, Iran, newly reborn as the first Islamic fundamentalist state, had sent approximately 650 Revolutionary Guards (Pasdaran) to assist them, setting up headquarters in the Syrian-controlled Bekaa Valley where they formed a camp in guerrilla tactics. Several Shia groups received training there: Hezbollah, Jundallah, Husayn Suicide Commandos, the Dawah, Islamic Jihad (Collelo 1989, p. 209). Members of these groups at first were presumed to be acting independently but, as we now know, were under the dictates of the government of Iran; they became central to the terrorist campaign against America, carrying out the massive suicide bombing attack against the US Marines and grabbing US citizens on the streets of Beirut, taking them hostage, and holding them for years.

Israel decided to launch a major invasion in early June 1982, sending troops into Lebanon to fight Palestinian forces. The intervention transformed the country's civil war to an international one: the long-running Arab–Israeli conflict was officially added to the complex dimensions of the Lebanese dispute. By mid-month, the Palestine Liberation Organization (PLO) fighters were trapped in Beirut, held under siege for ten weeks. Finally, through the efforts of an American special negotiator, Philip Habib, who brokered an agreement to separate the parties peacefully and to reduce the chances of a wider war, the PLO departed from Lebanon under the watchful eye of a Multinational Peacekeeping Force composed of US, Italian, and French troops. The exodus of around 10,000 Palestinians occurred without incident and ended September 1 (Collelo 1989, p. 205). About a week later, the 800 American Marines and their Western force compatriots left too, their job finished. Afterwards, serious violent activity resumed. Within days, the recently elected Lebanese President, Bashir Gemayyil, was assassinated by a Syrian agent; Lebanese Christian militiamen, with the permission of Israeli troops, entered two refugee camps searching for PLO forces left behind, massacred nearly 800 Palestinian men, women, and children.

The Multinational Force was invited by the Lebanese government to return. This time, their task was to help bring stability to the country by restoring the authority of the central government over Beirut, and separating the remaining Israeli troops from the people of Lebanon. The key to success would be peacekeeper neutrality. US Marines came ashore again on September 29, 1982. Their fate on this third visit would differ sharply from previous experience. The Lebanese government had assured Habib in writing that various factions would refrain from hostilities against the Marines (Collelo 1989, p. 207), but within six months Shia militant groups had launched their anti-American terrorist campaign. From their perspective, the US presence merely represented another foreign invader. Shiis had suffered heavy casualties since the 1975 conflict started. Now, the Americans, ally of Israel, had entered the picture with a military show of force. The first big hit, the American embassy in Beirut, resulted in a mass explosion in April 1983. Sixty-three people died, including a half-dozen CIA agents, among them the agency's national intelligence officer for the Near East (Baer 2002, p. 67).

The US Congress, in September 1983, sanctioned a continued American military presence in the country for an eighteen-month period and promised defense assistance and economic aid (Schiff and Ya'ari 1984, p. 293). An additional 2,000 Marines were dispatched and deployed in Beirut. Harwood (2003) claims a secret National Command Authority Order issued on September 11 allowed the United States to engage in offensive acts of war in direct military operations and also in support of another belligerent. They engaged firepower in direct support of Lebanese Army forces in the mountains east of Beirut on September 19, 1983, signaling a shift in American policy. Following this action, hostile acts against the US Multinational Force increased and the Marines began taking significantly more casualties, leading up to the large-scale suicide bombing attack on their sleeping quarters in October 1983, when 241 died. The Defense Department Commission report (1983, p. 42) investigating the suicide attack, stated that the US Multinational Force "in the eyes of the factional militias, had become pro-Israel, pro-Phalange, and anti-Muslim," concluding that while a direct cause and effect linkage between Marines' actions in September and the terrorist bombing on October 23 could not be determined, the prevalent view within the US chain of command was that some linkage between the two events existed.

Alongside unrest in Lebanon, the emergence of Iran's Shia-based Islamic Republic, through the revolution and realignments in 1979–1980, caused concern among regional states. Iraq, a secular-run, Sunni-ruled, Muslim autocratic neighbor, decided to launch an invasion into the country in September 1980, carefully picking a low point in expected combat response from the superior, but now disarrayed, Iranian forces, which until that time were heavily supported by a huge arsenal of sophisticated American weaponry. Both Saudi Arabia and Kuwait, viewing Iran's situation as threatening to their monarchical regimes, signed a secret agreement to raise oil outputs and contribute sales revenues to Iraq's war effort. Iran launched air raids on Kuwait borders for alleged involvement in the Iraqi military effort (Hiro 1991, p. 77). In December 1983, bomb explosions in Kuwait at the US and French embassies, the airport, and the compound of an American residential complex led to complications in the context of the Lebanese conflict. A Hezbollah terrorist team on behalf of Iran had carried out the attacks; several were caught and taken prisoner, including the brother-in-law of Imad Mughniyah, the chief Hezbollah leader in Lebanon. Later known as the "Kuwait seventeen," their release became a consistent demand of kidnappers of Western hostages in Lebanon. The government of Kuwait refused, however, to free them. (They somehow managed to escape during the 1990–1991 Gulf crisis. This issue was essentially an aside in the central negotiations in the Iran–US conflict, as were later demands to release Israeli-held Muslim prisoners.) The Iran–Iraq war continued for eight years, exacting a toll of up to one million people.

Lebanon throughout the 1980s was in anarchy, "an epicenter of terrorist activity" (Collelo 1989, p. 226). Assassinations, car bombings and suicide bombings were frequent, heralding the future in global terrorism activities. The spate of attacks carried out in 1983 and 1984 (in addition to the American embassy and Marine barracks, other targets included the French military base, the Israeli Defense Force headquarters, and the new US embassy building used to replace the one destroyed earlier) was an impressive demonstration of terrorist "power of the weak" force. As the frequency of suicide attacks increased, their impact waned, argues Collelo (1989, p. 228), who says Lebanese groups abandoned the tactic to concentrate on a more effective technique: hostage-taking.

Anti-American terrorist incidents in Lebanon and those related to Iranian policy are listed in Table 4.1. As O'Leary (2006) points out, terrorism threat assessment should be based on the number of attacks rather than the number of victims harmed in individual acts of violence, since attacks provide real evidence of a campaign strategy. A terrorist organization plans the number and frequency of incidents, rather than casualty levels that cannot predict in advance the degree of suffering.

The kidnapping of William Buckley, US CIA station chief in Beirut, in March 1984 was one of the most significant events to occur. Eager that Buckley would not be tortured to release state secrets, three weeks later President Reagan signed National Security Decision Directive 138 outlining plans to get the American hostages from Iran (Cockburn 1987). Once Buckley had been taken hostage, the CIA devoted considerable energy and resources to get him released, including repositioning a military satellite over West Beirut normally stationed over the Soviet Union, telephone monitoring of the Iranian embassies in Beirut and Damascus, interception of Syrian communications, making plans for a rescue mission, and attempting to infiltrate Hezbollah (Hewitt 1991, pp. 98–99). Nothing worked. It was US frustration, perhaps, that led decision-makers to participate in negotiations with Iran in the arms-for-hostages trade. Buckley was tortured in an attempt by his captors to access US intelligence information. He died about fourteen months after being taken prisoner – an unfortunate situation for his captors, who had sacrificed a bargaining chip and were chastised for allowing it to happen (Sutherland 1996, pp. 137–138; Anderson 1999; Baer 2002, pp. 79–92, 100). Delaying public announcement of his demise for three months, Hezbollah kidnappers claimed he was killed in retaliation for an Israeli PLO bombing incident.

Imad Mughniya, the Hezbollah leader responsible for most kidnappings, embarked on a reign of terror in Lebanon and by 1987 had racked up numerous violent acts against persons and property. The kidnappings, assaults, and hijackings were announced by organizations with different names. Some proclaimed in the name of Islamic Jihad, others included the Revolutionary Justice Organization, Organization for the Oppressed on Earth – as many as eight overall. But in truth there was only one group responsible, the Hezbollah operational wing. The aliases were intended either to suggest widespread opposition to the West or to disguise the identities of the guilty parties (Jacobsen 1993, pp. 249–250; Ranstorp 1997, p. 64). Although some abductions of foreigners were initiated in alignment with individual interests of certain Hezbollah clans, all acts of hostage-taking coincided with the collective interest of the organization as a whole.

Negotiation history

American power and stature in the Middle East were falling, in part due to these terrorist incidents. The Soviet Union, however, was not plagued by these problems, having overcome Lebanese terrorism after just a single incident. To be sure, their resolution approach sharply differed from the American style. Three of four minor Soviet diplomats kidnapped in Beirut September 30, 1985, were released after only one month in captivity. (The fourth was murdered shortly after being abducted.) The speedy release came about in the following way. First, the KGB allegedly reacted to the terrorist event by kidnapping in turn a relative of a high-ranking Hezbollah official and after killing him, they mutilated his body and sent the package to his family with a warning. "Moscow spoke the language of the terrorists" (Shoumikhin 2004, p. 5). Second, the Soviet Union officially stated it would hold responsible not just the terrorists, but also anyone "who could have stopped the criminal action but did not do everything possible to this effect," for this was an "evil deed for which there can be no forgiveness" (quoted in Zakaria 1989). Syrian, Palestinian, and Shiite militias helped round up at least seventy-five individuals for interrogation. The Syrian chief of military intelligence came to Beirut to manage the search. On October 30, 1985, the hostages were freed. To their enemies, America appeared weak and impotent (Boot 2003) while the Soviet Union seemed strong.

In the mind of American leaders were questions of how to regain US foreign policy stature in the Middle East. This meant freeing Beirut hostages, a problem, they decided, that had to be considered in a broader light linked to US–Iran relations. Iran, engaged in a tough struggling war with neighboring Iraq, badly wanted additional military weapons to continue fighting. The price of reestablishing cooperation would be tied to joint needs between the parties. Signal and back-channel communications led them to begin arranging an exchange: US citizens held in Beirut would be released, said Iran, if America could arrange the sale of armaments – currently prohibited by US law – to Iran. Origins of the entire scheme trace back to late 1984 (Tower Commission 1987, pp. 23–25). The

Table 4.1 Anti-American terrorist events of Iran–Lebanon linkage, November 1979–November 1991[a]

Date	Type of event	Nature of incident
1979		
November 4	Hostage barricade	Sixty-six US citizens at American embassy in Iran taken hostage, fifty-two held 444 days, released January 20, 1981, in exchange for US arms and financial assets returned to Iran
1982		
July 19	Kidnapping	US citizen David Dodge, Acting President, American University of Beirut, taken hostage, imprisoned in Iran
1983		
March 16	Attack	Raid on US Marines (by hand grenade) in Beirut, five wounded
April 18	Bombing	US embassy in Beirut, sixty-three killed, 120 wounded
October 12	Suicide bombing	US Marine Corp barracks in Beirut, 241 killed, 146 wounded
December 12	Bombing	Bombing of US embassy and American Residential compound in Kuwait (plus French embassy, airport and other targets), six killed, eighty wounded
1984		
January 18	Assassination	US citizen Malcolm Kerr, President of American University of Beirut
February 10	Kidnapping	US citizen Frank Regier, Chair, Electrical Engineering Department, American University of Beirut, taken hostage, imprisoned in Lebanon
March 7	Kidnapping	US citizen Jeremy Levin, CNN reporter, taken hostage, imprisoned in Lebanon
March 16	Kidnapping	US citizen William Buckley, CIA station chief, US embassy, Beirut, taken hostage, imprisoned in Lebanon
May 8	Kidnapping	US citizen Benjamin Weir, clergyman in Beirut, taken hostage, imprisoned in Lebanon
September 20	Suicide bombing	US embassy annex outside Beirut, twenty-four killed, twenty-one wounded
December 3	Kidnapping	US citizen Peter Kilburn, Librarian, American University of Beirut, taken hostage, imprisoned in Lebanon
December 3	Hi-jack	Kuwait Airways flight 221 en route from Kuwait to Pakistan, 162 aboard, including six Americans, two killed (USAid workers)
1985		
January 5	Kidnapping	US citizen Lawrence Martin Jenco, clergyman in Beirut, taken hostage, imprisoned in Lebanon
March 16	Kidnapping	US citizen Terry Anderson, Associated Press reporter stationed in Beirut, taken hostage, imprisoned in Lebanon
May 28	Kidnapping	US citizen David Jacobsen, hospital administrator, American University of Beirut, taken hostage, imprisoned in Lebanon

June 9	Kidnapping	US citizen Thomas Sutherland, Dean of Agriculture School, American University of Beirut, taken hostage, imprisoned in Lebanon
June 14	Hi-jack	TWA flight en route from Rome to Athens, eight crew members and 145 passengers, thirty-two Americans held for seventeen days, one killed (US Navy)[b]
1986		
September 9	Kidnapping	US citizen Frank Reed, Principal, Lebanon International School in Beirut, taken hostage, imprisoned in Lebanon
September 12	Kidnapping	US citizen Joseph Ciccipio, Comptroller, American University of Beirut, taken hostage, imprisoned in Lebanon
October 21	Kidnapping	Kidnapping. US citizen Edward Tracy, salesman and writer in Beirut, taken hostage, imprisoned in Lebanon
1987		
January 24	Kidnapping	US citizen Alann Steen, Professor of Journalism, Beirut University College, taken hostage, imprisoned in Lebanon
January 24	Kidnapping	US citizen Robert Polhill, Professor of Business, Beirut University College, taken hostage, imprisoned in Lebanon
January 24	Kidnapping	US citizen Jesse Turner, Professor of Mathematics, Beirut University College, taken hostage, imprisoned in Lebanon
June 17	Kidnapping	US citizen Charles Glass, ABC news reporter in Beirut, taken hostage, imprisoned in Lebanon
1988		
February 17	Kidnapping	US citizen Lieutenant Colonel William Higgins (US Marines), US chief of UNTSO
December 12	Bombing	Pan Am flight 103, 270 killed
1989		
March 10	Bombing	Car of wife of captain of USS *Vincennes* in San Diego, CA; she escaped
1991		
November 7	Bombing	American University of Beirut of College Hall and clock tower, the main administration building, symbol of the institution; completely demolished, four wounded, no one killed

Sources: Mark (1992): 13–30; Jacobsen (1993: 23, 96; Sutherland (1996): 356, 424; PBS Frontline (2001): 223–229; Buhite (1995): 223–229; Jewish Virtual Library (www.us-israel.org/jsource/Terrorism/usvictims.html).

Notes:
[a] A US ambassador to Lebanon, Francis Meloy, and embassy economic counsellor, Robert Waring, were kidnapped by a Palestinian faction (PFLP) on June 16, 1976, and killed on their way to meet President-elect Elias Sarkis. The assassinations, though connected with the Lebanese civil war, are not linked to Hizballah or Iran.
[b] Passengers with Jewish names were taken to secret sites in the Shia part of Lebanon and ultimately rescued by a US Delta Force unit (Faure 2003: 478).

"escape" of hostage Jeremy Levine in February 1985 (who one day discovered his chains unshackled, realizing it was a deliberate act by his captors to encourage his leave-taking) constituted evidence that Iran had presented their "bona fides" and wanted a serious deal.

Starting in August 1985, there were six transaction arms sales from the United States to Iran that in total cost around $30 million (a large sum absolutely, but relatively meager when placed alongside 1970s deals made with the Shah); some of these trades were managed through a third party, Israel, that helped camouflage the international transport of money and goods. The United States delivered the first set of 100 TOW man-portable anti-tank missiles in August. A second transaction, 408 TOW missiles, was delivered under the same routing on September 14. A Beirut hostage, Benjamin Weir, was released September 15. The third transaction, eighteen Hawk ground-launched anti-aircraft missiles, was delivered November 25, but due to their obsolescence, Iran cancelled the deal and refused to pay for them. The shipment was returned. No deal, no hostage exchanges. In the fourth sale, 1,000 TOW missiles arrived in Iran on February 17 and 27, 1986. Although a hostage release had been agreed upon, the plan fell through. No hostage was freed (Tower Commission 1987, p. 41). Instead, the Iranians indicated they wanted a high-level dialogue covering issues other than hostages. The US position was to meet provided the hostages were released during or before the talks. (Tower Commission 1987, p. 42). Transaction No. 5 resulted in the replenishment of 508 TOW missiles delivered to Israel on May 16 and May 19. Again, no hostage released followed. A small American delegation led by former US National Security Special Assistant Robert McFarlane, arrived in Tehran on May 25, carrying a planeload of Hawk missile spare parts. McFarland demanded the release of all hostages, and when no releases occurred he and his party departed, but not before the pallet of Hawk spares had been removed from their aircraft by the Iranians. The United States, in turn, ordered the plane carrying the remaining Hawk shipment to turn back in mid-flight when hostages were not released. On June 20, the President decided no further meetings with the Iranians should occur until the hostages were released. A US representative met his Iranian contact in London on July 21, 1986, to discuss promised release of hostages in exchange for the Hawk spares that remained undelivered from the May mission to Tehran. July 26 – less than a week later – a second hostage, Father Lawrence Martin Jenco, was freed. The additional Hawk parts were subsequently delivered to Iran on August 3.

Overall, the disappointing results of the trade from the US perspective – only a few hostages had been freed – pushed the Americans to open a second contact channel with Iran. In autumn 1986 meetings, the United States laid out a proposal for the provision of weapons in exchange for all remaining US hostages. The Iranians presented a six-point counter-proposal that promised the release of one hostage following receipt of additional Hawk parts, making clear they could not secure the release of all the hostages. Iran proposed exchanging 500 TOWs for the release of two hostages. The US side agreed. Subsequently, the President authorized the shipment of 500 TOWs on October 29, which arrived in Iran on

October 30 and 31. David Jacobsen, the third and last Beirut hostage to be freed under this trade and, as it happened, the concluding bargaining chip in the entire arms-for-hostages episode, was released on November 2.

The next day, November 3, 1986, *Al Shiraa* (The Sail), a pro-Syrian Beirut-based magazine, disclosed that America had sold arms to Iran in secret and that a US group of negotiators had visited Tehran earlier in the year to meet Iranian officials. Iranian Premier Hashemi Rafsanjani went public, confirming the visit. After a period of initial denials by US decision-makers, questions of policy and also violations of law came to the surface. The Attorney General ordered an investigation. What led to public disclosure, causing the trade program to disband? At least three stories emerged: one blames the Iranians; one blames the Israelis; the third argument blames the Syrians, who were pressured by the Soviet Union. The Tower Commission (1987, p. 51) and Cave (1994) reported the arms-for-hostage deal was leaked to the press by dissident Islamic Iranian sources to embarrass Rafsanjani for the skimpy payoff they received in the final transaction, the one conducted through the "second channel" of contact; it was lower: $8,000, rather than $10,000 per TOW. The Israeli source story is similar. According to Ben-Menashe (1992) the second opening of Israeli third-party involvement in the US arms exchange, following the first, which begin shortly after Reagan took office in January 1981, carried a different price structure and payoff margin. A third story says the KGB, aware that US–Iran arms sale profits were being sent to support the Nicaraguan contras and countering Soviet-backed Sandinista forces, tipped off the Syrians, who used terrorist coercion threats to force the news magazine editor to print the story (Jacobsen 1993, pp. 239–240).

The entire $30 million in sales – with attendant profits to Iranians, Israelis, and Americans – did not result in any long-term improvement of US–Iran relations. The trade released few Beirut hostages. Eight remained in custody a few more years awaiting their freedom; they were released in piecemeal fashion over a twenty-month period starting in mid-1990, the last one gaining freedom on December 4, 1991. The Iran–Contra affair chided the US administration for violations of law, but its public scrutiny also inhibited further government-based efforts to resolve the hostage crisis. The report of the President's Special Review Board (Tower Commission 1987, p. 1), a three-member appointed panel with John Tower, Edmund Muskie and Brent Scowcroft assigned to investigate the problem, concluded that:

> The secret arms transfers appeared to run directly counter to declared US policies. The United States had announced a policy of neutrality in the six-year Iran–Iraq war and had proclaimed an embargo on arms sales to Iran. It had worked actively to isolate Iran and other regimes known to give aid and comfort to terrorists. It had declared that it would not pay ransom to hostage-takers.

The Reagan administration had publicly adopted a tough line against terrorism, adamantly opposing any concessions to terrorists in exchange for the release of hostages – whether by paying ransom, releasing prisoners, or changing policies – most likely not imagining their future troubles with Iranian-based terrorism. In July 1982, in the midst of intense factional fighting in Lebanon, the United States became aware of evidence suggesting that Iran was supporting terrorist groups, including groups engaged in hostage-taking in Lebanon when David Dodge, acting president of the American University of Beirut, had been kidnapped, and through intelligence sources, discovered imprisoned in Tehran (Baer 2002, p. 74; PBS Frontline 2002). More important, the official report released at the end of 1983 investigating the Marine barracks attack confirmed Iran's complicity in it. On January 20, 1984, US Secretary of State George Schultz added Iran to the list of states sponsoring international terrorism. The sale of arms to countries on the list was prohibited.

Why did the Reagan administration decide to violate its own declared policy, by not only conducting negotiations with terrorists but also engaging in a scheme that appeared to provide ransom to the hostage-takers? The origin of the problem can be traced to the decisions and experiences of the Carter administration that preceded it, reflecting relations largely involving extensive, expensive business deals between the United States and Iran that had developed through the 1970s, culminating in a disastrous end: the US embassy seizure. America froze Iranian assets and broke diplomatic relations, imposed an embargo on all arms shipments to Iran, including arms that had been purchased under the Shah but not yet delivered. The Algiers Accord lifted many of the restrictions on Iran; a substantial portion of funds returned to Iranian control, although a large amount of money, billions of dollars due Iran, was held back for later distribution to be decided through the Claims Court channels.

Growing evidence suggests the Reagan campaign, during the 1980 election period, had secret contacts with the Iranian regime, where a trade plan involving arms-for-hostages had been agreed: hostages would be held until President Reagan's inauguration and arms shipped to Iran soon thereafter (Sick 1991). Waas and Unger (2002) reported that weapons and related supplies worth several billion dollars flowed to Iran each year during the early 1980s. After Iran was placed on the state-sponsored terrorism list, an arms–hostages clandestine deal was again in the works. This time, the focus would be on hostages held in Lebanon.

Who originated the negotiated plan to exchange people for missiles? At one point, General Scowcroft, a Tower Commission panelist, asked Michael Ledeen, a National Security Council staffer: "Do you have any notion how this thing got transformed from a research project into an action program over a very short period of time and who made the transformation?" Ledeen responded: "The Iranians came forward ... these ideas did not come either from the Government of the United States or the Government of Israel or arms merchants" (Tower Commission 1987, p. 127). The US presidential covert action finding of January 17, 1986, specified that the United States would sell TOWs to Iran, but would cease further arms transfers if all the hostages were not released after delivery of the first 1,000 TOWs. Still, the United States continued the program in spite of the policy clause to discontinue it (Tower Commission 1987, p. 41). Oliver North, a member of the National Security Council staff, who emerged as one of the most important driving forces behind the arms-for-hostages initiative, prepared a number of operational plans for achieving the release of all the hostages. Each plan involved a direct link between the release of hostages and the sale of arms.

Given the manner in which the Iran initiative was conceived and conducted, there is no mystery in why it failed, only in why it continued, particularly when promise after promise was broken by the Iranian side, the US Congressional Committee (1987, p. 277) concluded in its investigation report, adding that by the end of the initiative the administration "had yielded to virtually every demand the Iranians ever put on the table." Wanis-St. John (2006) summarizes the perils of back channel negotiations; had his work appeared twenty-five years earlier, perhaps the following might have been avoided. (1) At least four hostages were to be released in September 1985 after 504 TOWS were shipped, but only one was. (2) All of the hostages were to be released after the Hawk missiles were sent, but none was. (3) All of the hostages were to be released when the United States completed the delivery of Hawk parts in 1986, but only one was. (4) Iran was to release one hostage and exert efforts to release another after 500 more TOWS were shipped in October 1986, but only one was, and Iran demanded more weapons before making efforts to release another. Interestingly, in meetings held that month, Iran made it clear they wanted the relationship with the United States to extend beyond its merchant, trading character into broader foreign policy matters. But once the arms-for-hostage trade was made public, and the plan had to be abandoned, they turned to a new avenue for trading commodities, never abandoning their merchant-like approach: the hostages would only get their freedom through an exchange. Negotiating with terrorists was required.

The negotiated terms for Iran grew over the encounter, shifting from encouraging the United States to supply arms to encouraging speed-up to solve outstanding financial issues of Iran–US relations that originated with US decisions implemented to protect the United States and punish Iran, set in motion in November 1979. How much money did America owe Iran? When would payment be forthcoming? The final eight hostages were set free by a series of Iran–US Claims Tribunal awards granted to Iran and coordinated with mediation efforts through the UN Secretary General's office. Interestingly, two hostages, in memoirs of their ordeal, suggest the US–Iran conflict of the 1980s could have been solved earlier if America had simply paid back Iran what it was due. Sutherland (1996, p. 340) described how, in 1991, the still detained hostages viewed the situation after becoming aware of it:

> Our objective conclusion was that impounding all these funds was neither legal nor fair. It had really stung the Iranians as a matter of principle. The United States was deliberately taunting the Iranians for their humiliating actions in taking embassy personnel hostage. The more we thought about all these international shenanigans, the more it resembled grade school politics.

Jacobsen (1993, pp. 291–292), another hostage, argues that the "big bucks involved and the failure after more than eleven years to reach an agreement most definitely affected the status of the hostages.... Restoration of what legitimately belongs to a country could hardly be classified as ransom." Even the US attorney assigned to the tribunal, Abraham Sofaer (1999, p. 193) has commented:

> I once had the privilege of arguing before the entire tribunal a very important case involving the Iranian goods, armaments that were in the United States to which Iran had title. We refused to return those armaments and we refused to pay for them, an extraordinary set of positions for a major nation to take. The fact is we delayed that case as we have successfully delayed every case that the Iranians have tried to push.

When George Bush came to office in January 1989, pressed into the middle of his presidential inaugural address was this statement: "There are Americans who are held against their will in foreign lands, and Americans who are unaccounted for. Assistance can be shown here, and will be long remembered. Good will begets good will. Good faith can be a spiral that endlessly moves on." It was a signal directed at Iran, indicating the United States was prepared to work to resolve the Beirut hostage issue. US tribunal representative Sofaer (1999, pp. 196–197) says negotiating with Iran became a big issue for the administration but the appearance of trading hostages under any conditions became so sensitive he issued a memo saying that "if we negotiate our cases and we settle them, and if they [Iran] feel good about that, and they start releasing hostages, why should we object to that? Are we supposed to say that we will negotiate with you only if you don't release our hostages?" But the United States had been stung: on the domestic front, the Iran–Contra investigation proved embarrassing; internationally, the United States had come up short in its negotiated bargains with Iran – while making good its promises, the Iranians had not always reciprocated and very few hostages had been released. Negotiating with terrorists was sticky.

Through tribunal deliberations, the United States and Iran turned to small claims settlement in November 1989. By May 1990, the United States had agreed to pay $50 million (Sofaer 1999, p. 197). Hostages Reed and Polhill (incidentally, both were married to Arab Muslim women) were released at the end of April 1990. The next year, the United States agreed to pay Iran $278 million in compensation for seized Iranian military equipment at a meeting in February 1991, but the payment was delayed, it was said, by Iran's refusal in several subsequent negotiation rounds (in March, June, the end of July and early October) to accept the US demand that some of the money be used to replenish an Iranian account from which US claims are paid. Finally, on November 29, 1991, Iran notified the United States "fairly abruptly" that it would accept the US position, clearing the way for the award (Oberdorfer 1992). The final six hostages, two each held by three separate groups of Hezbollah (Hoffman 1989), were freed between October and December: the Revolutionary Justice Organization released Tracy on August 12, and Ciccipo on December 2; The Islamic Holy War for the Liberation of Palestine released Turner on October 21 and Steen on December 3. The Islamic Jihad released Sutherland on November 18 and Anderson on December 4. The latter group originally held CIA chief Buckley and also Weir and Jenco (the two clergymen) and Jacobsen (a hospital administrator), released years earlier in the arms-for-hostages exchange.

With respect to UN involvement, Perez de Cuellar, the Secretary General, began in earnest in March 1991 to seek a solution to the hostage issue. Deputy Picco was responsible for the details, including secret meetings with Hezbollah terrorists. Iranians showed great interest, for the Secretary General was responsible for issuing a report on the Iran–Iraq war by December 10 indicating which party had been the aggressor. If Iraq were declared to be so, the Iranians would be due war reparations; if they themselves were guilty, they would have to pay. On December 9, after the release of the last British hostage in Beirut, the United Nations issued a formal finding stating that Iraq was responsible for starting the war. While the United Nations denied these actions were hostage-related, many US officials believed otherwise. In the final composite agreement, by December 1991 all Western hostages were released, the US government had returned around $300 million to Iran and provided compensation to families of victims of the Iranian Airbus shot down by USS *Vincennes* in July 1988; Iran paid up to $2 million to Hezbollah of Lebanon for each of the eight hostages released (Oberdorfer 1992). Since the tribunal started work, about 4,000 cases have been resolved, the overwhelming majority in favor of US claimants (Katzman 2000, p. 5). A press report in 1998 (Opall) said that if the United States were found liable in claims submitted by Iran, America might have to pay at least $10 billion.

Negotiation analysis

The intricate web of US-targeted terrorism events related to the Lebanon setting through the 1982–1992 period is essentially a story of continued conflict dotted with negotiated bargains in the America–Iran relationship. A list of interaction outcomes related to the conflict is one way to infer the negotiated exchanges, since full public recording of the precise process is unavailable. Informally, aspects of the proceedings can be located in Iran–Contra affair testimony, and also in the memoirs of Giandomenico Picco (1999), the UN mediator brokering final details in the hostages' release in 1991.

What were the goals of each party, the United States and Iran, that action signals and talked-out bargaining were designed to achieve? What power pressure tactics did each side use? In essence, the objectives consisted of two sets of opposing positions. First, the United States, as a superpower, wanted continued presence and influence in Middle East politics. By contrast, Iran, a richly endowed rising power of the Middle East Islamic world, wanted the United States to extract itself from Middle East politics and withdraw from the region. Some of the anti-American violent incidents in Lebanon, particularly suicide bombings, are related to these opposing objectives, buttressing Robert Pape's (2005) argument of the strategic logic of suicide terrorism. Second, Iran wanted its money, owed by the United States, returned; the United States, however, was determined to reduce the actual amount due and delay payment through policies and legal maneuvering, in part as punishment for the terrorism against it. Iran-instigated hostage-taking became a leverage instrument at this level, as did US sanction decisions taken against Iran.

Linking the various incidents of anti-American terrorist events (see Table 4.1) with information on US punitive acts against Iran, arrayed in Table 4.2, and data in Table 4.3 showing the fate of American hostages and US assets returned to Iran, in a related chain of activity across the volatile decade, it is possible to see how nested sets of intense two-party bargaining in the complex conflict and allegiances involving America Iran, Syria, Israel, and Lebanese Shia militant groups unfolded, and, perhaps more important, to understand how Iran controlled the timing and flow of negotiated deals that resolved the terrorism campaign. It set the terms.

After gaining freedom in November 1986 as barter in an arms-for-hostages exchange, David Jacobsen began in earnest to think about ways to help his fellow prisoners, offering solutions to the US government. Some time after the end of the Gulf war, in the spring of 1991, he came to believe "that the real reason for the kidnappings was still secret. Something was missing." He began to wonder if the American delay in returning the last of Iranian assets, frozen in the United States since 1979, was the missing link in the puzzle. A highly placed contact with deep Iran–Lebanese connections confirmed his suspicions (Jacobsen 1993, pp. 309–314). He asked the US Department of State to provide a brief accounting of the billions in frozen Iranian assets and their disbursement, noticing a correlation between returned assets and hostage releases. With Iran–US Claims Tribunal award data, from 1984 onward, he tracked the chronological relationship between repayment to Iran and the abduction or release of American hostages. These data with updated corrections augmented by additional pieces of relevant information shown in Table 4.3 account for the fate of most of the eighteen hostages.

Jacobsen's (1993, pp. 315–316) argument about hostage exchange suggests the US government, angry over the Marine barrack attack and American embassy bombings in Beirut in 1983, was not in any hurry to return the Iranian assets called for in the Algiers Accord signed in January 1981. He is curious why no media investigation, in its full analysis of the Iran–Contra affair, had picked up this probable cause behind the kidnappings. In August 1992, he says, the Department of State claimed that all of the accounts with Iran had been closed and money dispersed, yet the dispute continued, since Iran was claiming entitlement to interest on the billions of dollars that had been frozen – a position the United States opposed. Jacobsen concludes that the "interest dispute" could be motivation for more anti-American terrorism.

From Table 4.3 it appears that Jacobsen is partially correct in the hostage–asset exchanges, but other exchanges were occurring too. The types of terrorist

Table 4.2 US punitive acts against Iran, October 1977–July 1988

1977	October 28	Creation of the International Emergency Economics Power Act (IEEPA)	The rapid rise in the price of oil in the 1970s and the extensive deposits of petrodollars by the wealthy nations of OPEC in US banks created concern in the banking community about potential effects of a sudden withdrawal of these funds. This issue had surfaced when lawyers from Iran met with US bank officials to argue that four major loans to Iran in 1977–1978 by Chase Manhattan syndicate banks had been questionably obtained. The Iranian constitution stated, "no state loans at home or abroad may be raised without the knowledge and approval of the National Consultative Assembly." This was violated in the Shah–Chase Manhattan dealings. Still, the banks went through with the loans (Bill 1988: 346–348). The IEEPA act gave the US President the right to declare a national emergency in the case of an unusual and extraordinary threat coming from outside the US that affected the security of the US, and power to stop any withdrawal of foreign assets from the US
1979	February	Department of the Treasury considers freezing Iranian assets held under US control	The alternative came under consideration several weeks after the Shah and his family left Iran in mid-January. The strategy, widely known, had its origins in the 1977 Iran–US bank loan decisions. With the new government in Tehran, it was possible that loans to the Shah could be declared illegal; the government could repudiate them, which would expose Chase Manhattan Bank to legal suits for fiduciary responsibility failure. Freezing Iran's US-held assets would get around this problem
1979	May 2		Foreign Minister Ibrahim Yazdi announces that Iran has requested the US freeze the assets of the Pahlavi Foundation and agree not to allow the Shah, who had taken large amounts of personal wealth out of the country, to enter the US
1979	October 22		The Shah enters the US. The Department of State announces the decision had been made on humanitarian grounds. The Iranian government officially protested this decision on October 26, 30 and 31 and November 1, and raised it directly with National Security Assistant, Zbigniew Brzezinsky at a meeting in Algiers on November 1
1979	November 13	Ban on importing oil from Iran	In response to the hostage crisis of November 4 with the seizure of the US embassy in Tehran along with sixty-six (later reduced to fifty-two) diplomatic personnel who were held hostage

continued

Table 4.2 continued

1979 November 14		Freeze of Iranian governmental assets in American banks and their branches abroad, estimated between $8 billion and $12 billion (forcing Iran to default on its loan interest payments, due November 15) Executive Order 12170, by President Carter, invoked IEEPA for the first time (applied quickly after learning Iran intended to remove all of its deposits from US banks)
1979 December	Ban on exports to Iran, except food, medicine and medical supplies	Iran has paid $300 million for military supplies currently being held in the US – about $50 million non-lethal, no sensitive items: tyres, trucks, routine spares; $100 million of "grey area" equipment; about $150 million of bombs, missiles, sensitive technology and software (Sick 1991: 98–99)
	Ban on new extension of credit to Iran	
	Ban on new service contracts for Iran	
	Ban on sending military equipment to Iran	
1980 April 7	Breaking diplomatic relations with Iran	
	Expulsion of Iranian diplomats	
	Restrictions for Iranians seeking US visas	
	Announcement of a census of all Iranian assets and claims against Iran under US control (a signal that these assets could satisfy US claims if future events made it necessary)	

1980	April 17	Ban on imports from Iran
Discontinuation of remittances to people living in Iran, except for family members
Revocation of operating licences for all non-bank Iranian entities in the US
Ban on travel to Iran
1980	April 24	US aircraft and helicopters land in Iranian desert in the south to rescue the American hostages (mission failed, two aircraft collide, eight soldiers killed)
1981	January 19	Algiers Accord signed

The negotiated outcome of the US–Iran hostages crisis returned fifty-two US hostages held in Tehran in exchange for unfrozen Iranian government assets of $7.955 billion held under US control. Iran must pay $3.67 billion for principal and interest due US bank loans and keep $1.42 billion in escrow as security against payment on disputed claims, with $500 million maintained in the account. The remainder, $2.88 billion, would be paid directly to Iran. An international arbitral tribunal, the Iran–US Claims Tribunal, was established to decide the claims of nationals of either country and counter-claims, including property rights, expropriations. "It will consist of nine members, consisting of one-third appointed from each government, and the group of six shall appoint the remaining third. The tribunal will conduct its business using the arbitration rules of the UN Commission on International Trade Law. All decisions and awards of the tribunal are to be final and binding." The US agreed to revokes trade sanctions, directed against Iran since November 14, 1979. The issue of returning the arms supplies Iran had paid $300 million for was not part of the agreement. (Ten years later, in 1991, the material was still in storage in the US. Iran had not received the goods nor compensation for the $300 million it had spent (Sick 1991: 190, 265). In February 1991 the US agreed to pay Iran $278 million. Iran delayed acceptance of the terms until November 14) |

continued

Table 4.2 continued

1983	December 27	US issues report on Marine bombing investigation, strongly hints Iran complicity	President Reagan in a press conference said "... this terrorism isn't just some fanatical individual who gets an idea and goes out on his own. There is evidence enough – even if you couldn't go into court with it – that it has at least a kind of tacit encouragement from various political groups and even from some states." The Department of Defense commission report suggested Iranian connections to the bombing – "Iran operatives in Lebanon are in the business of killing Americans" – but did not directly accuse Iran of sponsoring the attack. The report noted the official Defense Department definition of terrorism, which was limited to "revolutionary organizations" and excluded government sponsorship. The Long Commission concluded that DOD now "needs to recognize the importance of state-sponsored terrorism and must take appropriate measures to deal with it"
1984	January 19	US declares Iran a state sponsor of terrorism	Based on evidence of Iran's involvement in the bombing of US Marine barracks in Lebanon, Secretary of State George Schulz designates Iran a state sponsor of terrorism. Any country on the list is prohibited from receiving US foreign assistance and credits, including programs of the Export–Import Bank, the Peace Corps, or assistance authorized by the Agricultural Trade and Development Act
1984	September 28	US denies licence applications of exports to Iran, including aircraft, helicopters and related items on national security export control list	
1986	August 27	US Arms Export Control Act prohibits sending military arms to countries on the state-sponsored terrorism list	Department of Defense also ordered to deny contracts of $100,000 or more to firms that were owned or controlled by Iran, and tax credits were denied to US businesses paying taxes to Terrorism List countries
1987	October 29	Ban on imported Iranian goods and services	In retaliation for Iranian attacks – mining, small-boat assaults – on US-flagged tankers in the Persian Gulf, Iranian exports to the US drop from $1.6 billion to zero in 1987
1988	July 3	Shooting down of Iran Air (Airbus) flight 655 by USS Vincennes, a cruiser stationed in the Persian Gulf, 290 killed	

Sources: "US–Iran Relations," *passim*; Bill (1988): 343–348; Carswell and Davis (1985): 175–234; Sick (1991): 98–99, 190, 265; Department of State www.state/gov/s/ct/14151; Katzman (2000): 6–8; Institute of International Economics (www.iie.com/research/topics/sanctions/iran); Fayazmanesh (2003): 222; *New York Times, passim*.

messages and negotiated bargains in the US–Iranian conflict, largely played in the Lebanon theatre, can be identified using additional information from Tables 4.1 and 4.2. Iran followed two strategies. First, *fatality-driven non-bargain-chip* terrorist acts: several dramatic acts of terrorist violence were directed against symbolic targets – the US embassy bombings, Marine barrack attack, and assassination of the AUB President, committed between April 1983 and January 1984; and the *quid pro quo* violent reaction to the Iran Airbus shot-down in July 1988 that killed 290 travelers: the contract-for-hire Pan-Am 103 in-flight bomb explosion six months later, in which 270 people died. Second, *non-fatality-driven bargain-chip* terrorist acts: the common pattern of hostage-for-goods exchange – both military armaments (the Iran–Contra 1985–1986 deals) and owed assets from US accounts (1989–1991 settlements) fall into this category – explains thirteen of the eighteen US kidnap incidents, and Libya's $3 million purchase of an American hostage (and two British compatriots) adds a fourteenth case to this category. The remaining cases – there are two – no doubt involved a negotiated bargain, but do not show direct links to particular ending points marked here: Dodge was freed by his Iranian captors in July 1983 one year after being abducted, once it was clear the United States was not linked to the kidnapping of four Iranian diplomats on the highway in Lebanon in 1982, and only after US intelligence had discovered his whereabouts in Iran and appealed to Syria to intervene to free him. What did Iran or Syria gain in this process? Glass, kidnapped along with the son of the Lebanese Defense Minister, was free after two months (his Lebanese traveling partners were kept just a week), apparently again with Syrian assistance. The abduction may have been related to internal Lebanese politics, disconnected from the US–Iran conflict. Two hostages, Buckley and Higgins, were eliminated in the exchange proceedings, lost as bargaining chips when they died. (Although their captors claim they had been executed, evidence indicates that Buckley most likely died from torture injuries, while Higgins was probably inadvertently asphyxiated during car trunk transport (Jacobsen 1993, p. 179). Bodies of all three dead hostages were released in the final 1991 UN-brokered deal. Although Kilburn had been shot by a Libyan purchase-for-murder, the other two autopsied bodies show no signs of alleged execution.)

Why did Iran shift tactics in its anti-American campaign? Early terrorism against US targets in Lebanon applied to meet particular objectives consisted of a strategy to kill people, hence the use of explosives, including suicide bombing attacks, and assassination. Pape (2005) argues that suicide terrorist bombing campaigns against foreign occupiers are strategically geared to create massive fear and force the occupier to physically withdraw. Although his analysis is limited to suicide attacks and campaigns, the logic fits Iran's strategy. Iran wanted the Americans out of the Middle East – this was the first principle of the Algiers Accord – and that meant out of Lebanon, a necessary first step before it could begin to address the asset return problem with the United States. Forcing the Americans to withdraw their military presence, and scale back their diplomatic mission, would help level the playing field between the two sides, putting them on a more equal footing.

Table 4.3 The fate of American hostages and US assets returned to Iran, 1984–1992

Date	Hostage fate	Assets flow to Iran
1984		
January 18	Malcolm Kerr assassinated	
January 25		$218,666.31+ interest returned
February 10	Frank Regier kidnapped	
March 7	Jeremy Levin kidnapped	
March 16	William Buckley kidnapped	
April 15	Frank Regier freed	
May 8	Benjamin Weir kidnapped	
June 8		$7,933,951.31 returned
December 3	Peter Kilburn kidnapped[a]	
1985		
January 8	Martin Jenco kidnapped	
February 14	Jeremy Levin freed	
March 16	Terry Anderson kidnapped	
May 28	David Jacobsen kidnapped	
June 9	Thomas Sutherland kidnapped	
August 30		100 TOW missile shipment
September 14		408 TOW missile shipment
September 15	Benjamin Weir freed	
1986		
February 17		1,000 TOW missile shipment
May 25		508 TOW + Hawk parts shipment
July 26	Martin Jenco freed	
September 9	Frank Reed kidnapped	
September 12	Joe Cicippio kidnapped	
October 21	Edward Tracy kidnapped	
October 30		500 TOW missile shipment
November 2	David Jacobsen freed	

1987		
January 24	Robert Polhill kidnapped	
January 24	Alann Steen kidnapped	
January 24	Jesse Turner kidnapped	
May 4		$63,000,000 returned
May n.d.		$454,000,000 returned
November 30		$140,060.17 returned
1988		
February 17	William Higgins kidnapped	
April		$37,900,000 returned
May 18		$325,000 returned
July 3	US shoots fown Iran Air flight 655; 290 dead[b]	
December 21	Pan Am 103 bombing, 270 dead	
December 23	Iran pays $10,000,000 for Pan Am bombing (PFLP carried out the job)	
1989		
May 25		$28,500 returned
November 7		$567,000,000 returned
November 22		$55,999 returned
December 6		$7,800,000 returned
December 8		$400,000 returned
December 19		4,368,750 rials returned
December 26		$3,000,000 returned
1990		
January 24		$125,000 returned
January 29		$700,000 returned
February 21		$96,000 returned
April 22	Robert Polhill freed	
April 30	Frank Reed freed	

continued

Table 4.3 continued

Date	Hostage fate	Assets flow to Iran
1991		
February 14		$278,000,000 award: Iran refuses terms
March 28	Negotiations: Iran refuses US terms	
June 5	Negotiations: Iran refuses US terms	
July 29	Negotiations: Iran refuses US terms	
August 12	Edward Tracy freed	
October 7	Negotiations: Iran refuses US terms	
October 21	Jesse Turner freed	
November 14	Iran declared innocent in Pan-Am bombing[c]	
November 18	Tom Suthnd freed	
November 29		$278,000,000 award: Iran accepts terms[d]
December 2	Joe Cicippio freed	
December 3	Alann Steen freed	
December 4	Terry Anderson freed	
1992		
February 19		$134,128.65 returned

Sources: Antokol and Nudell (1990) 102; Jacobsen (1993); Oberdorfer (1992); Rainwater (1997); Goodenough (1999); Scharf (2001); *New York Times, passim*; *Washington Post*, November 7, 1989.

Notes:

[a] Hostage Kilburn was purchased for execution by Libya three days after the April 14 US air strike against Libya that killed Gaddafi's daughter. Reportedly, Gaddafi approached Hezballah and purchased three hostages (including two British citizens) for a total of $3 million. All three were shot in the back of the head.

[b] Reported in *Developments Concerning the National Emergency with Respect to Iran*, May 16, 1996, the survivors of each victim of the Iran Air shoot-down will be paid $300,000 (for wage-earning victims) or $150,000 (for non-wage-earning victims) under terms decided during the Clinton administration.

[c] Until mid-1990 the US implicated Iran in the 1988 Lockerbie air bombing, accusing Libya of the disaster. Libya did not release the two suspects until 1999. A trial was held in 2000, one of them was declared guilty. By August 2003 a deal had been struck for awards: a $4 million payment to each victim's family once UN sanctions were formally lifted (additional award if the US lifted sanctions and removed Libya from the state-sponsored terrorism list). Libya was taken off the US state-sponsored terrorism list in May 2006.

[d] The payment was delayed after the US had agreed in February by Iran's refusal in four more rounds of negotiations (on dates listed above) to accept the US demand that some of the money be used to replenish an Iranian account from which US claims are made. Iran notified the US "fairly abruptly" that it would accept the US position, according to Edwin Williamson, Department of State legal advisor. The money returned was in payment for military equipment Iran had purchased under the Shah. It is listed in Table 4.2 under December 1979 US actions.

Later, hostage-taking terrorism designed not to kill victims but to enhance terrorists' bargaining power became popular as a way to meet demands. In addition to the Beirut kidnapping sprees, at least two aircraft hi-jackings, in 1984, involving Kuwait, and 1985, involving the United States, fall into this category. The mechanisms of exchange were set in motion: kidnappers usually demand ransom. The Iran regime was not seeking ransom in its pure sense, but payment on US debt. The logic was the same. In May 1984, according to Sutherland (1996, p. 36), who later was taken hostage, officials at the American University of Beirut learned of the new strategy and reported it to faculty members in the following message:

> Hezballah will execute kidnapping operations at American University of Beirut and the US Embassy. The targets will have American identities. Have prepared 100 people for the operation, from which 20 are inside the university...
> Hezballah is watching all movements and are [sic] waiting for Zero hour. The plan is prepared and its execution is soon... First axis is from inside AUB. The second axis is from the Corniche. The third axis is from a civilian building which overlooks the new embassy...

The timing of the plan is important. The last Marine departed Lebanon March 31, 1984. Iran was suffering: placed on the US list of states sponsoring terrorism at the end of January, its trade was interrupted. A lot of its assets were tied up in the United States. The tribunal was handling US claims first. Iran was in the middle of a major war with its neighbor. It was stretched financially and militarily. (The country resorted to child conscription, sending thousands of young boys into battle.) It was ostracized from the international community. The United Nations had taken nearly a week to condemn Iraqi aggression against Iran when war broke out in September 1980, yet Iraq's invasion of Kuwait brought immediate and sharp reaction from the Assembly.

Evidence of a plan of hostage barter that Iran consciously followed can be found in several important messages: the first issued in July 1988, another in October 1989, and a third in March 1990, after the end of the Gulf War (Mark 1992, pp. 19–22; *New York Times*, November 7–8, 1989). The first two statements, both from Iranian Majlis speaker Rafsanjani, said Iran would intercede with the captors holding US hostages in Lebanon if the United States would release Iranian assets frozen during the hostage crisis of 1979–1981. Shortly after the second public message, on November 6, 1989, the United States agreed to return to Iran about half a billion dollars it had held to pay claims of US banks. It was a joint agreement by the United States and Iran within the special claims tribunal, but without independent tribunal involvement. The later statement, planted in *Al-Sharq al-Awsat*, the London-based Arabic-language newspaper, reported that Iran's conditions for assisting in a hostage release were (1) drop Iran from list of terrorist countries, (2) persuade Iraq to withdraw from Iranian territory, and (3) release the frozen Iranian assets in the United States.

From Table 4.3, it is clear that, throughout 1989 and until the end of February 1990 the United States was returning substantial sums of money to Iran, just prior to the March statement. In April 1990, two hostages were sent home (publicly, it was said, by "goodwill," implying the absence of any exchange, which was false).

In February 1991, the United States agreed to a major reimbursement award for Iran: payment for the nearly $300 million worth of military equipment bought more than twelve years earlier, which set the stage for the gradual releasing of the final six hostages. In retrospect, it appears that Iran was holding off this exchange until it was cleared of any involvement in the Pan-Am 103 bombing – a plan that worked out to its liking when the United States and Britain announced on November 14 that Libya was the guilty party (though, by many accounts, the evidence was slim; Iranian and Syrian complicity was far more substantial). Gaddafi waited nine years to hand over the two Libyan nationals for trial, a factor that suggests behind-the-scenes bargaining that may have involved numerous parties, including the United States and Iran. The decision to point at Libya freed Iran from owing the United States any reparation money for its documented act of violence.

In January 1992, it was announced that Iran paid the captors of Western hostages in Lebanon between $1 million and $2 million for each of the ten (six American, three British, one Irish hostages) released since early August 1991, a charge Iran officials deny, accusing Israel, a sore loser who did not get the return of Israeli captives or their remains, of planting the story. The payments, traced by US intelligence to various bank transfers, were in addition to regular financing that Tehran had provided for years to Hezbollah. Two German hostages were not freed, pending negotiations with Germany to release two Lebanese brothers of the Hamadi family in Hezbollah, convicted and imprisoned for shooting the American military officer Robert Stethem during the June 1985 TWA aircraft hi-jacking. They subsequently gained their freedom, and the last held Hamadi prisoner was exchanged in December 2005 for a German hostage abducted in Iraq (Goodenough 2005). As for five French hostages held in Iran, France agreed to pay $1.8 billion to Tehran in 1991; in addition, a $3 million ransom was paid for the release of its citizens, a scandal that emerged in the February 2002 elections (Karoui 2002). Iran, rather than the Lebanese terrorists, was in complete control of all hostage releases, a view shared by Picco, the UN mediator in the process.

The entire set of strategies played by Iran seems to fit Sofaer's (1999, p. 194) assessment about Iranian behavior at the Claims Tribunal: they did not know how to advocate their positions well. "The Iranians feel tremendously disadvantaged in the Tribunal because they don't know how to litigate and they are not willing to pay the money to retain good lawyers to take over the task of handling their litigation." Sofaer's remarks, presented at a conference held at New York University Law School in 1996, were echoed in comments by Thomas Shack (Sofaer 1999, pp. 209–210) stressing that Iran, unlike the United States, was not a nation of lawyers. Rather, they have few personnel trained in Western adjudication or international arbitration processes, and the Revolution removed people familiar with the history of contracts and history of negotiations between the two contending sides. The cultural divide mattered. That added to their difficulties. They were disadvantaged. Perhaps that explains, to some extent, why they chose an alternative negotiation strategy where they might be strong enough to influence outcomes in their favor: a sparing based on terrorism might weaken the other side; fighting based on verbal barbs would intimidate them. It seemed to work. Sandler and Scott's (1987) research on various forms of hostage-taking incidents between 1968 and 1984 found terrorists scored negotiated success in just 27 percent of the incidents; kidnappings were somewhat more likely to reap negotiated rewards. The Iranian outcome is consistent with that result. Donohue and Taylor (2003, p. 542), analyzing skyjacking and barricade seize events, conclude that terrorists who spend time negotiating and indicate concession willingness may secure their demands.

As for the US strategy, it also worked. Most of the hostages were freed. Lucrative weapons sales lined the pockets of arms merchants. Financial repayment to Iran had been delayed, benefiting American banks and business. Tribunal processes brought settlement relief in many cases. UN mediation intercession meant the United States never had to confront Iran direct or to admit America negotiated with terrorists, after the Iran–Contra scandal. The American government was not forced to deal with terrorist thugs – actual kidnappers and hostage holders – or with the terrorist mastermind leadership of the new Islamic Republic of Iran.

If both sides were successful – for the terrorists, achieving some of their real, not stated, objectives, and, for the target side, the liberation of hostages are two important criteria to apply in determining success (Faure 2003, p. 490) – why is it such an ugly story? Terrorism affects the innocent, striking at those who least expect it – noncombatants, the ordinary, and the peacekeepers – creating fear in the process. Fear implies unpredictability and lack of control for targeted parties. For the terrorists, however, the use of violence for extortion appears to be executed with precise strategic expression, which has come to light in this analysis. But the outcomes are not clean. The process resembles a sloppily fought war, that comes with unpalatable negotiated ends. What could be done to stop it?

The US Congress, in a search for various tools to combat international terrorism, passed a law in 1996 that for the first time permitted lawsuits against foreign countries specifically designated as "state sponsors of terrorism." In the fall of 2000, Congress passed legislation to enable certain US citizen victims of terrorism to collect on judgments they had obtained in civil lawsuits. It meant that terrorist acts sponsored by the Islamic Republic of Iran could carry substantial restitution payment to Beirut hostages and members of their immediate families. The amount for compensatory damage for an individual hostage was standardized at $10,000 per day in captivity, and money would be borrowed from the US Treasury as credit against frozen Iranian assets still held in the United States, unless Iran was willing to pay directly (Martinez and Newberger

2002, p. 5). A total of $23.2 million in diplomatic property plus $400 million in a Department of Defense account were remaining Iranian assets held in the United States in 2001 (Katzman 2002, p. 36). Many Beirut hostages sued. The law firm Crowell & Moring, of Washington, DC, has handled a large number of their cases: Anderson, Sutherland, Polhill, Kilburn, Regier, Weir, and Dodge. In 2003, favorable judgments were issued in cases that had been considered. Others are currently pending as of this writing (www.crowell.com/content/Expertise/ VictimsofTerrorism). Moreover, a ruling by US district Judge Royce Lamberth, on May 30, 2003, said the suicide bombing carried out against the Marines in Lebanon in 1983 was sponsored by Iran, giving wounded plaintiffs (and their families) in the case a right to seek compensatory damages. This conclusion supported the Department of Defense commission findings reported twenty years before. It is not clear to what extent actual payment has been made since these rulings, but the policy objective is very clear: from the US–Iran terrorist negotiations, it was evident that money talks. Thus, placing extreme financial burden on the perpetrators will be a way to provide sufficient punishment to deter them from further acts of terrorism. The intended deterrent can only work, however, if the United States has an ample supply of foreign-based assets on which to draw. Blocked assets of other Middle East countries on the US "state-sponsored terrorism" list tallied as follows on January 1, 2001: Iraq, more than $2 billion; Libya, about $1 billion; Sudan, about $33 million; Syria – none (Katzman 2002, p. 36).

Of all the states on that list, there are currently five: Iraq, North Korea and Libya are off, Cuba has been on it for a long time; the only designated "active supporter of terrorism" is Iran, the remaining are categorized as "passive or less active supporters of terrorism" (Perl 2006, p. 4). Iranian sponsorship is attributed to specific institutions, the Revolutionary Guard and the Ministry of Intelligence and Security, not the government of the Islamic Republic as a whole, according to Katzman (2002, p. 30) in a report for Congress. A small contingent of the Revolutionary Guard remains in Lebanon, assisting Hezbollah. The group, along with Iran, was indicted for terrorism against Israel, including bombing the Israeli embassy in Argentina in 1992 and bombing a Jewish community center there in 1994, which resulted in eighty-five deaths. Arrest warrants for four Iranian diplomats was issued by a Argentinean judge in 2003 (Katzman 2006, p. 21). Still classified as a terrorist group by the US government, Hezbollah expanded its efforts into legitimate politics: by 2005 it held fourteen seats in the Lebanese parliament (a 128 member body) and netted a Cabinet post, the Ministry of Energy and Water Resources.

Assessment

The techniques of terrorism witnessed in Lebanon in the 1980s – large-scale suicide bombings against military troops, major attacks on Western embassies, kidnapping – spread to other places in the 1990s and beyond. The diffusion of terrorism originating from Lebanese borders showed its mark in Saudi Arabia and Egypt, Spain and Indonesia, in suicide bombings; Somalia, Rwanda, Congo and Bosnia experienced attacks on foreign peacekeeping forces; and in 1998, the American embassy explosions in Kenya and Tanzania indicate, in retrospect, the launching of al-Qaeda, the singular most feared terrorist organization of the twenty-first century. Suicide bombing, a continuing problem for Israel, was introduced into the Palestinian conflict in the 1990s; 9/11, a spectacular terrorist event using planes, not trucks, for missile effect, is a glaring illustration of terrorist copycat application. Iraq is a nest of kidnappers preying on security holes, hoping to extract financial gain and, often, to influence the political process. These developments are notable, for beyond death and destruction the particular tool of attack tells us the terrorists' goals: bombings (including suicide bombings) and assassinations, are part of a fatality-driven non-bargain-chip repertoire. This approach is not part of a negotiation strategy but has one intended end – getting the intruder to leave. Hostage-taking, hi-jacking, and kidnapping, however, do signal an interest in bargaining and fit the non-fatality driven bargain-chip category. By American experience in Lebanon, destruction should come first, hostage-taking will follow for financial extortion as a further means to achieve power. The risks of terrorism against oil and gas pipelines in Central Asia show a similar profile: bombings of oilfields, offices of national oil companies, and the pipelines, are carried out in conjunction with kidnap episodes (Karmon 2002). In a terrorism campaign, the pattern of violence technique matters; it signals the prospects for negotiation, a process that may save lives but not save face for its targets.

Who will be open to the new techniques of conflict resolution negotiation strategies, targeted victims or terrorists? Terrorists' power and incentives make them rely on hard-bargaining tactics; yielding plays absolutely no role in the process, and interest-based bargaining would have to be initiated from the other side. Lewis (Lake 2003) tells of negotiating with Hezbollah while preparing a report to be aired on PBS Frontline: "[They] were true to their word, and what they said went. When they said no to me, it meant no; when they said yes to me, it meant yes. They don't negotiate, they set the terms." Target negotiating power, however, is such that hard bargaining will not work – it is not an option in the conflict structure. That leaves two strategies: submitting to terrorist demands, and discovering common interests in order to produce something close to a win–win outcome. Straight yielding is usually rejected on moral, as well as policy grounds, at least at the first level. Pursuing the interest-based solution falls entirely to the target – already a weakened player in this game – a rough-road process. Research shows (Donohue and Taylor 2003, p. 530) negotiators who see themselves with fewer options compared to their opponent will try to regain power through competition, often attacking the other side and attempting to force submission. The side with more options has greater latitude to show openness and conciliatory gestures. Both the Iran–Contra affair and restitution resulting from the Claims Tribunal are examples of how these features worked. Three short vignettes of Americans negotiating with Iranians illustrate different approaches. The first example shows the United States in power-dominant position; the second shows both sides feel power depleted, and third shows Iran in top power position.

1. *William Casey, National Republican Campaign chair, 1980, in a clandestine meeting in Europe concerning an exchange of arms-for-Tehran hostages deal.* The meeting opened with a tirade against the United States, its past involvement with the Shah, and actions of the Carter administration. Casey remained perfectly cool, betraying no hint of emotion; he did not respond to the charges. Instead, he presented a lengthy, well informed history of US–Iranian relations under the theme that relations were good under Republicans but deteriorated when Democrats were in power. Iran was in no position to fight the United States and would be better advised to come to terms. Once in power, the Reagan administration would be willing to return financial assets frozen, return Iran's military equipment, and give Iran its strength back. What, he asked, were Iran's intentions about the hostages? Was the Islamic Republic ready to deal with the Republicans? The Iranians promised to release hostages to the Republicans, the Americans promised to release Iran's assets and permit indirect arms shipments to Iran through a third country, Israel. At the end of the meeting an Iran negotiator remarked, "We are opening a new era; I am talking to someone who knows how to do business" (Sick 1991, pp. 84–87).

2. *Robert McFarlane, US National Security Advisor, 1986, in a clandestine meeting in Iran concerning an exchange of arms-for-Lebanon hostages deal.* McFarlane demanded the prior release of all hostages and the Iranians insisted on the immediate delivery of all Hawk spare parts, as conditions for the meetings. The group traveled to Iran without any hostage releases. On arrival, the Iranian official said, "Everything depends on good will and restored confidence. But there are some things that cause doubt. We were told that one-half of the equipment would be brought ... You did not bring it, this behavior raises doubts about what can be accomplished." McFarlane says, "Let's be clear. I have come. There should be an act of good will by Iran. I brought some things along as a special gesture. So far, nothing has happened on your side ..." When no hostages were released, McFarlane and his party departed (but not before the half-delivery of Hawk spares had been removed from their aircraft by the Iranians.) McFarlane forced the plane carrying the other half, in mid-flight, to turn back. He later reported, "The incompetence of the Iranian government to do business requires a rethinking on our part of why there have been so many frustrating failures to deliver on their part" (Tower Commission 1987, pp. 45–46, 300–319).

3. *Abraham Sofaer, US State Department Legal Advisor, 1996, in an open meeting at the Iran–US Claims Tribunal at The Hague concerning financial claims awards.* "These negotiations were very well prepared. They were very systematic. If people have a notion that they were like bazaars, they were in the sense that of course the Iranians always came in and either demanded ten times more than they eventually settled for, or offered ten times less than they eventually paid. But that was routine. You learned how to deal with that kind of negotiating strategy.... We had our troubles with the attacks on the oil tankers, the placement of US flags on third-country tankers in the Gulf, and Iranian attacks on some of our ships. We destroyed half their navy within two days. I would go back to The Hague and expect my counterpart to be very upset about everything,

but he was calm as can be. He said, 'Well, I see you are saying all those terrible things about us again.' And I said, 'Well, obviously we're not saying terrible things about you that aren't true.' And he said, 'Well, of course they're untrue, but let's get to work, let's do our work here'... We are bombing them when they do something wrong, we blow up their ships when they attack us, we are overwhelmingly powerful, they have run away from us on every occasion, why should we be so upset if they are willing to talk to us after we keep winning these encounters?" (Sofaer 1999, pp. 194–195).

The use of hostage-taking has been a common phenomenon in civil wars worldwide since the 1960s, using a common set of demands: to force government regime change or policy change, including territorial secession and liberation of prisoners; or in kidnapping, to squeeze financial rewards through ransom payment. The proximate aim dictates the type of individuals to be targeted, according to Elster (2004, pp. 15–17). Need money? Take someone wealthy who can meet ransom demands. For publicity seekers, take someone famous. To free prisoners, kidnapping a state official or diplomat is most appropriate. To reduce foreign presence and discourage foreign development projects, take expatriates, primarily working professionals (teachers, doctors). Elster (2004, pp. 4–5; see also Dolnik 2003) distinguishes the two terrorist acts by a temporal feature: kidnappers demand that the government act *after* the release of victims or as a condition for their release while hostage-takers demand that the government act or refrain from acting *during* the period of victim detention. The American experience with Iranian-sponsored terrorism in Lebanon suggests that both features were in place. In the arms-for-hostage exchanges, the kidnap definition applies; in the financial dealings in 1990–1991, the hostage definition applies. The terrorists wanted money and also reduced US presence in the Middle East: their kidnap pattern fits Elster's classification.

What appropriate counter-terrorism recommendations follow from the preceding analysis? First, identifying the exact purpose behind the terrorist acts, namely the contextual setting and set of political and financial demands clarifies the nature of the conflict and presumably indicates what type of negotiations may be necessary, and what commodities could be exchanged at what price. Second, recognizing the trade-offs between counter-terrorism measures applied in one domain that may have negative consequences in another. Enders and Sandler (1993) discovered that metal detectors installed in 1973 decreased skyjack terrorism but increased other kinds of hostage-taking incidents, with about a one-for-one trade-off; US embassy fortifications reduced the likelihood of future attacks, but were tied to an increase in assassinations of officials and military personal outside protected compounds. The US retaliatory attack against Libya in 1986 led to the killing of three Beirut hostages. They suggest in a later analysis (Sandler and Enders 2002) that terrorists may be encouraged to shift their strategy into legal protests and other non-violent actions to air grievances if the price of modes of terrorism acts is raised significantly. Ideology may sustain terrorist operatives, but not for long when the well runs dry. This means freezing finances. But American experience in the Lebanon hostage-taking episode seems to show this strategy may have backfired. Third, official government reaction to acts of terrorism committed against it should probably be played down rather than played up. Mueller (2005, p. 18) believes the United States exaggerates and overreacts to threats, a dangerous policy, as the Lebanon hostage crisis demonstrated. When President Reagan personally announced the release of one of the hostages, it demonstrated:

> that the actions of a few scruffy hostage-takers were of such monumental significance, that he, the leader of the world's greatest power, should interrupt his schedule and take it upon himself to announce to the world what they had done for us lately. Hardly a way to discourage terrorism. Rather it's likely to make it even more fashionable, giving the perpetrators prestige and recognition far beyond their objective strength.... To feed their egos and to play to their already inflated self-importance was unwise and undignified.

The public needs to understand that US prestige and magnificence are not at stake whenever an American is kidnapped by a faceless little band of foreign fanatics, says Mueller, who argues that dealing with terrorism can be an issue that is at once "to hot and too unimportant" to handle.

In the end, whether and how to negotiate with terrorists will be determined by mutual perceptions of power, persuasion, and pride, alongside desired outcome. A current dilemma, the West's efforts to disarm Iran of its developing nuclear power, shows how factors of negotiation turn into a complicated calculation. The United States could launch a large-scale pre-emptive conventional strike against Iran. In reaction, Iran, with the help of Hezbollah, a well trained force with a good network, could initiate a large-scale anti-American terrorist campaign in Iraq (Hersh 2006). Yet there is an argument for pursuing diplomacy, though this is likely to occur only after brinkmanship, when both sides may be more willing to adopt a pragmatic approach, taking a lesson from negotiation: governments might push a hard line to call the other's bluff, believing toughness produces concessions, but in the end back away if appropriate incentives are presented. In social exchange, says Baldwin (1998, p. 123) each party offers rewards or punishments to induce the other to behave in a particular way. The exercise of power means the user has to consider the other side's disincentive to comply. The greater the reluctance, the more resources have to be expended by the other side to bring about a change.

A reciprocity response in negotiator action is one strategy for doing so. Kim (2005) summarizes reciprocal strategy advice this way: (1) cooperate irrespective of what the opponent does if mutual cooperation is preferred over any defection; (2) follow reciprocity if mutual cooperation is your best outcome and unrequited cooperation is the worst; or if you believe the opponent prefers mutual cooperation. While this displays a clean theoretical picture, its application will depend on mutual perceptions that may lead in opposite directions, either conflict escalation or its diffusion, limiting practical usefulness. Further, different degrees of reciprocity within a bargaining setting become important and can only be understood in context. For example, the cost of freeing the American hostages held in Beirut changed over time. In the arms-for-hostage exchange, $30 million in weapons sales liberated three men; two hostages released in 1990 cost more, around $25 million each, the price for the last six was close to $50 million per person. These terms were not necessarily set unilaterally. Iran–Contra deals were cut short; the claims settlements had a jagged finish.

Lessons

The American tale of negotiating Beirut hostages' liberation perfectly illustrates how incentives can be structured for each side, what reciprocity meant, and also the impact of the entire negotiation episode in both prolonging and ending a terrorist campaign. Among the lessons taken from this experience, a few points stand out with respect to negotiating with terrorists:

1. *Terrorists think strategically.* Acts of violence and moves in negotiation processes are clear and goal-directed, focused on concrete issues, not abstractions or vague desires. Terrorists set the terms and the pace of negotiations.
2. *Terrorists choose alternative techniques of violence for different purposes.* The tool of illicit violence indicates whether negotiations will happen: fatality-driven events (bombing and suicide bombing, assassination) mean no negotiations while non-fatality driven events (skyjacking, hostage barricade, kidnaps) signal negotiation willingness or eagerness.
3. *Terrorists follow reciprocity in negotiations.* Attack begets attack, goodwill begets goodwill, illustrated with the *quid pro quo* exchange of airliner blow-ups, Libya's hostage purchase, and armaments and debt repayment exchanged for hostage releases.

Where is the other side's advantage? It lies in reciprocity moves, recognition of non-negotiable conditions, and conflict prevention measures. The latter is most important, although few methods, according to Lum *et al.* (2006), have been systematically evaluated for their effectiveness. Negotiation requires problem-solving skills, strategic analysis, imagination, and intuition. Rapoport (1960) constructed three different forms of human conflict based on behaviors and participant objectives and alternative intellectual tools to understand the nature of dispute management and resolution: fights, games, and debates. A "fight" is an exchange of deeds – players seek to bring harm to one another through a direct exchange of hostile acts in an action–reaction process; conflict is managed through reciprocal responses and conflict resolution means yielding to the opponent's demands or withdrawing from the conflict arena. A "game" consists of moves and counter-moves in a strategic interaction context in order to outwit the opponent; it is based on calculations of interests. Conflict resolution is equilibrium, a balance of power between sides. "Debates" are composed of verbal exchanges designed to convince the other side to alter their beliefs. Here, conflict resolution becomes belief convergence among the protagonists. Analyzing the Vietnam War, Walker (2004) found the American use of the "fight" model and its reciprocity approach was effective in resolving conflicts with a bully player who employed exploitation and bluff strategies. The episodes of US–Iran negotiations conform primarily to the "fight" model with occasional movement into a "game" perspective. Throughout this period, conflict resolution goals by each side seem to have been quite consistent: to bring harm to the other side and force them to submit to your goals. The contours of a conflict negotiation transformative "debate" were never realized. In this sense, negotiating with terrorists is the means neither for communicating broad overtures of peace or for achieving integration between parties; rather, for both sides, it will remain power-based bargaining.

5 Negotiating in Beslan and beyond

Adam Dolnik

On September 1, 2004, a group of terrorists took more then 1,200 hostages on the first day of school in the North Ossetian town of Beslan. The deadliest hostage crisis and at the same time the third deadliest terrorist attack in history was about to unfold. After a fifty-two-hour stand-off, detonation of explosive devices inside the school triggered a chaotic rescue operation, in which 331 victims and thirty-one terrorists were killed, 176 of them children. The Beslan school hostage crisis was an unprecedented terrorist attack, both in its scale and targeting. Much more grand than the 1974 Democratic Front for the Liberation of Palestine attack in Ma'alot, Israel, or the 1977 take-over of a school in Bovensmilde in the Netherlands, this was the largest ever terrorist take-over of a school (Mickolus 1980, p. 494). In addition, following 9/11 and the 1978 torching of a movie theater in Iran (still unresolved), Beslan is the third deadliest terrorist attack in history (tied with the 1985 Air India flight 182). And finally, with the exception of the 1979 hostage crisis in Mecca and the 1996 Chechen take-over of a hospital in Kizlyar, Beslan involved the largest number of hostages in any similar crisis in history. Stemming from the above facts, it is clear that understanding the lessons of Beslan is one of the key prerequisites of designing counter terrorism strategies for the twenty-first century.

Despite notoriety, the Beslan school tragedy still remains an incredibly misunderstood phenomenon. What really happened during the incident? Who were the attackers, and what was their goal? What was the treatment of hostages like? Was it possible to resolve the crisis via the process of negotiation? How did this incident reach such a tragic end? All of these questions are yet to be satisfactorily answered. Based on exhaustive open source research in three languages, examination of thousands of pages of witness testimonies and court transcripts, analysis of available video footage, and extensive field research in Beslan, Chechnya, and Ingushetia, including the examination of evidence left behind in the school, visits to the perpetrators' home villages, reconstruction of their trip from their training camp to Beslan, and dozens of interviews with hostages, witnesses, relatives, negotiators, and investigators, this chapter will analyze the myths and facts of the attack, with the clear purpose of identifying successes and failures. Particular attention will be devoted to an analysis of the events that took place in terms of negotiability, in an attempt to provide an analytical perspective on the possible alternatives that were available to the Russian authorities as the incident progressed. A critical inquiry into the incident is especially important, as lessons learned from past hostage crises are an invaluable tool in developing future response frameworks. Further, there are concrete indications that similar hostage-takings are likely to take place in the future, and not just in Russia. The globalizing trends in terrorism as well as the publication of a very concrete and analytical terrorist training manual,[1] which builds on the lessons learned and "best practice" of previous hostage incidents, present us with new challenges.

From the first glance, it is obvious that we are not prepared. While there are many trained crisis negotiators around the world, almost none of them has ever had contact with a terrorist hostage-taking incident. Further, the entire training program of most hostage negotiators focuses on resolving crises that do not take into consideration issues such as ideology, religion, or the differing set of objectives and mindsets of ideological hostage-takers. This is especially true in regards to the terrorists of the "new" breed, who have become less discriminate, more lethal, and more well prepared. Further, many of the paradigms and presumptions upon which the contemporary practice of hostage negotiation is based on, do not reflect the reality of Beslan-type incidents.

For example, here is a list of the characteristics of a negotiable incident, which are currently used by the FBI and other crisis negotiation bodies as the basic guideline to determining whether a given hostage incident has a chance of being resolved through the negotiation process:

1. The desire to live on the part of the hostage-taker.
2. The threat of force by the police.
3. The hostage-taker must present demands for release of hostages.
4. The negotiator must be viewed by the hostage-taker as someone who can hurt but desires to help.
5. The negotiator needs time to develop trust with hostage-takers.
6. The location must be contained and stabilized to support negotiations.
7. The hostage-taker and negotiator must have a reliable means of communication, either by phone or face-to-face.
8. The negotiator must be able to "deal" with the hostage-taker, who controls the hostages and makes the decisions.[2]

Additional checklists and criteria are used as well. As will become apparent throughout this chapter, most of these conditions were not satisfied in Beslan, and numerous additional obstacles and indicators of volatility were also present. Further, the conditions to follow many of the standard FBI guidelines for crisis negotiations were simply not present. Hence, if one were to follow the current "cookbook" of crisis negotiation teams, the only possible conclusion would be that the Beslan situation could only be resolved through a tactical resolution. However, how does one do that if there are more then 1,200 hostages inside, the opposition is ready for death and has made numerous preparations to make an assault as costly in terms of human life as possible? Under such conditions, is a full breach really the preferable option? Or even a plausible worst case alternative (BATNA)? Do other, less costly means exist? This chapter will explore some of these issues using the Beslan case study as a model.

The greatest limitation of this chapter stems from the fact that most available accounts of the hostage crisis differ significantly in their description of virtually every aspect of the incident. This is further complicated by government secrecy, vested interests, and media censorship, as well as the fact that even eye-witness accounts are often contradictory. Some details are still being disputed, and therefore some aspects of the crisis cannot be determined with absolute certainty. For the sake of completeness, alternative interpretations of events (or author's comments on the uncertainty of certain pieces of information) are included as endnotes. For a complete picture, it is important to pay particular attention to these.

The first part will provide a chronology of the crisis, with specific focus on the negotiation aspect. The second part will then analyze the negotiability of the incident, incorporating an analysis of the strategic calculus behind the attack, indicators of volatility and de-escalation, and the failures of the strategy employed in Beslan. And finally, the conclusion will look at the lessons learned and prospects for the future.

Negotiation analysis

This section will provide a basic chronology of the events that unfolded in Beslan. Given the limited space of this chapter, it is impossible to include many fascinating details of the crisis. However, other excellent and highly detailed descriptive accounts exist and an interested reader is strongly encouraged to consult them for additional information.[3]

Day 1

On September 1, 2004 just after 9:00 AM, a group of terrorists arrived at the School No. 1 in Beslan, and with swift action took over 1,200 people hostage, also deploying 127 home-made explosive devices around the school building. The initial response to the incident consisted of a brief shoot-out of armed parents with the hostage-takers. An hour and a half after the take-over, soldiers and policemen finally started arriving at the scene. This is amazing considering the fact that the main police station is located a mere 200 m from the school.[4] The initial telephone contact was reportedly handled by a local Federal Security Service of the Russian Federation (FSB) negotiator, whose identity is being kept secret.[5] He spoke to a man who on the inside was known as Ali but for the negotiations used the name "Sheikhu." From the very start, it was clear the terrorists were instructed by their leadership to speak only to high-level officials. According to hostages that sat close to Ali, he spoke with someone on the phone ending a conversation by saying, "I will only talk to the President." His phone rang again in fifteen to twenty minutes. "President?" "No, his aide." Ali interrupted the talk at once.[6] In the meantime, the authorities compiled their first list of hostages, and publicly announced that there were only 120 of them.

Around this time, doctor Larisa Mamitova was treating two of the hostage-takers who were injured in the initial take-over. Mamitova offered her help in communicating with the authorities, and was eventually sent outside by the leader of the group, Ruslan Khuchbarov (a.k.a. "Polkovnik") with the following hand-written message:

> 8-928-738-33-374[7]
>
> We demand for negotiations President of the Republic Dzhosokhov, Zaizikov, president of Ingushetia, Roshal, children's doctor. If they kill any one of us, we will shoot fifty people to pieces. If they injure any one of us, we will kill twenty people. If they kill five of us, we will blow up everything. If they turn off the light, even for a minute, we will shoot to pieces ten people.

From early on, the terrorists selected out two groups of men and led them outside the gym. One group had the task of barricading windows, while the other was forced to kneel in the corridor with hands behind their backs facing the wall. The first group never returned. Once its job was finished, they were led to a classroom on the second floor, lined up against the wall and shot. Their bodies were thrown out of the window.

As the incident progressed, tensions grew even higher. In the afternoon, the hostages overheard an argument between the terrorists and their leader, in which particularly the two female attackers present expressed their displeasure with holding children hostage. Around four o'clock in the afternoon one of the suicide bombers detonated, killing five or six of the men lined up in the hallway and injuring many more.[8] Those injured were later sprayed with gunfire, and their dead bodies were thrown out of the window. At this point, the number of dead hostages already reached twenty-one.

In the meantime, negotiations continued. According to the now former President of Ossetia, Alexander Dzasohov, a deal to exchange the children for the release of the thirty-one terrorists arrested in the Nazran raid had almost been made, but at the last moment the terrorists backed down. When Mikhail Gutseriev – the former speaker of the Russian State Duma and president of the Rusneft' oil company, asked the terrorists about specific demands, Sheikhu suggested that they be handed over in writing.[9]

After 7:00 PM, one of the men demanded by the terrorists for negotiations, Dr Leonid Roshal, entered the picture. Never requested by the authorities, he flew to Beslan on his own initiative after being informed of the situation by journalists. Once he reached the school, Roshal called the terrorists expressing his readiness to enter with water and medicines, but was told that he could only enter the school with the other three men demanded earlier; if he approached alone he would be shot.

Day 2

In the early morning of September 2, Mamitova overheard a radio broadcast reporting that only 354 hostages were held inside the school, and that the telephone number provided by the terrorists was non-operational. She asked to see Polkovnik and informed him of the report, also suggesting to send another note with a new telephone number. Polkovnik tore a piece of paper from a notebook and handed it over to Mamitova. "Write again," he said. "Our nerves are at a breaking point...."

As the day progressed, the terrorists were becoming increasingly angry and frustrated, mainly due to the repeated government claims made in the media that the number of hostages was 354, and that the hostage-takers had not presented any demands. The hostage-takers saw this as a deliberate attempt to obstruct negotiations, and to justify the launching of an armed assault on the school. Infuriated, around noon of the second day, the terrorists called a "dry strike" and stopped giving the hostages water. From this point on, the hostages really started to suffer from the lack of food, water and deteriorating conditions inside.

Just before 2:00 PM, the terrorists' mood suddenly changed and they became visibly excited. From the top floor they announced on a megaphone that "big person" was coming in for the negotiations. This "big person" turned out to be Ruslan Aushev, Afghan war general and former Ingushetian President. Aushev and Khuchbarov held a discussion in the staff room,[10] and at the end of the meeting, Aushev was handed a handwritten note dated on August 30, 2004, addressed to President Putin from "Allah's slave" Shamil Basayev:

> Vladimir Putin, you were not the one to start the war, but you could be the one to end it, that is if you find the courage and resolve to act like de Gaulle. We are offering you peace on a mutually beneficial basis in line with the principle "independence for security." We can guarantee that if you withdraw the troops and recognize Chechen independence, then: We will not strike any political, military or economic deals with anyone against Russia; We will not have any foreign military bases even temporary ones, we will not support or finance groups fighting the Russian Federation, we will join the Commonwealth of Independent States, we will stay in the ruble zone, we could sign the Collective Security Treaty, although we would prefer the status of a neutral state; we can guarantee that all of Russia's Muslims will refrain from armed methods of struggle against the Russian Federation, at least for ten to fifteen years, on condition that freedom of religion be respected ... The Chechen nation is involved in the national liberation struggle for its Freedom and Independence and for its preservation. It is not fighting to humiliate Russia or destroy it. As a free nation, we are interested in a strong neighbor. We are offering you peace and the choice is yours.

The terrorists set a deadline for the Kremlin to respond by the morning of September 4.[11] Aushev promised to hand over the letter, and asked for the release of kids.[12] Khuchbarov agreed, and the nursing mothers were released along with one baby each, some of them having to leave their other children behind. After leaving the school with the twenty-six released hostages, Aushev immediately transmitted the text of the letter to the Kremlin with an urgent plea for negotiations.[13] In addition, a list of specific demands was also handed over in writing. These demands were never made public, but available evidence suggests that the list corresponded to the one later provided by Basayev himself:

- We demand that the war in Chechnya be stopped immediately and that the withdrawal of forces be carried out.
- We insist that Putin immediately resigns from his post as President of the Russian Federation.
- We insist that all hostages, be it children or adults, go on hunger strike in support of our demands.

In the evening of the second day, Aslanbek Aslakhanov, Putin's advisor, who was one of the negotiators demanded by the terrorists, called the school. He was informed that he could come to Beslan to negotiate, only if he had the authority to do so granted by Putin. Aslakhanov answered affirmatively and added, "Some demands are unrealistic and you know it. Some we will fulfill. I'll talk to the President." Sheikhu replied: "If you do, then see you tomorrow at 3:00 PM, we'll hold an official meeting." According to his own account, Aslakhanov then spoke to President Putin, who allegedly stated that "the children's lives must be saved at all costs. Agree to everything. But the first two demands cannot be met."[14] This is an extremely interesting point. If Aslakhanov did indeed talk about the possibility of satisfying some of the terrorists' demands, it clearly contradicts the official claim that no demands were made. Similarly, Putin's comment about the unacceptability of the "first two demands" confirms their existence. It is not clear, however, what the President meant by "agree to everything"; if the first two demands – withdrawing of troops from Chechnya and his own resignation – were unacceptable, then there was nothing else to agree to but the demand that hostages go on a hunger strike. So while the statement "agree to everything but the first two demands" by itself may be interpreted as evidence of the Russian leadership's willingness to offer almost any concession in order to save the lives of the hostages, in the context of the actual list of demands it translated into agreeing to absolutely nothing.

The terrorists' desperation to speak to the authorities was evident inside the school. Polkovnik even sought out Mamitova and told her that if there were any members of parliament or other politicians that she knew, she should call them. Mamitova remembered hearing from someone in the gym that the children of the North Ossetian parliament speaker Mamsurov were also among the hostages. Before they were summoned to the teachers' room, Ali took aside the boy, hugged him and kissed him on the head. "Don't worry. Nothing bad is going to happen to you. We just need you to help us jump-start the negotiations. Talk with your daddy and tell him what's going on."[15]

When Mamitova and the children finally managed to get through to Mamsurov, he replied: "The government has ordered me to leave my parental emotions at home." Visibly upset, Khuchbarov then turned on the television, where the government media were still reporting that there were only 354 hostages, and where Dr Roshal was claiming that kids were not in immediate danger, and that they could survive eight or nine days without water. Khuchbarov then sent Mamitova and the kids back to the gym. "Go, nobody needs you."

On the evening of September 2, Ali came into the gym visibly distressed. When asked by Larisa Kudzyeva what had happened, he replied: "I don't want to lift my foot from the trigger,[16] but I'm forced to do it. They don't want to talk. The answer is no. They told me that Russia will never talk to terrorists. That the problem does not exist." When she asked what that meant, Ali replied: "I don't know what that means. They told me I have a day and a half to sort it out." Kudzyeva countered: "That can't be; maybe you didn't understand." Ali: "No, I understood. I understood everything."[17]

The authorities have a different story. According to official sources, Roshal called the terrorists in the evening of the second day and offered them free passage. The offer was allegedly bluntly refused.[18] In the evening of the second day, Aushev suggested to engage Aslan Maskhadov, the last elected president of the separatist government, for negotiations. Maskhadov had publicly condemned the attack and this gave a glimpse of hope.[19] By midnight, at the civilian segment of the local crisis staff, an agreement was allegedly drafted, with key components oscillating around negotiations between Russian leaders and Maskhadov, a plan for Chechen autonomy, and a gradual troop withdrawal.[20]

Day 3

The morning of September 3 brought some optimistic news: Maskhadov had sent a message confirming that he was ready to fly to Beslan to negotiate. The local authorities responded by announcing: "Important new faces are about to enter the negotiation process, they will arrive soon."[21] Only an hour after this announcement the storming started, leading some sources to speculate that the explosions that triggered the mayhem were no accident, and that their purpose was to deny Maskhadov the chance to come in and save the day.[22] The federal authorities in turn, categorically denied Maskhadov's willingness to come to Beslan to negotiate in the first place.[23]

The small glimpse of optimism that was present outside following the morning announcement, however, was not shared by the people inside the gym. Conditions were increasingly deteriorating with some of the children resorting to drinking urine to survive, and at least two of the kids already reaching the verge of death. The terrorists were acting increasingly aggressive, became even less responsive to hostages' anxious pleas for water, and their anger grew with their inability to quiet the hostages down.

At 1:02 PM, following a morning agreement with the terrorists to allow the collection of bodies of the hostages killed on the first day, a lorry approached the school and suddenly, several shots were fired. Almost simultaneously, the first explosion inside the school ensued, followed by a large explosion exactly twenty-two seconds later. Shortly thereafter, all hell broke lose. By this point the firefight had become irreversible. At 6:13 PM, there was one last contact with the hostage-takers. "It's all your fault. Say 'Hi' to you, Putin!" Around 2:00 AM, more than twelve hours since the initial explosions, the last shots were fired.

Assessment

This portion of the chapter will assess the potential of negotiations as the best possible tool for the resolution of the incident. Firstly, the motivations and strategic calculus of the attackers will be examined. What were they trying to achieve? What was the desired outcome? What was their best alternative to a negotiated agreement (BATNA)? Without understanding these questions, it is impossible to design an appropriate negotiation strategy. Secondly, traditional analytical framework for assessing the negotiability of hostage incidents will be used to identify the negative indicators of volatility, as well as comparatively positive indicators of de-escalation that were present. Simultaneously, the weaknesses of a mechanical application of this framework to Beslan-style incidents will be identified. And finally, this section will analyze the successes and missed opportunities in the handling of the Beslan incident, in order to draw lessons for the resolution of similar crises in the future.

Goals of the attack

In order to understand the terrorists' calculation behind launching the Beslan operation, we must examine several aspects, namely the selection of target, tactic used, and overall strategy.

The target was indeed striking, and it was clearly designed to raise the stakes. In the 2002 Moscow theater hostage crisis, the Russian leadership did not shy away from storming a theater full of hostages in the middle of Moscow, killing 129 people in the process.[24] Taking hundreds of schoolchildren hostage would introduce even greater decision-making dilemmas and greater public pressure to not storm the school, leaving the Kremlin with few options but to negotiate. According to Basayev's own words, Moscow or St Petersburg would have been more attractive locations for the operation, and he allegedly even considered attacking two locations at once. However, due to operational and financial limitations, a target substitution had to be made. Ossetia then provided an ideal substitute because "it is Russia's fort post in the north Caucasus, and all bad that comes to [Chechens] comes from the territory of Ossetia, with the silent consent of its population."[25] The selection of Beslan in particular made sense, as the School No. 1 is one of the largest in the region, to which even the Ossetian elite send their children.[26]

The tactic that was used in the attacks was also striking. Obviously, there was the idea of taking hostages as a means to create a "good," which could then be used to "trade" for political concessions. As mentioned above, taking a large number of children hostage significantly raised the stakes. Fortifying the location, placing a large number of explosive devices throughout the school, booby trapping possible entrances and monitoring them with remote control surveillance cameras,[27] deployment of snipers in strategic positions, use of gasmasks and sentry dogs in order to prevent the use of anesthetic gas, and other protective measures taken, were designed to overtly minimize the perceived chances of success of a rescue operation. Few hostage crises in history have presented the response teams with such a formidable adversary.

The apparently suicidal tactic selected for the operation was significant as well. First of all, the repeated expression of determination to die during the incident was aimed at denying the counterpart threat level: the proclamation of the desire to die weakens the deterrent value of threats by the government to resolve the situation forcefully.[28] Further, the seeming irrationality of suicidal operations is useful in attracting extensive media coverage which triggers popular attempts to comprehend the motivations of such an act, leading to worldwide debates about the systemic foundations of the enormous dedication and hatred demonstrated by the attackers. In the eyes of many people, the group then gains the image of committed believers willing to do anything to reach their goals, also implying that the present *status quo* of their constituency is so humiliating and so unacceptable that death is preferable to life under such conditions. This is especially true in cases where the suicide attackers include women, as has frequently been the case in Chechen operations. This was apparently the element that the terrorists were trying to capitalize on in Beslan as well, as on numerous occasions they engaged the hostages with questions like "You know why our women sacrifice themselves like that?" or "Do you think our women blow themselves up because they like it?" In addition, it is also clear that featuring images of female suicide bombers in their video footage from the site was particularly important for image purposes; after the original two bombers died on the first day, one of the terrorists approached Larisa Kudzyeva with an offer to release her children if she agreed to put on the *hijab* and a suicide belt.[29]

Overall, the goals of the operation were multiple. Basayev's success in the 1995 hostage crisis in the hospital in Budyonnovsk had convinced him that large-scale hostage-takings can be instrumentally successful in forcing the Russians to the negotiating table.[30] At the same time, he also learned from past incidents that the Russian leadership can always be expected to launch a rescue operation – typically around the end of the third day of the crisis – and that these actions produce on average more than 130 deaths. In light of these experiences Basayev's explanation of the goals of Beslan was logical: "We came there not to kill people but to stop the war, and if it works out that way, to force the Russian leadership to kill its own civilians, if only through this to force the lying and vain world to understand what is really going on, to lay bare our wound and pain, because people don't see what is happening in Chechnya. They see it only when huge actions like this one occur on the territory of Russia itself."[31] From a negotiation perspective, this logic is highly disturbing, as Basayev has been able to convert barricade hostage scenario that under normal circumstances is not so favorable to the hostage-takers into a "win–win" situation. The logic is simple: If the Russians satisfy the demands, Basayev wins. If the Russians storm the building and a large number of hostages die, he also wins. Finally, the desire or at least the acceptability of dying a martyr's death on behalf of hostage-takers then erases any possible down side.

There was yet another strategic goal that would be fulfilled in Beslan regardless of the outcome of the incident: the provocation of violent retaliations by the predominantly Orthodox Christian Ossetians against the Muslim Ingush minority in the province.[32] These were then supposed to provide a spark for a large-scale Christian–Muslim confrontation in the entire Caucasus, not only taking the pressure off Chechnya, but also creating a nightmare scenario for Moscow.[33] In light of this purpose and in consideration of Basayev's long-term strategic goal of expanding the Chechen conflict throughout the region, attacking in Ossetia with a team featuring a majority of Ingush attackers was a logical strategic choice, since more than 600 people had already died in ethnic clashes between both groups in 1992.[34] The resurrection of such historical conflicts may only need a small spark. Although official versions deny this, an armed group of Ossetians heading to Ingushetia to revenge Beslan was actually stopped by the federal troops at the Nazran checkpoint shortly after the incident. Since Beslan, the tensions between the two ethnic groups have followed an escalatory pattern.

Besides understanding the strategic calculus of the master minds of the operation, it is also important to examine the profiles and backgrounds of the executors, as they are essentially the ones who will make the very final decision in terms of executing hostages, dying, surrendering or taking up an offer of free passage. And although ideological hostage incidents typically feature little independent decision-making on behalf of the executors, based on analysis of Basayev's claim of responsibility it seems that in case of Beslan this element was present, as the demand to release the imprisoned attackers from the Nazran raid[35] appears to have been the executors' own initiative.[36] Understanding the personality and group dynamics of the hostage-taking team inside the school is therefore vital to designing suitable negotiation strategy.

This chapter is not the appropriate place to provide the life saga of each of the Beslan terrorists, which by itself presents enough material for a separate book. As a result, only a basic overview can provided. The official number of terrorists was thirty-two – two of them women – although hostages claim the actual number to have been much higher.[37] Published reports, interviews with investigators, hostages, and the terrorists' family members reveal the following scope: Some of the terrorists had a long history of fighting in the separatist struggle, others were violent criminals who escaped punishment to the lawless regions of Chechnya or Ingushetia, only to later join the rebels. Some were fanatical Islamists, others seem to have been driven by more personal grievances and revenge, one was an Orthodox Christian who converted to Islam under the influence of his brother. Most of the terrorists had some family members either killed or kidnapped and tortured by the Russians in Chechnya and Ingushetia. Some had a history of conducting terrorist attacks against civilians, others had previously only killed soldiers. Their roles in the crisis were apparently different: while some attackers were clearly destined for sacrifice, others were almost certainly meant to survive. Some held important positions in Basayev's Riyadus-Salikhin Battalion of suicide fighters (RAS) and participated in the planning of the operation, others were only marginal players who didn't even have advance knowledge of their target. This fact even resulted in a serious argument among the terrorists about the idea of taking kids hostage.[38] This overall diversity of background, prior experience, rank, division of labor, and differing fates brings an important element into the analysis of negotiation options and strategies. Did the schisms inside the group perhaps provide an opportunity for the negotiators to drive a wedge between the hostage-takers?

Volatility. From the perspective of the traditional crisis negotiation framework, it was clear from the beginning that Beslan would be incredibly challenging to resolve. In fact, as mentioned in the introduction, traditional analytical checklists would place Beslan into the category of non-negotiable incidents requiring a tactical resolution. However, upon closer inspection it becomes apparent that there were a number of dynamics present in the crisis that made the applicability of the commonly used generic incident assessment forms obsolete. This section will identify the traditional indicators of volatility, as well as some of the shortcomings of their mechanical application.

The first volatile factor was represented by the fact that the incident was obviously premeditated and carefully planned. Such deliberate hostage crises are naturally more difficult to negotiate, and the process is likely to be significantly longer in duration than in the case of spontaneous hostage incidents, such as surprise police intervention during a bank robbery or a domestic violence situation. Quite simply, if the hostage-takers are mentally and physically prepared to be in the given situation, the less likely they are to start second guessing their decision to take hostages. This, however, does not mean that we should automatically conclude that this shift will not take place. It only means that changing the terrorists' expectations and resolve will need much more time than is the case in most other hostage incidents. Further, while the Beslan terrorists did bring with them vitamin supplements and rations for at least three days, not everyone was comfortable with the idea of taking children hostage. This provided some window of opportunity for planting a seed of doubt in the minds of at least some terrorists.

Secondly, the presence of multiple perpetrators available to handle the negotiations made the situation even more unpredictable: building rapport with hostage-takers is much more challenging if they are under direct pressure from their peers and if they can effectively negate the formation of a personal relationship with the negotiator by simply switching representatives. This was also the case in Beslan, where the negotiations were handled by at least two different terrorists. Further, they also cleverly employed the "deferment of authority" principle, in which the person who speaks is never the one who can make the final decision. This is one of the principles employed by hostage negotiation teams, and is designed to allow the negotiator to never fully commit to any deals without consulting his superior as Combalbert emphasizes in his chapter. The negotiator can then deny an agreement previously reached without losing face, by pointing to the decision-maker as the one responsible for the change of heart. This makes negotiations more difficult than when the decision-maker is confronted directly. Another reason why the presence of group hostage-takers is considered an indicator of volatility, is the fact that due to the psychological process known as "groupthink," group hostage-takers in general tend to be more decisive when in comes to killing hostages than individuals.

Another, volatile element of the crisis was the fact that the hostage-takers were well armed and heavily brutalized. Security precautions taken by the militants made an assault on the location without a significant loss of life virtually impossible, and the history of ruthlessness on the part of a number of the terrorists in this group made their claims of preparedness to kill the hostages in cold blood quite persuasive. Further, the fact that hostages died in the initial take-over was also a highly negative development, as deaths of hostages in the early stages usually complicate subsequent negotiation efforts by tarnishing the hostage-takers' "clean record," which is one of the strong persuasive elements negotiators use to facilitate the surrender or free passage in the final stages of an incident. Further, the commanders of hostage response teams become less amenable to pursuing the negotiation option once hostages have been killed, and greater legal and public opinion obstacles to letting the terrorists leave arise as well.

Another worrying factor right in the beginning of the incident was the fact that the stronger male hostages were separated out of the group and transferred to another location. This filtering process not only signaled the anticipation of a tactical assault – holding hostages at different locations makes an assault more difficult, as multiple tactical teams must attack all locations simultaneously in order to limit the risk to hostages held at other locations – but also allowed for a quick "discriminate" execution of hostages if it became necessary to pressure the authorities. The slaying of the males, who were perceived not only as dangerous to the hostage-takers due to their muscular build but also as morally "involved" in the violence in Chechnya and Ingushetia, would have been psychologically easier and also less politically dangerous for the terrorists than killing women and children. Tragically, this proved to be the case during the afternoon of the first day, when the terrorists did in fact execute several men in cold blood just to make a point. Later, additional people died in the suicide blast, and the ones injured were also finished off and thrown out of the window. This extremely bold measure rarely seen in historical hostage crises constitutes one of the most important dilemmas for the future. The current *modus operandi* of crisis response teams goes by the rule that until hostages start dying, negotiations take priority. Once hostages start being executed in cold blood, the last resort option of a full-scale rescue operation is activated. But as discussed earlier, in cases like Beslan, the rescue operation has only a miniscule probability of success. Is it preferable to risk more deaths resulting from the rescue which by itself is far from guaranteed to free the hostages, or to continue negotiations? Does the execution of several hostages really constitute a sign of absolute non-negotiability? Because of the historical rarity of such a development, we really do not know. Similarly, could the absence of executions of women and children be interpreted as a positive sign of possible restraint in terms of *indiscriminate* executions on behalf of the terrorists? What does the absence of executions on the second and third day tell us about the prospects of successes of an eventual negotiated settlement? These questions are not by any means meant to suggest a moral relativity of the issue, or to imply that lives of male hostages are less precious than that of the women and children. But on utilitarian grounds, crises response teams need to ask themselves: which approach can result in the deaths of the fewest people? Storming of the location of further negotiations? All of these questions need to be analyzed and the premises upon which the current hostage rescue "cookbooks" rest, need to be re-evaluated.

The third possible volatile element was the absence of change in the terrorists' demands over time. In "negotiable incidents" hostage-takers typically start bidding high but reduce their demands as the incident progresses and as their exhaustion triggers a regression to a hierarchically higher set of needs such as hunger, thirst and sleep. If such a process does not occur over a growing period of time, the contemporary paradigm suggests that the chances of a negotiated solution decrease considerably.[39] However, this paradigm is again based on past experience in non-terrorist hostage incidents where ideology is not involved, and where many of the demands made are not thought out beforehand. In such cases, it is not surprising that hostage-takers modify their demands over time? With terrorist hostage-takers, who have received a clear set of demands from their leaders and who lock themselves in their position by stating their demands publicly, this process cannot be expected to occur on the same timeline as non-terrorist incidents, as the one thing the image-conscious terrorists fear the most is the perception of failure. Also, the presence of multiple hostage-takers in cases like Beslan prolongs this process significantly, as the hostage-takers not only have the option of resting some of their crew by working in shifts, but also are able to feed from energy and determination of their colleagues. As a result of these factors, in combination with the lack of sufficient experience and data on terrorist hostage-takings *à la* Beslan, we simply do not know if and when a change in the hostage-takers' demand can be expected to occur. Implicitly we should not tie ourselves down to specific time horizons and limit our options based on this indictor alone.

Another potentially volatile element was the alleged use of drugs on behalf of the hostage-takers. In general, the presence of psychotropic substances makes the situation less predictable, sometimes giving the hostage-takers the courage to resort to more radical measures than they normally would. This is one of the reasons why providing drugs or alcohol to hostage-takers is considered as a "non-negotiable demand." Following the autopsies of the dead Beslan terrorists, investigators claimed that tests revealed that twenty-one of the thirty-one gunmen had heroin or morphine in their bloodstream. Another six allegedly used light drugs ranging from codeine to marijuana.[40] According to local prosecutor Nikolai Shepel, tests even revealed levels exceeding lethal doses of heroin and morphine in most of the thirty-two terrorists, suggesting that they were drug addicts. Alexander Torshin who heads the federal investigative committee even claimed that the terrorists used some kind of a "new generation" drug that allowed them to continue fighting despite being badly wounded and presumably in great pain.[41] However, all of these allegations are being strongly disputed by the hostages, as well as the North Ossetian parliamentary commission which in its report stated that "no traces of strong narcotics were found in the bodies of the hostage-takers." In Beslan the assertion about "drug addicts" has long been dismissed as Moscow's attempt to cover up the failure of the authorities to negotiate.[42] Fascinatingly, even the Beslan terrorists could predict this development; in one of the conversations with Larissa Mamitova, Khuchbarov asked whether she saw any drug addicts among them. When she shook her head, he replied, "Remember my words: they will call us drug addicts..."[43] Another similarly manipulated story are the reports that the terrorists raped young girls inside the school. It all started by a rumor coming from a boy that heard from a hostage that some girls were taken to another room and then a scream could be heard. As the story passed from source to source, it snowballed into a version in which the laughing terrorists raped young girls with bayonets, while capturing the act on video.[44] However, actual hostages, even those who have absolutely every reason to hate the terrorists for killing their children, vigorously deny the rape story. On the contrary, they claim that whenever girls revealed any skin in an attempt to relieve the immense heat that formed in the gym, they were ordered by the gunmen to cover up immediately. Similarly, Khodov when asked by one of the hostages whether he was going to rape her, replied defensively, "We did not come here for this. We don't need it. There's a greater reward for us with *Allah*. The other stuff is simply not interesting to us."[45]

This is not to say that the behavior of the terrorists toward the hostages was not unusually brutal. After the terrorists stopped giving the hostages water on the second day, the children were forced to drink their own urine in an attempt to survive in the immense heat of the packed gym.[46] Despite numerous pleas from the hostages, this policy was never changed. Further, at least some of the terrorists clearly demonstrated that they had no psychological trouble killing hostages. One of the men who died on the first day from injuries suffered during the initial take-over was taken away before his death and shot through the knees and his skull was broken into pieces with rifle butts.[47] Some of the terrorists even psychologically tormented the children. For instance they placed boxes of chocolate in everyone's view to tempt the hungry kids, but simultaneously telling them, "Whoever even touches it will be shot."[48] In addition, Vladimir Khodov, one of the most brutal of the terrorists, would occasionally beat some of the older boys with his rifle butt.[49] And while there were no executions of women and children, the overall behavior of some of the terrorists did not bear the marks of a forming Stockholm syndrome, or the mutually positive relationship between hostages and hostage-takers which typically makes it psychologically more difficult for the latter to execute the former in cold blood. Again, in this regard there was no uniformity among the members of the team. Hostages agree that only about five or six terrorists behaved especially cruelly, while many others were remembered as "decent" or even "kind" and "nice." Many of the terrorists secretly gave the hostages water and chocolate, or at least looked the other way when they saw some of the hostages violating the ground rules. One of them almost paid for this with his own life: when he offered a bottle of water to Marina Khubayeva, another terrorist walked up and shouted at him, "Do you want a bullet in your head?"[50] At least two of the terrorists even guarded the kids from the hail of bullets in the final storm, risking their own life in the process. Several others, on the other hand, shot at the backs of the children running away.[51] The unfortunate fact was that, despite their numerical inferiority, the hostage-takers that were the most brutal, such as Khodov and Khuchbarov, were the leaders of the group. The absence of psychological barriers to killing hostages on the part of these men in charge made the situation extremely volatile.

Finally, and perhaps most important, the terrorists' repeatedly declared desire to die and become martyrs suggested a high level of volatility. One of the identified preconditions of negotiability of hostage incidents is the desire on behalf of the hostage-taker to live – if the hostage-takers are indifferent to staying alive, it is difficult to make them focus on personal safety thereby drawing attention away from their original demands. Also, the threat of force posed by the hostage rescue unit becomes much less powerful as a bargaining tool when survival plays no part in the hostage-takers' calculation of the outcome. Under circumstances in which the captors see it as their primary objective to kill themselves and take as many of their victims with them as possible, negotiation has very little chance of success. However, such situations are extremely infrequent. After all, the whole point of taking hostages is to protect one's own safety during the stand-off.

Contrary to popular opinion, the terrorists in Beslan were indeed concerned about their safety.[52] One of the themes that kept being repeated during the crisis was the threat to kill fifty hostages for every terrorist killed, and twenty hostages for every terrorist injured. Throughout the conversations with hostages, it also became apparent that some of the terrorists did expect to survive. For instance, at one point Khodov, who was injured on his right arm, was told by doctor Larissa Mamitova that he needed to see a doctor as soon as the crisis ended, as he was in danger of developing gangrene. Khodov asked specifically what type of doctor he should go and see, suggesting that in his case the question of survival was still open-ended.[53] During the same conversation, Khodov also changed his behavior to become very unfriendly once Mamitova told him that she worked in the village of Elkhotovo. It wasn't known to her at the time that Elkhotovo was Khodov's home village, where his mother still lived and worked, coincidentally also in the medical field.[54] The change of behavior toward Mamitova could then be interpreted as a signal of fear of being identified, an issue that would not matter to a terrorists who had already discarded even a remote possibility of survival.[55] In short, while there is no question that members of Khuchbarov's unit were *prepared* to die during the Beslan operation, it is questionable whether their death was truly designed as the operation's only *preferred outcome*. The real challenge was to come up with a solution that would be more attractive to the terrorists than their own demise. For this reason, the declared preparedness to die on behalf of the terrorists might have made negotiations extremely difficult, but certainly did not exclude the possibility of a nonviolent resolution altogether.

Indicators of de-escalation

Besides the above-stated indicators of high volatility, signs of de-escalation[56] were also present as the incident progressed. Unfortunately, compared to the indicators of volatility, these were very few in number.

One possibly positive indicator was the fact that the attackers let several deadlines pass, and that they failed to follow through with some of their threats. Experience shows that once a deadline is breached, it is easier to break through future deadlines and to prolong the incident.[57] And while the prolongation of the incident by itself does not automatically guarantee a peaceful resolution, it does strengthen the chances for such an outcome. At the very least, it provides the tactical unit with more time to study the behavioral patterns of the perpetrators and to prepare for an assault. In that sense the Beslan terrorists' failure to follow up some of their threats with action constituted a positive development. For instance, since the very first day the terrorists were concerned about the authorities turning off the lights or shutting off communications, so they threatened to kill twenty hostages if the cell phone was turned off, if it was on but no one answered their call, or if lights were shut off. Late in the first day, the cell phone number Khuchbarov passed outside for communications was in fact turned off, but no executions followed. On the second night of the crisis, lights were shut off during a thunderstorm but no hostages were killed. And while these facts constitute bright points that are only very minor, in crises like Beslan where there are almost no good news they provide at least a glimmer of hope.

Another encouraging element of the crisis was the release of the nursing mothers with their babies following Aushev's intervention on the second day. This move demonstrated the willingness of the terrorists to make agreements and to release hostages. Fascinatingly, it was not so difficult for Aushev to convince the terrorists to release the nursing mothers. He simply agreed to convey the terrorists' demands to Putin, and asked for the kids to be released.[58] This suggests that the principle of *quid pro quo* was clearly understood by the terrorists. In addition, it also appears that they were in fact prepared to release more people if the negotiations made some headway. According to the hostages, on the first day the terrorists compiled a list of all kids under the legal school age, presumably to provide quick reference to the hostages to be released in future deals. And since a precedent for the release of a small number of hostages had already been set, it could have been used to pave the road to further small agreements at the end of which other small groups of hostages would be freed. Moreover, the terrorists had multiple demands, which presented an opportunity to dissect the discussion in the negotiation into many small pieces and small agreements to facilitate this process.

Negotiations: missed opportunities

The negotiability or non-negotiability of the Beslan crisis will always be an issue of much contention. Throughout the crisis, the federal authorities kept denying the existence of any demands whatsoever on behalf of the hostage-takers, implying that there was nothing more that could have been done to save the lives of the hostages but to storm the location. According to the head of the investigative group of North Caucasus directorate of the Russian Prosecutor General's office (RIA 2005), "proof exists that the terrorists who seized the school in Beslan did not intend to negotiate with anybody." How could one negotiate with a group of suicidal drug addicts who have no demands?

However, these statements are an evident manipulation of the reality. The terrorists did come to Beslan to achieve certain political objectives. They presented a clear set of demands. Throughout the crisis the terrorists were eager to speak to the authorities but, according to hostages, no one would talk to them (*Chechnya Weekly* 2005). At every moment they waited for someone to get in touch with them, telling the hostages to "be quiet, [we] can't hear the cell phone. If they call, maybe things will get better for you" (Khuzmieva 2005). Some of the terrorists also told the hostages, "We will not kill anyone, we have a plan. If it is fulfilled you will go home." Yes, it is true that the terrorists also kept repeating that they came to Beslan to die, that they would blow up the school, that the hostages are "not needed by anyone," that "no one will leave alive," and that the hostages would be "killed by their own." But that does not change the fact that it is beyond reasonable doubt that the terrorists' primary objective was to achieve a specific set of political concessions. In addition, not only did the attackers put forward a clear set of conditions and demands, they also specifically stated what they were willing to offer in exchange. Yes, their stated demands were by themselves difficult to achieve, both logistically and politically. However, the fact that their proposal included multiple demands and specific conditions provided much room for discussions without necessarily giving in.

With regards to the key demand to end the war in Chechnya, the main mistake was to mislead the focus of the authorities on the *substantive* nature of the demand and on the political unacceptability of fulfilling it. The situation was basically seen as a zero-sum game, leading many to mistakenly conclude that there was no possibility of a negotiated resolution. However, the main focus should have been placed not on the instrumental but rather on the *expressive* nature of that demand, as discussed in the preceding chapters by Combalbert and others, and to ask the question "Why?" "Why do you demand the end of war in Chechnya?" "Why should Putin resign?" These are obvious questions that have obvious answers, but in crisis negotiations such questions need to be asked, as they provide the terrorists an opportunity to clearly state their grievances. This in turn gives the negotiator an opportunity to engage the spokesperson on the other side on a more personal level, by asking about his or her *personal* experience with the alleged injustices and abuse. This in turn provides an opportunity for the negotiator to express empathy. In ideological hostage situations, it is always very difficult to move the discussion away from ideology toward a more personal level, and this approach provides one of the possible ways. Forming personal rapport between the negotiators on both sides is a critical principle which the crisis negotiation practice is based upon. Another reason why asking the question "Why?" is important is the fact that answers can provide an insight into the hostage-taker's underlying interests. If these interests are understood, new options that would address the terrorist's root motivations and concerns, but would stop short of their original demands, can be introduced. Through this process the hostage-takers' expectations can be changed. Also, shaping the militants' perception of having achieved some success gives them a stake in the outcome, and can prevent them from taking radical steps that would waste everything that had already been accomplished. This is why it is important in the beginning to focus on the demands that are easier to fulfill. Specifically, the demand about the release of the hostage-takers' imprisoned comrades from the Nazran raid provided hope, as this was something that could have feasibly been discussed. According to Aslakhanov (2004), trading these prisoners for child hostages was acceptable to President Putin as well.

Beslan was, of course, an extremely challenging situation, with huge stakes, executed hostages, extremely well prepared terrorists who seemed to be holding all the cards and who had an obvious knowledge of the hostage negotiation playbook. However, this by itself was not a sufficient reason to give up on the possibility of a negotiated settlement altogether. The terrorists' demands should have been broken down into smaller pieces, which would then be discussed in more detail. For instance, the demand of the President issuing an edict that would end the war in Chechnya. The negotiators should have focused on asking about the language of the text. Would the Russian word "Chechnya" or the Chechen separatist term "Ichkeria" be used? What else was to be included? Simply a commitment to a pull-out of troops, or apologies for the past? Does the pull-out of troops mean just the army or all *federal* troops? Which district should be "freed" first? Is there an understanding of the logistical issues involved in such a massive operation? What sort of guarantees are the terrorists prepared to propose, to prove that they will keep their promise and release the hostages once the pull-out is completed? What gestures of good faith were they ready to offer? Perhaps providing water to the children? Or even releasing kids under seven years of age, the list of which the terrorists collected on the first day with apparent intent to release them in future agreements? This is just an example of some of the issues that could have been raised and discussed in order to engage the terrorists. Further, on day two it was clear that the number one priority of the negotiations had to be the improvement of the conditions inside the school to improve the survivability of hostages. Clearly the situation in which the hostages were not being given water could not have lasted much longer, and some children already started dying. The authorities should have worked step by step to offer some small concession to facilitate the improvement of the conditions inside, and then work toward the prolongation of the incident in an attempt to wear out the hostage-takers, while at the same time working to get as many hostages as possible out of the school in the process. The terrorists stopped giving water to the hostages on the second day, after the officials repeated their claim that there were only 354 people held in the gym. Perhaps publicly admitting the actual number of hostages could have been exchanged for water for them?

Another opportunity was presented by the demand for the four negotiators specified by the terrorists to come to Beslan. Individually they were unacceptable; the terrorists ominously wanted to face Dzosokhov, Zaizikov, Aslakhanov and Roshal all at the same time. According to the testimony of the sole surviving terrorist, Khuchbarov offered to release 150 people for each negotiator. When asked whether these men would be executed, Khuchbarov gave a guarantee of their safety.[59] Importantly, Khuchbarov had previously given the same guarantee for Aushev and had kept his word. On the other hand, it is true that the situation of the other four men was a lot less predictable. Basayev had previously issued a *fatwa* calling for Zaizikov's execution and criticized and condemned Roshal for the statements he made after the Moscow theater hostage crisis in 2002. Dzosokhov and Aslakhanov were obvious targets by their title alone. All of these facts suggest that they would have probably been killed had they entered the school. Nevertheless, just summoning all of them to Beslan, and showing their presence near the siege site on television, would have put more pressure on the terrorists to reciprocate in some way. It could have also facilitated the discussion about possible confidence-building measures by both sides. These attempts might not have led to anything, but still could have kept the communications going.

Overall, the biggest mistake in Beslan was the failure of the authorities to even talk to the terrorists. True, the political reality cannot be overlooked. Putin, who had won his first presidency based solely on a tough stance on Chechnya, could hardly afford being seen as negotiating with terrorists. Allowing Maskhadov to enter the negotiations, and perhaps succeed, would also have been a huge political and personal blow to Putin. Moreover the Kremlin's fear that giving in to the terrorists' demands would only encourage further acts of terrorism is also understandable. However, an unpublicized, small-scale behind-the-scenes negotiation effort described above could have worked to contribute toward saving the lives of hostages while at the same time limiting the negative impact associated with the public perception of terrorists' success.

In the end, it would be difficult to argue that Beslan could have been resolved without the loss of life. The chances of negotiating a complete surrender or free passage for the terrorists unfortunately remained in the realm of wishful thinking, especially given the Russian government's track record of deceiving the militants with false promises of safety in similar situations in the past. Nevertheless, even if the incident was bound to end in bloodshed, maximum effort should have been made to get as many hostages out of the school as possible before resorting to a violent solution. Not only did the federal authorities fail in this task, they failed to even seriously try. Even more disturbingly, the official reactions and statements on television, such as the deliberate and clearly false downplaying of the number of hostages inside, added even more fuel to the fire. As in past hostage crises in Russia, the Kremlin seems to have had only one goal in mind – to discredit the separatist leadership and to teach Basayev a lesson. Many people may applaud Putin's "courage" and argue that the "no negotiations with terrorists" policy should be upheld at all costs, and that the "national interest" should come before the fate of individual hostages no matter how painful the decision. It is not the issue here to debate the pros and cons of this argument. The point is to recognize that in the handling of the Beslan crisis political realities played the main part, and that the lives of hostages inside the gym were considered only secondary to the "national interest." As a result the *worst* possible lesson we could learn from Beslan is that it is impossible to negotiate with the "new terrorists."

Lessons

In the aftermath of Beslan, Basayev (2002) – in his typical fashion – tried to put all the blame on Moscow by stating that he regretted that "so many children died at the hands of the Russians," but also emphasizing that he did not regret the seizure of the school itself. Unlike in the aftermath of the Moscow theater hostage crisis, however, he did not make an attempt to plead for international sympathy; on the contrary, Basayev threatened to attack "citizens of states whose leaders support Putin's Chechen policy," also proclaiming that "this world will sooner be set on fire than we refuse to fight for our freedom and independence!" In another interview conducted in January 2005, Basayev (2005) confirmed his intention to launch more "Beslan-style" operations in the future.

On July 10 2006 Basayev was killed in the possibly accidental explosion of a truck filled with 220 lb of explosives in the Ingush village of Ekazhevo. Since then, the Chechen separatist movement has suffered many setbacks. However, Basayev did leave behind a network of militants of the Caucasian Front, which now has a presence in Dagestan, Chechnya, Ingushetia, North Ossetia, Kabardino-Balkaria, Karachaevo-Cherkessia, Adygea, Stavropol, and Krasnodar. A future Beslan-style operation on Russian territory may be only a matter of time. Even more disturbingly, contemporary developments suggest that we may witness similar operations carried out by other groups outside of Russia as well. Basayev is now a prominent figure in international *jihadi* circles, and other groups around the world have taken note of his signature tactics. For instance, in issue No. 10 of al-Qaida's online manual *Al Battar*, the late Abdul Aziz al Muqrin offers detailed instructions on carrying out barricade hostage operations, making numerous references to the tactics used in "Shamil's operation in Moscow." This manual is quite revealing with regards to what we might expect in the future, especially in light of the increasing importance of online materials as an operational blueprint for the newly formed independent cells, that are behind the majority of today's spectacular terrorist attacks worldwide.

Overall, incidents like Beslan as well as manuals such as the *al-Battar* 10 suggest that while we can certainly expect the resolution of future hostage incidents to be extremely challenging because of the hostage-takers' extensive knowledge of operational procedure, security precautions designed to limit the probability of success of a rescue operation, and a high level of distrust in the authorities intentions, there is still likely to be room for a negotiated settlement.

1 *Terrorists are susceptible to negotiation.* Whether we will succeed in this endeavor in the future will largely depend on the political sanction of the use of negotiations to resolve hostage situations, as well as on our ability to think outside the box and adapt to the different circumstance and requirements of situations involving ideologically inspired hostage-takers.

2 *Terrorists reciprocate, negatively and positively.* As long as there is an understanding of the principal of *quid pro quo* on behalf of the hostage-takers, negotiations are possible. The ideal situation, of course, is to end a hostage incident without the loss of life. However, such an outcome is becoming gradually more unlikely with the terrorists' increasing sophistication and know how of our operational procedures, as well as their lower level of restrain in terms of execution of hostages. For the lack of a better option, we will need to redefine our own measures of success and increase our tolerance for casualties in terms of not giving up on negotiations based solely on the fact that hostages have died during the incident.

3 *Negotiation benefits from a contrasting alternative against which to bargain.* At the same time, it is quite possible that some situations will ultimately need to be addressed by a tactical resolution. But even in such situations the negotiation element will still be crucial, as it can be used to get the maximum number of people out of the target location before the storming. Some of the suggestions provided in this chapter can hopefully provide guidance in this direction.

Notes

A more extensive version of the author's investigation and analysis of the Beslan incident was published as Dolnik and Fitzgerald (2008) and Dolnik (2007).

1 Issue No. 10 of al-Qaeda's online magazine *al Battar* features a highly analytical guide to carrying out barricade hostage incidents written by the late Abdul Aziz al Muqrin, the leader of al-Qaeda in Saudi Arabia.

2 McMains and Mullins, *Crisis Negotiations: Managing Critical Incidents and Hostage Situations in Law Enforcement and Corrections*, 2nd edn (Cincinnati, OH: Anderson Publishing, 2001), p. 50

3 The best works on the Beslan events include: Uwe Buse, Ullrich Fichtner, Mario Kaiser, Uwe Klussmann, Walter Mayr, and Christian Neef "Putin's Ground Zero," *Der Spiegel*, December 27 2004, pp. 65–101; John B. Dunlop (2005), "Beslan: Russia's 9/11?" American Committee for Peace in Chechnya and Jamestown Foundation, October; C. J. Chivers "The School: The Inside Story of the 2004 Attack in Beslan," *Esquire* 145/6 (2006), available: www.esquire.com/features/ESQ0606BESLAN_140?click=main_sr; Adam Dolnik and Keith M. Fitzgerald, *Negotiating Hostage Crises with the New Terrorists* (Westport, CT: Praeger, 2008), p. 228; Adam Dolnik, *Negotiating the Impossible: The Lessons of the Beslan Hostage Crisis* (RUSI Whitehall Report 2-07, London: Royal United Services Institute, 2007).

4 It was later reported that the late arrival of policemen on the scene was caused by the fact that the duty officer with the key to the weapons locker could not be located for a full forty minutes.

5 Interview with Stanislav Kesaev, Vladikavkaz, July 2005.

6 Chief Beslan gunman described, *Caucasian Knot*, August 4 2005.

7 Mobile phone number.

8 According to one version, the woman was detonated remotely by Khuchbarov because of her disobedience. But, since the bomber detonated in a doorway, also killing the other suicide bomber and another terrorist in the process, it seems more likely that the detonation was an accident. Further, the other terrorists immediately afterwards prayed by the bodies of their dead colleagues, which is something that wouldn't happen if they were considered traitors.
 9 Buse et al., "Putin's Ground Zero."
10 RIA: Inquiry finds Chechen Separatist Leader was given Chance to intervene at Beslan, March 3 2005.
11 Henry Plater-Zyberk, "Beslan: Lessons Learned?" Conflict Studies Research Centre, November 2004.
12 Interview with Ruslan Aushev, Moscow, November 2005.
13 Ibid.
14 Aslanbek Aslakhanov, interviewed in Kevin Sim's documentary "Beslan: Siege of School No. 1," *Wide Angle*, 2005.
15 Interview with Larisa Kudzyeva, Beslan, November 2005.
16 The terrorists had a book that was rigged as a switch to the explosive daisy chain. One terrorist always had his foot on this book. If he lifted the foot, detonation would occur.
17 Interview with Larisa Kudzyeva, Beslan, November 2005.
18 Buse et al., "Putin's Ground Zero."
19 On the other hand, the Kremlin has tried to implicate Maskhadov in previous acts of terrorism, and providing him an opportunity to appear as a savior by engaging him in this crucial role was hardly going to be acceptable to the Kremlin. Nevertheless, both Dzosokhov and Aushev contacted Maskhadov's envoy, Zakayev, in London. The reply was that Maskhadov was ready to assume the negotiating role but asked for a guarantee that he would be allowed unhindered access to the school and that the Russians would not kill him.
20 Buse et al., "Putin's Ground Zero."
21 Statement by Lev Dzugayev, official spokesperson for the President of North Ossetia, September 3 2004.
22 "New Details emerge on Maschadov's Bid to Mediate in Beslan," *Chechnya Weekly* 7 1 (January 5 2006).
23 Further, after Beslan the federal authorities accused him of actually planning the attack and put a $10 million bounty on his head. Maschadov was then killed on March 8 2005 in the village of Tolstoy-Yurt, near Grozny.
24 For a detailed study of this incident see Adam Dolnik and Richard Pilch, "The Moscow Theater Incident: Perpetrators, Tactics, and the Russian Response," *International Negotiation* 8 3 (2003).
25 Basayev Interview for Channel 4 News, February 4 2005.
26 According to Senator Alexander Torshin, who heads the federal investigative committee, the terrorists also had a back-up school that would be easier to attack than Beslan in the village of Nesterovskaya, in Ingushetia, on the road to which the terrorists would not have to travel from Ingushetia across checkpoints.
27 Plater-Zyberk, "Beslan: Lessons Learned?"
28 William Zartman "Negotiating Effectively with Terrorists," in Barry Rubin, ed., *The Politics of Counterterrorism* (Washington, DC: Johns Hopkins Foreign Policy Institute, 1990).
29 Interview with Larisa Kudzyeva, Beslan, November 2005.
30 In this case Basayev was able to negotiate with then Prime Minister Chernomyrdin and was granted free passage out of Budyonnovsk, a refrigerated truck for the transportation of the dead bodies of several of his men, as well as an announcement of a temporary cease-fire and a declaration of the Russian commitment to serious negotiations with Chechen representatives.

31 Basayev interview for Channel 4 News, 4 February 2005.
32 Nur Pasha Kulayev, interviewed on Russian NTV station, September 4 2004.
33 Šéf teroristů z Beslanu uniká, tvrdí tisk, *Idnes*, September 10 2004.
34 Anne Nivat, *Chienne de guerre* (New York: Public Affairs, 2001), p. 92.
35 On 21 June 2004 Basayev personally commanded more than 200 of his fighters in the attack on the now former Ingushetian capital of Nazran. The attackers wore local police uniforms and set up roadblocks at which they stopped and killed the real police officers who raced to reinforce their colleagues. Nearly 100 people, including several ministers, died before the fighters withdrew and disappeared in the largest Chechen operation since 1999.
36 Plater-Zyberk, "Beslan: Lessons Learned?"
37 The official number is the result of thirty-one bodies being found, with one terrorist being captured alive. The hostages, however, report seeing between fifty and seventy hostages, suggesting that some were able to escape. In addition only seventeen of the bodies were positively identified, and consequently only a limited profiling sample is available.
38 Yekaterina Blinova and Anton Trofimov, "Beslan Hostage-takers may have Included Arrested Terrorist: Basayev Link Likely," *Nezavisimaya Gazeta*, September 8 2004.
39 Thomas Strentz, "Thirteen Indicators of Volatile Negotiations," *Law and Order* 39 9 (1991), pp. 135–139.
40 Nick Paton Walsh, "Mystery still Shrouds Beslan Six Months On: Theories and Rumours Fuel Relatives' Doubt and Anger," *Guardian*, February 16 2005.
41 "MosNews: New Drugs used by Beslan Terrorists puzzle Russian Experts," available: www.mosnews.com/news/2004/10/19/smoking.shtml (October 19 2004).
42 This would not be inconsistent with past cases, as the Kremlin has always attempted to portray Chechen militants as drug addicts, bandits and alcoholics.
43 Dunlop, "Beslan: Russia's 9/11?"
44 See, for instance, "Canticle of Deborah: They knifed Babies, they Raped Girls," *Sunday Mirror*, September 5 2004, available: www.freerepublic.com/focus/f-news/1208007/posts.
45 Interview with Larisa Kudzieva, Beslan, November 2005.
46 Drinking urine, unfortunately, further aids dehydration.
47 Interview with Larisa Kudzieva, Beslan, November 2005.
48 Interview with Aneta Gadieva, Vladikavkaz, July 2005.
49 Mark Franchetti and Matthew Campbell, "How a Repressed Village Misfit became the Butcher of Beslan," *Sunday Times*, September 12 2004, available: www.timesonline.co.uk/article/0,,2089-1257953_1,00.html.
50 Ibid.
51 Testimony of hostage Svetlana Dzheriyeva at the Kulayev trial.
52 "Beslan Hostage-takers did not Want to Die – Former Ingush President Ruslan Aushev," MosNews, 28 September 2004.
53 Interview with Larisa Mamitova, Beslan, November 2005.
54 Mamitova did in fact know Khodov's mother but never met the son before.
55 Similarly, when on the second day Larissa Kudzyeva approached Khodov with a request to wash her blood-soaked skirt he replied, "You'll wash it at home."
56 Strentz, "Thirteen Indicators."
57 McMains and Mullins, *Crisis Negotiations*.
58 Interview with Ruslan Aushev, Moscow, November 2005.
59 *Регина Ревазова, собственный корреспондент "Кавказского узла."*

6 Negotiating visible and hidden agendas

Victor Kremenyuk

Since the ancient times, terrorism was a policy of opposition to the authorities, who used threats to life, health, and property of individuals as the main method of achieving their goals. In this capacity terrorism continues to exist in the present and its magnitude has only significantly increased due to the increase of the destructive capabilities of the human race.

When we speak of terrorism, one major consideration should be kept in mind. It is one thing when terrorism appears in a society which gives all the chances to those who oppose the official policy or the policy supported by the majority – that is, in a democratic society. Democracy opens all the possibilities for the opposition to struggle in a constitutional and legal way against the policy it does not accept: creation of an opposition party, mass demonstrations and rallies, election campaigns, etc. It gives legal substance to these "anti-governmental" activities. And when in these conditions the opposition still prefers to use illegal and violent means it puts itself into the position of an outlaw with all the relevant consequences: police action, special units operations, military tribunals, and states of emergency.

A totally different thing is when the authorities push the opposition into the extremes by refusing to give it a chance of a legitimate and legal means to protest against the existing order. In this case the use of violence by the opposition, though it meets the understandable criticism and disapproval of society, can be labeled as "illegal but legitimate." The authority, through its inability (or unwillingness) to speak with the opposition, makes it violent and inclined to use terror. The history of nineteenth-century Russia testifies to this completely.

It is important to emphasize this aspect because of its consequences for the state of authority and law. In one case, when terrorism develops in the conditions of democracy it is treated, and with good grounds, as an illegal and criminal activity, and, understandably, as a subject of a resolute suppression. In another case, under the conditions of non-democracy or weak democracy when the opposition is forced into "marginal" status it may receive sympathy and even compassion. Yes, it uses unacceptable means taking hostages, killing dignitaries and ordinary people, destroying public facilities (with the people inside or without), but it is forced into it by the conduct of the authority.

These general remarks give a good argument for the study of the problem of the negotiation with the terrorists. All of them are outlaws and that is where the question whether to negotiate comes from: should a legitimate authority deal with outlaws or not, even if human lives are at stake? But, following the mentioned distinction, it may be said that there are "bad" terrorists who prefer violence to any other means of argument and thus are regarded as unacceptable partners (thus putting certain moral restraints on the freedom of negotiations with them) and "good" terrorists who act as terrorists because the authorities push them into that position. This consideration makes the question of whether to negotiate with them or not a hard moral and political choice.

It is well known that even without moral or political overtones, negotiation with terrorists is a special and rather difficult matter. Primarily, it is special and difficult because it is essentially a negotiation with an irrational partner. His/her irrationality comes from the fact that the terrorist makes his case on the basis of intimidation: s/he creates the situation in which something dear to the people is threatened: human lives first of all. And s/he proposes to remove this threat if the other side (the authorities) agree to meet his demand. This does not mean that because of that, negotiation with the terrorist is an irrational undertaking as a whole. It means that negotiation with the terrorist is essentially an attempt to engage an irrational actor into a rational process where the outcome depends on the results of an adequate and reasonable exchange with unusual commodities and priorities. But still the process itself and the conduct of the actors to a large extent, because of irrationality of the terrorist, are so hectic, spontaneous, and unpredictable that general rules of negotiation hardly work in this case. It emphasizes the importance of the study of this type of negotiation (Zartman 2006).

It is also important to emphasize that on the initial stage of the studies in this area the questions of the behavior of the terrorists were the focus of attention while in the next stages the problem becomes mainly "how to make irrational behavior rational." Disregarding a wall of moral, human, and sensual differences between the terrorist and his opponents, they have no other option but to make a deal. And the task of the negotiator in this case is to find the ways that will help to forge an appropriate solution without giving a sense of recognition of the legitimacy of the terrorist and his demands.

The terrorist usually acts either through a direct use of violence or the threat of it. His purpose is not so much a rational and comprehensible outcome (though this should not be excluded completely) but a propagandistic and political victory due to intimidation and confusion of those to whom his action is addressed. At least when the terrorist first appears as a party in negotiation, his purpose is not to make a deal but to cause damage to his opponent (Faure 1995). Later it changes: very often the terrorist disregards his harsh rhetoric and wants a deal. And it takes time and effort to convert what the terrorist wants declaratorily into a deal which may save people, property, or political order from destruction as the end of the encounter. Contrary to what is widely perceived today about the negotiation with the terrorist ("We do not negotiate with terrorists"), in reality this is a very delicate, responsible and hard mission that may be entrusted only to specially trained personnel or to the people with solid public reputation (Hayes 2002).

With all that, negotiation with the terrorist acquires the quality of something trivial because the amount of attacks worldwide grows, because some political parties and groups which originally rejected terrorism in principle have come to use terrorist tactics, and because the use of these tactics is regarded as the only way to make a breakthrough in a conflict under the conditions of a stalemate. In any case, terrorism and its impact on human behavior, including negotiation, sometimes requires the introduction of changes and modifications in the normal conduct of the political process (Kremenyuk 2004).

It relates to almost all cases of terrorist attack. But it is especially important when a terrorist attack is a part of the sustained political struggle of the opposition which, due to different reasons, turned to violent means. In this case it is evident from the very beginning that the case is much more complex than a simple police operation: it demands a political solution under the conditions of stress.

Contextual issues

Among the changes that follow the need to negotiate with the terrorist are the issues of the improved and updated structure of negotiation. Usually, the negotiation with the terrorist is considered a one-shot deal, rather specific, rather isolated, highly responsible but unique (Hayes 2002). Because of the "currency" of the exchange, i.e. human lives, health, and freedom, it resembles only the cases of the negotiations of the slave-traders in the past. But otherwise they, as a negotiation exercise, are unparalleled.

Both sides usually avoid shedding too much light on their interaction: the terrorist wants to be regarded as tough and uncompromising, and his opponent does not wish to be compromised by the fact of making a deal with an outlaw. But still important things like the lives of the hostages, the possibility of an armed clash, and the danger of destruction of public facilities are negotiated through concessions to the terrorists in the areas they indicate: payment of ransom, release of fellow terrorists from prisons, public excuses by the officials, etc. Very often, because of the usual secrecy, the scope of the issues discussed with the terrorists goes far beyond this list and includes issues of much higher political and administrative level: withdrawal of the military forces from specific areas, change of the policy of the government, recognition of the opposition and other aspects which turn the technical matter of negotiating with criminals into a matter of policy-making. And that demands a different approach.

An approach that may be suggested is to put the negotiation with the terrorist into a wider political, social and psychological context. The terrorist does not appear from nowhere, his/her existence is the result of a political/military conflict that exists in the society for years and has become a part of the life. Mainly, the opposing parties accept the situation of the stalemate and either do not have any sound resolution strategy or adhere to some unrealistic emotional positions which do not help to move to the end of the conflict. It is in these conditions that terrorists try to take over control of the conflict using inhuman means. When the other side, the authorities, is not prepared for this and is also satisfied with the *status quo*, the terrorist act is regarded as something which breaks the routine in an unacceptable way. But, if the other side is prepared politically and psychologically for the resolution of the conflict the terrorist regards it a good pretext to start a political offensive.

It is a general rule that "negotiation with the terrorist" concerns a specific situation when terrorists acquire the possession of some important values: hostages, outstanding personalities, children, priests, or the objects of some value (historical shrines, cathedrals, water supply centers, nuclear power plants, etc.) and use the threat to kill the people or destroy the shrines if their demands are not satisfied. This typical model of an encounter with terrorists is well known and more or less elaborated (Burton 1979). There are standard operation procedures for the force structures, and established patterns of engagement of experts in psychology, history, and culture who are recruited by the authorities to deal with the terrorists (Ragaini 2004). There are even such specific methods as involvement of some personalities close to terrorists: members of their families, friends, known public figures, clergy, popular actors who are engaged by the authorities in the quest of forging a deal with the terrorists.

And, of course, there are negotiations. Because of the widespread contempt and disapproval of the terrorists and their methods, socializing with them is regarded as disgraceful. And that creates the moral and ethical dilemma: to negotiate or not to negotiate. Currently most governments and political parties have overcome that impediment. Their conclusion is: if there is a chance to save even one human life, the negotiation should take place. All other considerations are irrelevant and immoral. Trained and competent people among the negotiators are entrusted a double and even triple role: on one hand, their task is to get an agreement with the terrorist in order to avoid public confusion and the loss of values and lives; on the other hand, they have to be discreet, avoid publicity, demonstrate both responsibility and tact, able not to make the other side feel uncomfortable and cheated, publicly stripped down or humiliated. A task of confidence-building and advancement. This is a hard job and some good pieces of analytical literature are devoted to it (Cristal 2006).

What makes the problem of negotiation with terrorists even more complicated is the fact that any terrorist attack sooner or later grows into a political problem. Speaking in general terms, each case of terrorist action is already an embryo of a political problem because it is an open challenge to the law, to the authorities, to the rules of civilized conduct, to everything which makes the life of a society regular. So, any challenge to it, especially if it is demonstrative, humiliating the norms of civilized life, human feelings, is a matter of policy because it is addressed, first of all, to the authorities and is intended to show to the public to which extent the authority is weak and unreliable. Since the first duty of any authority is to defend the law and order, the terrorist act is the revolt which has to be suppressed by any means. Or else, negotiated.

This is one side of the political nature of negotiations with terrorists. The other consists in the fact that terrorist attacks are very often a response to the policy of the authorities in a conflict in which the terrorists are identified with the opposition to the government. Either for propagandistic purposes or for some pragmatic reasons, terrorists add to their usual demands some political conditions such as release of prisoners, withdrawal of forces from specific territories, change of military or police commanders, sometimes even a change of government, or of its policy on some specific issue as has been, for example, in Chechnya (Dolnik 2006 and in the previous chapter).

There should be no surprise if we remember that terrorist attacks are not simple criminal acts. Somehow it has happened that in books and press reports the criminal side of terrorism overshadows all the others, as is understandable: terrorism is a crime and should be treated as such. But it would also be correct not to forget that this criminal activity has a strong and sometimes even dominant political overtone: a struggle against a regime, a demand for self-determination, a search for something which seems to the terrorists as "justice." In short, terrorism is also a tool in a political struggle, and it is a powerful tool because it forces the other side either to capitulate or to act even more radically than the terrorists.

If we go back to the origins of modern terrorism in nineteenth-century Europe, in Russia and the Middle East, it is easy to identify a strong political rather than criminal element in it. Terrorism was and is a function of the people who use intimidation, abduction, and threat of death to the innocent as a means of political struggle. According to their teachings there are no "innocents" in the struggle; all those who are not with them are the enemies. Also, terrorism was and is an instrument of those who want change but whose legitimate interests are bluntly ignored by the ruling classes. Terrorism was and is an act by those who have nothing to lose since they have already lost everything – homes, relatives, children, property, hopes for the future. And all this is terrorism. In this sense it comes from nineteenth-century Marxist revolutionary theory, which declared, "Workers of the world, unite; you have nothing to lose but your chains!"

In current literature it is mainly criminal terrorism that is studied and the means to deal with it which are discussed are also of the most primitive nature: police action (Kremenyuk 2004). But it is important to note that currently the notion of "police action" has also included a possibility and even necessity of negotiations. This is a result of a sustained effort by the rational elements in society which have resolutely rejected the bravado and irresponsibility of the adherents of the military action. The threat to deal a military blow to the terrorists almost does not work: the terrorists come from that cohort of the people who have already lost everything and do not care much for their lives; of those who are committed to the self-sacrifice and cannot be intimidated either by the prospect of death or by the threat of prison (Burton 1979).

Here comes the chance for negotiations because an experienced and capable negotiator can use even the slightest signs of a possible compromise in order to engage the other side into a productive dialogue. The cases where the deal has not happened and have led to a complete failure are not that numerous, though each of them – "Black September" in Jordan in 1970, the Olympic Games in Munich in 1973, the "Nord-Ost" theater in Moscow in 2002, Beslan in 2004 – left behind a train of bitter feelings, anguish, and reproaches to the governments. The cases where the deal with the terrorists was done and the lives of the innocent were saved are much more numerous though one of the conditions set by the terrorists in such cases is discreteness and an information smokescreen. They do not like it when the public learns that terrorists are capable of being predictable and their demonstrative irrationality is sometimes a part of the game.

Following the differences in the genesis and rationale of the terrorism in reality, there are two distinctly different types of terrorist performance. One is simply a "demonstration of flag," the demonstration of the existence of terrorists and of their ability to act. Usually this type of terrorist activity leads to the cases of hostage-taking for ransom, demands of money, threats of explosions in public transportation, and other cases when the main purpose of the terrorists is "money through intimidation." In the conditions of the growing insecurity, uncontrolled illegal spread of the weapons, growing popularity of different "revolutionary" or quasi-revolutionary movements this type of crime becomes rather attractive and even popular.

The other types of terrorist attack is connected to political struggle and is associated with attempts to achieve political goals through terror, through the use of intimidation, demonstrative readiness to sacrifice lives of innocent people in the interests of political movement. Both types are essentially an illegal use of violence and coercion but with striking difference between their goals and motivations.

It is helpful in this regard to go back to the thesis of the double nature of terrorism (a criminal act versus the only possibility to fight the authorities) and to try to understand that it has a direct impact on the problem of negotiation: in one case you conspire with the criminals, while in the other you have a chance of solving an important political conflict. While all is clear with the first type of negotiations, the second type is a demonstration of how a weakness of a political movement compared to the powers of the government may become its strength. The asymmetry permits the terrorists to abandon of all the existing rules of conduct and to behave like a "loose cannon" threatening to wipe out what exists of the political order. The asymmetry in capabilities of both sides is compensated by the asymmetry in their attitudes toward the general rules of human behavior and thus puts the two opponents on a more equal footing: "You don't want to consider my case, so I don't care about your rules of the game!" The balance between them is based on an equation: on one side, a threat to lives or freedom of innocent people; on the other, a demand of political concessions.

This was demonstrated in the case of Beslan: more than a thousand hostages, mainly schoolchildren on one side and demands of independence for Chechnya on the other. The terrorists even managed to send some of their demands to the authorities: withdrawal of federal forces from Chechnya, recognition of the regime of Aslan Maskhadov (who was elected President of Chechnya before the second war started in 1999), return to the Khasavyurt agreement of 1996 that recognized the right of the Chechens to independence. In a word, this was a terrorist attack (and thus the subject to the competence of the local police and military commander) and at the same time a political action which was a subject for the supreme authorities in the Kremlin.

From the point of view of negotiation analysis this aspect acquires a certain importance of its own. First, several independent negotiation encounters appear instead of one. What is on the spot and covered by the media is the negotiation between the terrorist group and the local authority, sometimes rather friendly, sometimes very hostile. Next is the negotiation between the local authorities and the supreme authority in which the local authorities play the role of the tape-recorder and adviser since they know better about the local conditions while the higher authority has a better general view of the situation. Very often this is accompanied by the negotiation between the supreme authority and the emissary of the terrorists (a "short-circuit").

Second, there is a certain division of responsibilities and of relevant subjects among these negotiations. Each of them has its own subject and agenda, its own pace and its own turf while together they are what we call "the negotiation with the terrorist." This creates a specific sub-system of negotiations which have to be somehow coordinated and regarded as parts of the same political process.

Third, the time element acquires special importance in all this sequence of negotiations because very often a success in one of them is a *sine qua non* for the outcome of the other. As a result, a certain structure of negotiations with different actors, agendas, locations, and responsibilities appear united by the whole situation and subject: release of hostages and satisfaction of the demands of the terrorists.

Dimensions of the structure

The immediate rationale for negotiations with terrorists is the release of hostages and other measures to avoid violence and to adhere to the law. The more substantial goal is to demonstrate that the law is always stronger than violence and can win even in the case of a terrorist attack. Even if sometimes the whole effort of negotiation may be regarded as a "capitulation" to the demands of the terrorists, still there are the highest values of society which are at stake: lives and freedom of its citizens, law and order of society. There are those who would not agree with such statement and will insist that "humiliation of the state" (a compromise with the terrorists) is an unacceptable price, a failure.

Much depends here not on the differences in the ways of thinking but on the differences in values: for political cultures where the state is an "absolute value" a possibility to make a deal to save the people through an agreement with the terrorist is unthinkable since it leads to the humiliation of the state (Russia); for the political cultures where rights and lives of individuals are the top priority (the Western tradition), everything is acceptable if it leads to salvation. And all this concentrated in the Hamletian question: to negotiate or not to negotiate?

Negotiating visible and hidden agendas 155

Against this background the substructure of the negotiation with the terrorist is constructed. The double nature of a terrorist attack requires two overlapping and complementary perspectives. The first – a so-called "narrow sense" – is the traditional one: a crime which demands adequate response, a case when the government is challenged but at the same time has a chance to demonstrate its negotiating capacity, its adherence to the universal values and, its readiness to work for the benefit of its people..

The second – a so-called "broad sense" – is to regard the whole case of a terrorist attack as part of a hard confrontation between the government and its enemies in which the opposition demonstrates its survivability (especially if the official propaganda declares it "destroyed"), its disregard of the accepted rules and norms, and its ability to attack the government and to demonstrate to which extent the authorities risk the lives, health, and property of their citizens if they ignore the demands of the opposition, and prefer to adhere to the chosen position in the conflict.

There is something like a propagandistic battle between the government and the terrorists concerning the heart of the issue. The government will always be interested to present the case as a "crime," as a result of the act by irresponsible "barbaric" people. Its position would be to minimize the political component in any terrorist attack and to maximize its criminal nature. The terrorists will always emphasize that they were "forced" to apply the terrorist methods because the authorities ignored their "just and legitimate" demands issued through regular channels. Much in the further struggle will depend on who wins this first round of the exchange. All the chances are usually on the side of the terrorists because very often the authorities try to reduce the free flow of information, citing the "gravity" of the situation, and that makes the news media hostile to them.

In the case of a terrorist attack this episode is only a preface, an introduction to a much more complex, multi-dimensional and important process. The task of the terrorists from the very beginning is to put the authorities on the defensive, to reduce their freedom of action thus giving to the terrorists a possibility to press, to insist on the immediate result and reduce to the minimum flexibility of the government as a tool of bargaining. It sets from the very beginning the high price of a failure to reach an agreement and a perspective of a collapse if the government does not carry out its obligations – freedom and security of its people. It also demonstrates – sometimes openly, sometimes through some Byzantian maneuvers – the real purpose of the terrorist attack: to force the government to agree to the solution of the disputed problem on their conditions.

What is important to emphasize in this context is that the structural analysis of the situation reveals not only what is on the surface (i.e. terrorist act and the response by the authority) but also a complicated and multi-dimensional structure of interests: in the terrorist camp (because there is always at least two, if not more, wings in any terrorist group which will use any failure or mistake of the other to strengthen its own position), on the government side (there are always at least two groups in any government which stand for either a violent solution of the situation or for diplomatic settlement), between the government and society, especially news media (because the society has all the legitimate grounds to know what the government does and why, while the government actively uses secrecy and closed information to avoid public criticism of its actions). The situation, though it may seen a zero-sum game, in reality is much more diverse and fragmented and contains chances for cooperation as well as strong elements of confrontation (Faure 1995).

One of the first sequences of such a development is the creation of a certain "tree of interests" around the whole event. On the terrorist side it is to demonstrate resolve, readiness to go to the extremes, and, at the same time, readiness for a compromise, the desire to win politically and psychologically, to humiliate the other side. Very often this interest is associated with a compromise between different wings among the terrorists. On the part of the government it is to demonstrate resolve and flexibility, readiness to destroy the terrorists and to negotiate on the primary role of law and order, readiness to make a deal but as an exception rather than a rule. The interests of both sides come into an interplay and form a certain "cone": from the agreement to probe for a possible compromise and up to the possibility to use this case for some breakthrough decisions on larger political issues.

This "tree of interests" forms an interdependent complex of purposes in a certain sequence: the solution of the status of the objects of intimidation (hostages, objects of culture and religion, supply stations, water, etc.), the negotiation on the political agenda, the structure and consequence of gradual advancement in the solution of the conflict (which decisions are conditioned by the others), the desirable outcome. Actually it sets the real ("invisible") agenda, priorities, and landmarks. And it is within this component of purposes that separate negotiation cases appear: the one where the counter-terrorist agents of the government try to contain the terrorists and limit the scope of destruction; the other, where the government tries to discuss in an appropriate form the political issues which the terrorists want to discuss and at the same time to synchronize it with the first; the third when the government has to explain its conduct and to sell it to the public and media (Hayes 2002).

This structure and the process that develops within it have two different dimensions. One concerns the whole task of making an agreement with a certain group of terrorists on the subject which has become the source of conflict: hostages or other threats which may lead if not solved, to a political crisis. The other is associated with the state and evolution of the political problem which is at the heart of the conflict between the government and opposition. The ideal solution is to find an agreement which will help both to save the lives of the people and solve the political controversy but ideal solutions are not achieved easily. There has to be an alternative.

Once the interests of the actors and the purposes based on these interests are set, it is the problem of method and mechanism which comes next in importance. Partly, the issue of the method is already clear: to construct such a chain of steps which will force the other side to move in a certain direction each time threatening to use force if it demonstrates skepticism, obstinacy, or desire to avoid commitments. What creates an asymmetry at this stage is the threat by the terrorists to walk out and to stop the negotiation while the government can hardly afford it: it knows it will be criticized by some political groups for the engagement in negotiation but, if the negotiation prematurely fails, it will be beaten for a "double sin": the negotiation with the criminals and failure to achieve success.

To make the situation more robust and resistant to a possibility of failure, an experienced negotiator builds a package which consists of different dyads (an issue and its solution) and is implemented in isolated negotiations, thus making it practically impossible to stop the talks: along with some difficult and questionable negotiations there will also be successful and tempting and if the overall balance at these negotiations is in favor of an agreement then there will be strong support for the negotiation even among the terrorists.

Depending on the complexity of the issues raised by the terrorists the amount of individual negotiations may be fragmented into two (at the best), three, four or even more separate encounters and there will be a problem to coordinate all of them, to keep them within one general line and to watch for the time schedule because the terrorists usually are not inclined to turn negotiations into an endless procedure; for them time limit is also a weapon. All these cases create one common negotiation space but they differ in subjects, levels of responsibility, participants, outcomes, and role in the whole counter-terrorist effort.

It would be wrong to perceive this structure as an anarchical decentralized system without any general leadership. On the contrary, each side tries to control what is going on in each part of the negotiation and to which extent the outcome corresponds to his/her long-term goals. But the reverse side of it is the growth of unexpected though logical happenings which may change significantly the course of events. To explain this point more extensively the case of the "Stockholm syndrome" may be mentioned: the emergence of something like sympathy and feeling of intimate understanding between the terrorists and hostages which is capable of reversing completely the events in a hostage crisis and bringing additional power to the terrorist making his position more comprehensible and acceptable for the public.

It is always useful to remember that a terrorist, especially in societies where the rights of an average citizen are grossly ignored or abused by the authorities, is always a much more sympathetic figure than the government. The tales about Robin Hood are the best example.

Managing complexity

The net result of all these structural efforts is that the negotiation with a terrorist is split into basically two parts: one under the spotlights of the media, the so-called "visible" part; and the other, somewhere in the shadows where the emissary of the terrorists tries to wrench concessions out from the bewildered government. It may be labeled as a "hidden" part of the negotiation. The "hidden" part is well known to the authorities and the public at large because it is a political conflict which exists for a rather long period of time. What is new and unexpected is that it becomes a possible source of a crisis because of the terrorist action.

Thus both the research task and the needs of practice prompt several points for analysis: composition of each part, its agenda, participants, goals, probability of an agreement and its contents; type of connections between the two parts, in which aspects they are united and facilitate the achievement of the final result, and in which they contradict each other and make the final outcome either impossible or hardly attainable. And, the last but not least, what is the management procedure for both, that is what is the negotiation strategy and who is responsible for it?

This chapter is not concerned with the larger "political/strategic" negotiations with terrorists that is the focus of another book (Zartman and Faure 2010). This chapter chooses two other elements: the "hidden" part of the negotiation with the terrorists where political issues are discussed because of the terrorists attack and their desire to raise these issues (as it happens rather often in the Middle East, the United Kingdom, France, and Spain) and the relation between the "hidden" and "visible" parts of the negotiation, their interplay and the role of this link in the whole conflict resolution effort. It means that mainly it studies the case of a negotiation with the terrorist where the hostage-taking or any other act is only a part of the strategy which seeks a solution of a larger problem on the conditions of the terrorist.

When the authorities, as an actor, run into a situation in which a group of hostages is taken by terrorists and demands of a ransom are issued, still they want to know whether that is the main purpose of the act or there is another "invisible" interest. No doubt it will have to become engaged in a hard and exhausting negotiation in order to reduce the risk to the people or other values and generally will work under the terms of a "damage limitation" strategy. Its goal will be to achieve the promise and (if possible) guarantees of the hostages' lives and freedom and to reduce the political effect of the deal which will testify that the terrorists have acquired power.

At this point it becomes clear that the two sides, even if they agree to begin negotiations, see the process itself and its purpose differently. For the authorities, what is important is the limitation of the damage caused by the terrorist attack (number one) and by the agreement to negotiate (number two). They will inevitably be mainly concerned with the issues of their own prestige and the prestige of the law. That is why they will try to concentrate on the issues of containment of the event, prevention of its spread, and eventual punishment of the crime. But everything sounds different when the authorities discover that all the bombast of the terrorists, threats to the lives of the people or to the important centers merely serve as an invitation to negotiate the hard political issue in which the official side is already in jeopardy (because it is pressed by time and by the threat to the lives of the hostages) and is encouraged to start negotiations both by the terrorists and by the media or different groups of the public.

Negotiating visible and hidden agendas

As for the other side, the terrorists, this is the case in favor of a solution of the conflict which for a long time was the main purpose of their struggle. Their attitude acquires the shape of the strategy of the conflict resolution. The two strategies meet and the logical question is: who wins? One strategy is directed to defend the positions of the authorities in the eyes of their own population and of their foreign partners, the other is oriented toward the solution of the conflict with the government and the continuation of the support on the part of its adherents. And the most distinctive feature of the whole situation is the fact that both depend on each other more than in other times.

In addition to the usual tasks of discretion, cautiousness, desire to avoid unnecessary victims, and general restoration of the situation back to normalcy, the government has to concentrate on difficult political issues where the situation is always fraught with both predictable and unpredictable dangers. In the terms of the negotiation process it means that both sides must work out an elaborated and multi-dimensional negotiation strategy: identification of purposes and desirable outcome, the scope of resources and assets which may be sacrificed for the satisfaction of the demands of the other side, the possible "rate of exchange" of the demands and concessions, possible pluses and minuses of an agreement which follows the negotiation. It concerns both the "visible" part of negotiation and the "hidden," the political one. Both strategies have to be prepared and interconnected because the terrorist will inevitably threaten the lives of hostages ("we shall kill one hostage every hour") as a tool of making the position of the government "softer" and more "cooperative."

The situation may turn out rather hopeless if we regard it in a certain perspective: the government adheres to a rigid position on the political issues, has no intention to change it, there is a stalemate in the whole process and, in order to defreeze it and to begin the process of conflict resolution, a strong incentive is needed. In this case the terrorist attack plays the role of such an "incentive." But this is not the only possible scenario because rather often (as may be noticed at times in the Israeli–Palestinian case) the governments on each side are ready to turn to political settlement but they need a pretext, something that will approve the change in their public position.

This side is important to understand that usually there is a complicated and mutually dependent structure of interests around any conflict, be it domestic or foreign. Political parties formulate their visions and strategies to deal with it once they are in office. Agencies of any government, power structures, legal institutions, and others take their positions. Non-governmental organizations, the Church, and groups of citizens have their positions. In the long run it means that any such conflict is surrounded by a whole sub-structure of interests and positions and the negotiation with the terrorist must be put somewhere into this dense network. In terms of negotiation strategy it also means that the outcome of the negotiations between the government and terrorists will depend on how successfully they will connect their intercourse with a larger political process.

The beginning of the negotiation with the terrorist may be labeled as a strategy of damage limitation. From any point of view a terrorist attack is a damage:

for the hostages, for the government, for the law, for the state of public morale. It is natural that the first goal in negotiation with the terrorist is the limitation of the damage caused by his action: liberation of the hostages, reinforcement of the prestige of the government and of the robustness of the law. All these subjects are the essence of the agenda and the starting point for the negotiation.

But when the negotiation starts and the two strategies meet – the damage limitation versus conflict resolution – the result is the case of complexity magnified by the shortage of time and intense pressure from the media. This is why the next and maybe even the final part of this negotiation comes under the heading of "managing complexity," which means that the negotiation on the fate of hostages gradually develops into a much wider and much more complicated undertaking. Hence, the initial subject (life and freedom of the innocent people) may become submerged under the avalanche of events, consequences and parallel considerations.

Even from the least dramatic point of view, the negotiation with terrorists is a crisis. It is a crisis because there are always time limits. It is a crisis because the stakes are high. It is a crisis because it puts an overload on all the existing mechanisms of the authority and demands an acceptable solution for both sides that means the necessity to court the terrorists. It is, of course, a personal crisis both for the hostages, their friends and relatives, and for the decision-makers. And from this understanding negotiation with terrorists is part of a crisis management strategy in which the freedom of the hostages is the most important and obligatory part.

Crisis management in the conditions of complexity and reduced time budget raises the academic and practical value of the negotiation with the terrorist up to the level of the war management and demands appropriate and responsible solutions. This very often puts the issue of negotiations into the category of national security with the relevant decision-making and decision-taking procedures. On the other hand, negotiation with terrorists is a complicated and difficult undertaking in which two different and specific things come together: management of the crisis caused by the terrorist and negotiation with the terrorist which is essential for managing this crisis.

Each side in such negotiations has chances to win or to loose and what becomes crucial for the outcome is how quickly they will agree on something that will bring them closer, and create a common interest between them. Despite different considerations which put them on the opposite sides, including desire to win, resentment of each other's policies, moral and legal disapproval, feeling of a challenge and its own justifiability, still they have something in common.

First, both sides want to put an end to the situation – it is unbearable for the authorities and exhausting for the terrorists. When the terrorists plan their action they usually try to limit the whole event in time and in participation. (Too many people involved means the risk of leakage is too high.) What helps to compensate these limits is surprise and high speed of development. But that exhausts them physically and psychologically. Second, both want to win public sympathies and public support (though this consideration also puts them at odds).

Third, both want to avoid bloodshed and massacre (though this was questionable in many cases, for example in the case of Beslan, as it appears that the Russian government was preparing for the military action from the very beginning of the crisis).

This is a very delicate point in the whole process of crisis management. It is clear that each terrorist attack begins with a direct conflict between the two sides. Then the sympathy to the victims and understanding that they have to be saved makes the government "softer" and open for a dialogue with the terrorists. Then the terrorists want to use this asset in order to impose their positions on the government and to get guarantees that its concessions will be respected even after the hostages are released. Besides, they want a guarantee that both their freedom and the outcomes of the negotiation will be respected by the other side. And all this, taken together, forms the escort to the process of hard bargaining between the two sides.

Negotiation analysis

Negotiation with terrorists is of the type in which a strong interdependence exists among separate elements of the negotiation process. Each of the elements exists as an individual matter with all the qualities of an individual negotiation, but only when assembled together do they become a "negotiation with terrorists." What makes this negotiation different from other cases when political settlement is discussed (end of the war in Vietnam or withdrawal of the Soviet troops from Afghanistan) is the visible human element associated with the need to free the hostages and the sense of emergence because life and freedom declare the time limits and the rhythm of the process. The interdependence here is strikingly visible: "If you want to liberate your subjects, be cooperative and meet our demands."

The first conclusion from a brief glance at this negotiation is that the terrorists acquire such a powerful position that the government has simply to agree to whatever they say and be happy if all the hostages are safe and in a good shape. But in reality this is not so: there are elements of vulnerability in the positions of the terrorists, not only in the government's. Physical and psychological strain, threat of exhaustion, growing feeling for the innocent hostages, especially children and old people, permanent threat of military action – all this makes the terrorists vulnerable and open to pressure. Besides, the government has always a much larger scope of temptations that may attract the terrorists: money, freedom, promise not to persecute after the episode is finished, threats to the relatives of the terrorists (Russian innovation). The government has enough proposals it may use against the only thing the terrorist possess – the lives of the hostages.

Typical alignment in the negotiation with the terrorist – lives and freedom of the hostages for the government's concessions – may be located in two different ways. One is devoted mainly to the primary subject of the case (hostages) and concentrates the effort only on the solution of this problem. A position typical for the Israeli negotiations (Cristal 2006) because for them it is impossible to go too far beyond this subject: their counterparts do not want to even discuss such issues as conflict resolution. For them the only possible solution of the conflict is destruction of Israel. But there is another possible way to negotiate with the terrorist and its essence is to put the whole case into a larger political context, to use the case of the terrorist attack in order to get out from the political impasse.

An experienced negotiator has all the possibilities to build a relevant negotiation strategy based on these premises. The initial position of both sides, though sometimes they seem as absolutely incompatible, in reality may be developed into the points for bargaining and in this sense the "hidden" agenda may play a role of a significant reserve for the negotiation process. No doubt it increases the range of interaction between the two sides but equally may allow them to turn the "must" into the virtue: to transfer the argument on the lives of the hostages into beginning the resolution of the political conflict.

Sometimes one of the major problems of the conflict resolution is not the absence of a relevant strategy (it always exists in the heads of the decision-makers and, if not, may be worked out by a group of experts) but the unavailability of political parties so deeply dug in that in order to unfreeze the situation, to start a process which may lead to a genuine solution, the real exploit is needed. There is a resistance by some groups of the public, there is a grounded skepticism by the rival parties, there is an opposition inside the ruling party and all this serves as an obstacle in the beginning of the conflict resolution effort.

From this point of view a terrorist attack, which usually breaks the existing blockade around the conflict, activates human feeling and establishes new links between the participants, and creates a crisis that may be regarded as a possible starting point for conflict resolution procedures. It may play the role of the central element of the negotiation strategy on the "hidden" agenda: if the "visible" agenda will concentrate on the dramatic issues of the salvation of the human lives or other values, the "hidden" negotiation may switch over to the solution of the conflict which has given birth to the terror.

The interrelation between the "hidden" and "visible" agendas in the negotiation with terrorists is the important element both for the negotiation analysis and conflict studies. In the negotiation analysis it permits a new vision of the negotiation process where the publicly known negotiation case may (or should) be followed by "hidden" conflict and the real outcome of the process will depend on the results of the parallel negotiation which is almost unknown to the public. As for the conflict analysis, the findings of this chapter may help extend the scope of possible scenarios of the evolution of any conflict where the possibility of terrorist actions may resolutely change the balance of assets between the two paths of the evolution of the conflict: continuation or resolution.

7 Negotiating the grand swap in Kandahar

P. Sahadevan

Negotiating with terrorists over hostages essentially signifies negotiating under threat. Hostage-takers face an imminent threat of commando action by the government whose citizens they have taken hostage. At the same time, terrorists use hostages not only as an effective shield against any coercive measure but also as a currency of exchange (Faure 2003: 476) or bargaining chips in negotiations (Zartman 2003: 446). Thus, both government and terrorists perceive threat or really threaten each other, with the innocent hostages bearing the brunt of it. If hostage-takers are non-suicidal contingent terrorists (Zartman 2003) with a steely and ceaseless determination to accomplish their demands of, for instance, collecting ransom or getting some of their comrades released, they invariably seek negotiations as the way out of a hostage crisis. Negotiations are the most preferred strategy of terrorists, who are as much interested in achieving their desired goals without endangering their lives as governments are in protecting the lives of the hostages. Since hostage-taking is a calculated interest-driven activity of terrorists, aimed at advancing their cause, they know too well that any military response by their opponent would not only harm them physically but also defeat their goals. At the same time, the affected government tends to avoid risking the hostages' lives while trying to defeat contingent terrorists and end the hostage crisis militarily. Thus, both parties tend to experience *almost* the same sort of compulsions and constraints providing the context and creating conditions for a common approach towards, and interest in, negotiations as a logical and practical method of resolving a hostage crisis, a point Kremenyuk has developed in the preceding chapter. This exemplifies the point that negotiation is inherent in a hostage situation (Zartman 1990: 165–166).

Yet, in comparison, governments are the reluctant negotiators in any hostage crisis. The reason is that a negotiated solution would require both parties' willingness to compromise on their respective positions and demands. In simple terms, their readiness to negotiate would imply their desire to give and take – better termed a trade-off. In this context, governments are faced with severe limitations and constraints. Since hostage-taking is a blatant criminal act by some unlawful people or an organization, governments tend to feel that giving into terrorists' pressure by accepting some or all of their illegitimate demands in the process of taking what is legitimate (the release of hostages) would amount to be bestowing legitimacy on them and approving their crime. In many negotiations, therefore, governments are seen as parties that "give", more or less, to terrorists, who are essentially the "takers". Thus the principle of compromise is expected only from governments, since they are forced to accept some of the demands of terrorists. On their part, under pressure, terrorists may extend concessions to their opponent by scaling down their demands (from their maximalist position to a minimalist one, which is still a maximum for governments, thus still not providing a Zone of Possible Agreement, ZOPA). This is truly an undesirable situation for governments. The entire process is very complex primarily in view of the differing nature and status of both negotiating parties – the state seeks to work within the politico-legal limits bound by established norms, whereas terrorists are wedded to violence as a means to achieve their desired ends and free of conventional restrictions – and the situation (marked by a hostage crisis) in which negotiations are conducted.

This chapter provides a critical analysis of the entire structure, process and outcomes of the Indian government's negotiations with the contingent terrorists who, in the last week of December 1999, hi-jacked an Indian Airlines (IC 814) plane and kept 161 people as hostages for eight days at Afghanistan's Kandahar airport. The treatment begins with an account of the hi-jacking and hostage-taking incident and establishes the terrorists' identity and goals. Then, in the subsequent section, some of the structural elements of negotiations are presented as a background for analysis of the protracted negotiation process between the Indian interlocutors and the terrorists. While assessing the outcome, the final section will highlight the theoretical implications of the Kandahar hostage negotiations.

Negotiation history

On the eve of Christmas in 1999, an Airbus A300 carrying 189 passengers and crew on a flight from the Nepalese capital Kathmandu to the Indian capital New Delhi was hi-jacked in mid-air by five Kashmiri terrorists at around 16.55 IST. A country with scenic beauty in the Himalayan region, Nepal is a major tourist attraction for middle-class people of neighboring India. All but twenty-three passengers were Indians. Most of them were tourists, including a large number of honeymooners.

In the first few hours of the hi-jacking crisis, the terrorists mercilessly unleashed their fury on the passengers and crew. They were desperate to protect themselves from an attack by the passengers or Indian commandos, ensure a smooth execution of their plan and find a safe haven to keep the hostages before seeking negotiations with the Indian government. Presenting a moving account of the entire in-flight experience in an informative book *IC 814 Hi-jacked* (Jaggia and Shula 2000), Flight Engineer Jaggia and his co-author said that the hi-jackers moved all nineteen executive class passengers to empty seats in the economy cabin; ordered the cabin crew to blindfold men; remove hand baggage from overhead bins in the economy class to the executive class cabin; separate women from their families and ask them to keep their heads covered. They threatened to blow up the aircraft if the crew or passengers refused to cooperate.

Having ensured the immediate safety and full cooperation of all on board, the hi-jackers now focused their attention on finding a safe place for landing. They asked the pilot to fly the aircraft toward the west, apparently to reach the Pakistani city of Lahore – a predetermined, and the most favored, destination of the hi-jackers. Pakistan refused landing permission and closed its air space to the Indian aircraft. As the hi-jackers insisted on taking the plane to Lahore and threatened to kill the passengers one by one if diverted to some other place, the pilot continued to fly the aircraft toward Pakistan, only to be told categorically by Delhi Air Traffic Control (ATC) that Lahore ATC declared it would shoot down the aircraft if it entered Pakistani air space. What created some anxious moments when the hi-jackers were haggling with the pilot was the fast depleting level of fuel reserve in the aircraft, with only twenty-five flight minutes remaining. At this stage the hi-jackers found reason in the pilot's argument that he needed fuel to fly the aircraft to any of their chosen destinations. They therefore agreed to land the plane at the Amritsar airport (an Indian town bordering with Pakistan) on the pilot's promise that he would arrange refueling within minutes of landing.

Landing at the Amritsar airport at about 19.00 hours IST, the hi-jackers ordered the pilot to keep the aircraft moving up and down all the time on the runway. Fearing a commando attack, they did not allow him to switch off the engines. When the Indian authorities tried to delay the refueling process, apparently with the intention of storming the aircraft, the impatient hi-jackers stabbed four passengers and ordered the pilot at gunpoint to take the aircraft off. They turned out to be suicidal terrorists in desperate and insecure moments; in response to the pilot's plea against flying without refueling, they wanted the plane either to be downed by a Pakistani missile or crashed for lack of fuel. They pressed a gun at the pilot and started counting down from 30. The plane took off to Lahore when they had counted down to 2. Again, it was forced to enter Pakistani air space. Lahore ATC repeated its warning that the plane would be shot down and switched off the runway lights. Finally, the Pakistani authorities relented only when the Indian political leadership made requests. The permission did not come through before the pilot averted a crash landing mistakenly on a busy road in Lahore and the aircraft was left with fuel for one and a half minutes of flying. The plane was refueled at Lahore but the airport officials did not allow the injured passengers to disembark. Within minutes of refueling, Lahore ATC promptly ordered the plane to leave the airport. Now, the hi-jackers asked the pilot to fly to Kabul, the capital of civil war-torn Afghanistan.

On being informed by Lahore ATC that Kabul airport was closed during the night, the plane headed for the Middle East. When it had entered Omani air space, Muscat ATC denied permission to land. The next available option was the United Arab Emirates (UAE). But the UAE ATC had initially rejected the pilot's request for landing. It was only when the US authorities, mainly Deputy Secretary of State Strobe Talbott, intervened at the request of the Indian government that the aircraft was allowed to land at the Al-Minhad air force base, 64 km from Dubai, at about 1.32 AM IST. Here again, the hi-jackers did not allow the pilot to switch off the aircraft engines. Instead they insisted that the plane remained on the runway and was kept moving up and down. On India's request, the US officials seemed to have explored with the UAE authorities the possibility of storming the aircraft. However, the plan was given up in favor of negotiating with the hi-jackers for the release of the sick, women and children. In return the UAE authorities agreed to refuel the plane and supply food. Fearing foul play, the hi-jackers insisted on refueling first before releasing some passengers. Finally, a compromise was worked out whereby refueling and release of twenty-seven passengers took place simultaneously. The body of a young man who was stabbed to death in Amritsar was dumped. The hi-jackers were apparently satisfied with the barter deal. But the presence of security forces at the air base made them worry about their security. Therefore, as soon as the refueling was done, at 4.00 AM IST, the hi-jackers hurried the pilot to take off. Their chosen destination was again Kabul.

Afghanistan under the Taliban rule welcomed the hi-jacked Indian plane. Since the Kabul airport was heavily damaged in the civil war, its battered runway could not accommodate a large aircraft like an Airbus. Kabul ATC therefore asked the pilot to proceed to Kandahar, another Afghan city, which the hi-jackers accepted reluctantly. On landing at Kandahar in the early Christmas morning, the hi-jackers established direct contacts with the Taliban men and seemed to have obtained their permission to stay there with the hostages until all their demands were met by the Indian government. Though the hi-jackers initially found themselves in the place of their choice, occasionally their difficulties with the Taliban officials made them to be very restive and forced them to think in terms of leaving Kandahar for a better place, preferably Kabul. However, in view of the air-unworthiness of the plane, they abandoned their plan and decided to stay on there for another week, until the hostage crisis was brought to an end through negotiations on December 31.

Who were these hi-jackers-hostage-takers? What did they want to achieve? As individuals they were all terrorists, since they unleashed violence (both mental and physical) in a premeditated way against unarmed and innocent civilian passengers. In terrorist situations an individual's identity as a terrorist is only partial. It becomes total only when the group to which he belongs is taken into account. Cadres who carry out terrorist activities submerge their own identities in the group and thus tend to carry a "group mind" (Post 1990: 33) or a kind of collective group identity to which they have provided the necessary organic structure. Thus as members of Harkat-ul Ansar (HuA), one of the terrorist outfits fighting against the Indian state in Jammu and Kashmir (J&K), the hi-jackers' group identity was far more prominent than their own individual identity.[1] They carried out the operation so meticulously, risking their life at the behest and in the name of their organization. The Indian government therefore laid the blame on the HuA for the hostage crisis. Though the group's immediate objective that the hi-jackers sought to achieve was to get some of its leaders and cadres (see below) freed from Indian jails, its larger goal had been to promote the cause of Kashmir's liberation from Indian rule (Ganguly 1997). As expected, the hostage crisis drew the world's attention to the Kashmir question.

The hi-jackers were not only Kashmiri nationalists but also religious fundamentalists. The combined influences of both political and religious ideologies made them hard-core, aggressive and resolutely uncompromising. The HuA's ideology is rooted in Deobandi religious tradition and its cadres are largely drawn from Islamic seminaries in Pakistan. In addition to theological teachings, the students were imparted practical knowledge of *jihad* in Afghanistan. Many of the HuA leaders and its cadres were trained in Afghanistan by the Harkat-ul-Mujahideen (HuM) during the heyday of the Afghan civil war (Swami 2000a: 14). Despite the strong influence of religion and Kashmiri nationalism, the hostage-takers remained contingent terrorists with a commitment to their group. They appeared willing to commit suicide only if they were threatened severely. They revealed occasionally their suicidal tendencies in some desperate situations viz. when they got tough responses from the Indian government and also when some unfolding developments and turning points in the hostage crisis became unexpected or contrary to what their original plans intended to produce. Thus, their commitment to advance the declared goal and desire to promote the HuA's immediate interests instructed them to suppress their suicidal tendencies in favor of forcing the Indian government to engage them in negotiations in which the hostages were used as a bargaining chip. Differently the expression of their desire to die could also be interpreted as a deliberate tactic of deception that hostage-takers invariably employ in order to counter any threat of use of force by their adversary (Dolnik 2003: 505) or even pressurize it to accept their core demands.

Contextual issues

Negotiations are a context-oriented phenomenon taking place in a particular situation for a definite purpose. A "negotiation situation" (Kremenyuk 2002) is characterized by a wide range of factors that constitute the basic structure, conduct the process, and produce some agreed outcomes. If structure conditions a negotiation process and provides "the enduring external constraints within which negotiations unfold" (Faure and Sjostedt 1993: 9). Structure refers to "a distribution of elements" (Zartman 1989c: 243), including the number of negotiating parties; their organizational apparatus for decision-making; the distribution of power between them, the nature and size of issues, and the role of third parties, as well as location and public sentiment as structural factors relevant to hostage negotiations.

Negotiating parties

In a hostage situation the principal negotiating parties are the targeted government/state of the hostages and the hostage-takers themselves. Strikingly, both enjoy different status. The state is endowed with an infrastructure for effective negotiations and the other is a non-state actor and illegitimate entity that has no machinery and institutional support base for conducting a negotiation process. In terms of skills, knowledge, training, and experience, terrorists forming a small team do not match government's mixed team of highly qualified and experienced professionals. Though they share a common terrorist background, they totally lack knowledge in theory and practice of diplomacy and negotiation. Yet they try to develop their own perspectives, skills and knowledge in the art of negotiations based on their clans' (other terrorists) experience in similar hostage situations elsewhere in the past. In this way one hostage-taker becomes a teacher to another, whose experience, in turn, is an invaluable lesson for new practitioners of the hostage-taking act. Terrorist negotiators tend to be extremely shrewd, cunning and manipulative; they know what they speak and what they want to achieve. They cannot be simply deceived by mere political rhetoric or convinced by their counterpart's oratory skills and diplomatic acumen. They are not a mixed group of negotiators, but may have a sufficiently broad knowledge to match their counterpart's. They perform simultaneously a dual task of hostage-taking and holding negotiations.

In the Kandahar hostage crisis a seven-member team of negotiators represented the Indian government. They were senior officials with an impeccable record of service. Though the team was led by a senior career diplomat (Vivek Katju), two intelligence officers (Ajit Doval and C. D. Sahay) played a significant role. While Doval did most of the talking with the terrorists Katju largely remained in touch with the local Taliban leaders and tried to secure their support for his government. By sending a mixed team of senior officials drawn from three different domains of government – diplomacy, intelligence and internal security – the Indian leadership sought to overcome the challenges of negotiating with the terrorists, who, in the same way, were keen to drive a hard bargain with their counterparts. The terrorist negotiating team was led by the chief hijacker-hostage-taker, known to the hostages as Red Cap (Chief), who was later identified as Ibrahim Attar. He had sufficient technical knowledge on the functioning of aircraft. He devised a sound security strategy to prevent an external commando attack and, above all, demonstrated his utmost skills and astuteness in negotiation as if he was professionally well trained in the field (Jaggia and Shula 2000). He was said to have done the talking alone, but discussed the strategies with his comrades at every stage of negotiations. All of them collectively made one thing pretty sure, i.e. their opponent team could not outsmart them in negotiations.

Issues

Issues are one of the principal structural elements in negotiations. Their recognition by both parties is a first step towards fruitful engagement in negotiations. At least in the early stage the tendency of one of the parties is to maintain a position of non-negotiability until it brings about a positive change in its perception.

Unlike other types of negotiations there are limited issues and a few parties in hostage negotiations. In this context, Zartman (1990: 166) observes that "items for trade are severely limited ... the drama is in the tension not trade ... Yet drama *is* the name of hostage situations." There are only two principal actors in the entire *drama* – one is a hostage-taker and the other is a custodian of hostages, viz. their government. The major issues in the *drama* are related to trade-offs and security – first, hostages are sought to be exchanged for terrorists' demands (publicity, ransom, and freeing their jailed comrades) and, second, the former in exchange for the latter's personal safety. Both are closely interconnected. No hostage-takers would ever agree to a grand swap-deal that accepted one or more of their principal demands but did not guarantee their safety in the post-deal phase. They do not risk or compromise on their security in order to achieve their demands.

Trade-offs, security, ransom and publicity were the major issues in the Kandahar hostage negotiations. As the analysis in the following section reveals, the first two demands were the toughest for the Indian government to consider. Both teams of negotiators focused entirely on these issues, and the other issues – ransom and publicity – were found to be the easiest to deal with. Of these, the last one was totally a non-issue since the terrorists earned enough international publicity to the cause of Kashmir's independence by their very hostage-taking act. Yet, as in the case of other hostage situations, their cause was not a direct issue in negotiations. Since both trade-off and security were tightly packed, together they demanded a combined solution.

Decision-making

Bargaining and decision-making are the important characteristics of a negotiation process (Kaufmann 1989: 7). In hostage negotiations terrorists tend to function both as bargainers and decision-makers. It is however, possible for them to gather intelligence, with the help of accomplices and patrons, as an input into their negotiating strategy and decision-making process. A terrorist organization delegates the task of bargaining to hostage-takers while keeping to itself the authority of decision-making if it is able to maintain communication links with its men on the ground. This is also true in the case of governments whose representatives engage terrorists in direct negotiations within the parameters and frameworks set by their political leadership. These "delegated negotiators" (Kaufmann 1989: 8) provide crucial inputs to decision-making under an institutionalized structure involving the targeted government's chief executive, Cabinet, opposition leaders, bureaucracy and intelligence agencies. Decisions made at the political level constitute an output to the negotiation process conducted by the delegated negotiators. Thus, the actual decision to reach a negotiated end of a hostage crisis is made far away from the location where the hostage crisis unfolds, but its implementation takes place in the crisis spot, which is typical for terrorist negotiations, as Combalbert discusses, in view of the criticality of issues involved and the nature of parties participating in negotiations.

In the Kandahar hostage crisis, negotiation and decision-making constituted two separate, yet integrated, processes involving two different sets of teams. Each process influenced and directed the other. In the case of the terrorists, although both the tasks appeared to have been undertaken by themselves at the same time, it is indeed a little known fact that their leadership played an important decision-making role. Throughout the period of hostage crisis, they kept in constant touch with HuA chief Facular Raman Khalid, based in Pakistan (Dixit 2002: 26). In addition, they received intelligence inputs and directions regularly from Pakistan's Inter Services Intelligence (ISI), whose role as the chief trusted patron in the hostage crisis became "so obvious and visible" (Singh 2006: 238) by the presence of some of its officials at Kandahar. However, it must be admitted that both processes were not neatly structured and strictly separated, as in the case of the Indian government, which, as stated earlier, delegated the task of negotiating to a seven-member team of officials.

Being delegated negotiators, Indian officials conducted the negotiation process according to the set limits and instructions given by their political leadership. They brought to bear upon the process their professional skills and experience, devised their own tactics, and made a proper assessment of the hostage-takers' interests, expectations, moves, and behavior. But, at every stage, they had to depend on the government leaders in New Delhi for guidance so necessary for making their timely responses to the terrorists' demands and decide about their next steps and strategies in the bargaining process. In New Delhi, the government set up a comprehensive institutional mechanism that followed a complex process for decision-making. At the bottom was the Crisis Management Group (CMG),[2] which undertook the heavy task of monitoring the hostage situation, issuing directions to the officials, reporting the developments to the political leadership, and implementing the government's decisions on the ground. Below it was the Central Committee (CC), headed by the Director General of Civil Aviation. Its members (about ten) are officials from various relevant government departments. Both the CMG and CC worked in close coordination. The Cabinet Committee on Security (CCS), a high-powered body comprising some important Ministers (such as Home, External Affairs, Finance, Defense, etc.) headed by the Prime Minister, assumed a major role in decision-making process. It met first on the day of hi-jacking and thereafter every evening till the termination of the hostage crisis, to make a comprehensive assessment of the situation and evaluate all options that were available before the government. In this process it received crucial inputs regularly from the negotiators, intelligence agencies and media.

At the highest political level, it was Prime Minister A. B. Vajpayee who played a key role in decision-making. Information received from various institutions and agencies formed a crucial input. The Prime Minister's Office (PMO), a powerful institution which exercises an overbearing influence on almost all central Ministries, headed by Rajesh Mishap, Principal Secretary and National Security Advisor to the Prime Minister, effectively undertook an advisory function. Besides, the Prime Minister had a small coterie of his trusted Cabinet and party colleagues who participated in several brainstorming sessions and advised him. In order to obtain the military's input into the decision-making the Prime Minister held a meeting with the three service chiefs (army, navy and air force). Realizing the need for a bipartisan approach to the crisis termination, he held a series of political consultations with the Opposition leaders and coalition partners of the right-wing Charity Ajanta Party (BJP) that led the National Democratic Alliance (NDA) government at the time of the hostage crisis. Thus, the Prime Minister emerged as the single most dominant figure in the decision-making process and toward the end of the crisis the PMO became the real venue for this exercise, rendering the CMG control room virtually inactive. Indeed, it was he who, in consultation with some of his close associates/advisors, and with the approval of the Cabinet, took the final decision to end the hostage crisis.

Power

A major structural ingredient in negotiations is the parties' power, defined as their "relative ability to make their options prevail (or to counter the other's efforts to make its options prevail)" (Zartman 1989: 243). Power changes "opposing positions" held by both parties into "a joint position" (Zartman 2002: 66) – an essential precondition and a basic principal of conflict resolution. This is said to be possible in a symmetrical power situation, which seemingly marks a hostage crisis (Zartman 1990: 184), in that terrorists tend to neutralize the targeted government's countervailing power by using hostages as a shield against any coercive action. However, power symmetry does not characterize all hostage negotiations. In many hostage crises, governments are rendered weak *vis-à-vis* terrorists by two major factors – the latter's issuance of threats to hostages' life and constraints facing the former in undertaking military action to release hostages perhaps due to non-cooperation or denial support by the country (where hostages are kept) and opposition by foreign governments and kin of hostages to any such measure. Thus, any calculation of a targeted government's power should be based not merely on its military strength but also such factors as the role of third parties, the crisis location, and public sentiments. Why are negotiations hard even in asymmetrical power situations? Asked differently, why doesn't a targeted government easily give into terrorists' pressure and accept their core demands? The answer lies in prevalence of power symmetry even in an asymmetrical power situation (Zartman 2002: 66–70) exemplified by the government's inherent ability to retain an option of exercising its veto over an agreement. Symmetrical negotiations between parties with asymmetrical power relations are therefore a significant feature of a hostage crisis. Governments may enjoy asymmetrical power *position*, yet their tough *behavior* tends to disguise it. Both parties tolerate each other's behavior in view of the fact that there is no best alternative to a negotiated agreement (BATNA) (Fisher *et al.* 1991).

This was best illustrated in the Kandahar hostage negotiations in that the terrorists seemed to have gained the upper hand *vis-à-vis* the Indian government, whose strong military power became ineffective and inconsequential. First, the terrorists posed a direct threat to the hostages' life by declaring to kill them one by one or blow up the aircraft if the government rejected their demands. Though all these threats sometimes appeared to be a tactics of deception, there was every possibility of them becoming real. The terrorists were heavily armed with 17 kg of RDX, a box of HE 36 grenades, Uzi machine pistols, knives and an assault rifle. They retrieved a bag containing explosives and arms from the rear cargo hold of the plane just before the start of negotiations. Second, in a way of enhancing the hostage-takers' coercive power and at the same time neutralizing India's offensive capability, the Taliban officials openly extended to them security cover against an Indian commando attack. Third, the Taliban firmly rejected India's repeated plea for their support and co-operation in a commando operation to release the hostages. By this, they removed one of India's preferred options of seeking a military end of the hostage crisis.[3] Once India abandoned its military option under the pressure of both Taliban and Indian public, power tilted toward the terrorists. Thus it was a typical case of a powerful party negotiating from the position of a weak and weaker party possessing greater tactical power to be stronger. Even in such asymmetrical power situation, however, a condition of power symmetry marked the negotiation process, since India was able to exercise its veto over the terrorists' demands and a deal that they sought to conclude according to their terms.

Third parties

In hostage negotiations third parties assume greater salience and significance in view of difficulties in establishing and maintaining communication between parties. A third party trusted by both sides makes a significant contribution to a negotiation process (Zartman 1990: 186–188). The involvement of third parties in Kandahar hostage negotiations followed a multi-track process. Despite its official position revealed by External Affairs Minister Jessant Singh against any form of "third-party interference" (*Hindustan Times*, December 26, 1996), the Indian government sought external support in conducting the negotiations.[4] It began with a request to Erik de Mull, the Islamabad-based UN Coordinator of Humanitarian Affairs in Afghanistan, to visit Kandahar to ascertain the hostages' conditions (*Hindustan Times*, December 27, 1999) without, in the words of Singh, claiming it to be an "intermediary or a negotiating role" by the United Nations (CNN 1999).[5] Notwithstanding the fact that India wanted the United Nations to maintain a low profile, it was the world body's representatives who played a crucial role in establishing first a communication link with the hostage-takers in the pre-negotiation stage (see the section below).

Simultaneously, India mobilized international support. On December 25, the day after the hi-jacking, Singh got in touch with several of his counterparts, including prominent UN member states and countries whose nationals were on board the hi-jacked plane. In addition, the Indian Foreign Secretary spoke to many of his counterparts abroad and heads of diplomatic missions in New Delhi (Singh 2000). Subsequently, several countries issued official statements in support of India and condemning the hostage-taking. "These left," in India's assessment, "no room for doubt that the hi-jacking of IC-814 represented an unacceptable act of international terrorism and that any action undertaken by the Indian government would receive full [international] support" (Singh 2000). A desirable action that India had initially in mind was a commando attack to free the hostages, for which the international help was crucial, particularly since there were many foreign nationals aboard the plane. However, once this option was given up in favor of negotiations, the expected role of external parties was to put pressure on the hi-jackers, their patrons and the Taliban to end the crisis.

This role, undertaken in three ways, was important since it would make an impact on the negotiation process. First, some of the prominent stakeholder countries (whose nationals were among the hostages) urged Pakistan to use its influence over the Taliban authorities to protect the hostages' life and terminate the crisis at the earliest (ENS 1999). Pakistan was considered to be an important source of help not only because of its proximity to the Taliban regime[6] but also its intelligence agency's complicity in the hostage crisis (Dixit 2002: 25–27). Second, some of the Western nations whose citizens were aboard the plane directly urged the Taliban to play a constructive role in ending the crisis.[7] Third, India reached out to the UAE and Saudi Arabia for their help to isolate the terrorists and win the support of the Taliban. India's approach was to get closer to the very forces that the terrorists regarded as their patrons or allies. In this context Pakistan's cooperation was also directly sought (Jessant Singh 2006). Besides, India asked the United States to exert pressure on the Taliban government, both directly and through Pakistan and Saudi Arabia, to play a positive role in ending the hostage crisis.[8]

Thus the major target of external influence was the Taliban, a dominant third party in the hostage crisis.[9] Needless to say, all the stakeholders (Indian government, governments of foreign national hostages and terrorists) were forced to depend on them to achieve their goals. This gave them an indispensable position in the crisis, leading them to behave in the manner of their own choice and preferences. In accordance with their own decision and India's expressed desire, the Taliban started their role as a facilitator of the negotiation process, only to be seen expanding its role soon as a biased intermediary who, in Minister Singh's assessment, "consistently and clearly had their sympathies with the hi-jackers and their supporters and acted accordingly" in a partisan manner (Singh 2000). The hapless and traumatized Indian government could not question, challenge or disown them. It had no choice except cultivating the Taliban who, besides virtually playing the role of judge and jury, became the guarantor to implement the deal reached at the end of negotiations. In executing their role the Taliban had to keep changing their tactics to suit their interests and plans. They tried to present to the world a positive outlook of them being an impartial intermediary deeply and genuinely interested in a negotiated termination of the crisis. But their actual role behavior in Kandahar negotiations showed discreetly their pro-terrorist proclivities, as explained in the following section, was in contrast to its projected image internationally and the impression they created in India that their support and cooperation to the government was genuine and total. This led Singh to repeatedly thank the Taliban.

Location

Singh's (2000) statement, that Kandahar was "the most adverse location" for India to tackle the hostage crisis, has emphasized the importance of location as a major factor in negotiations with terrorists, as frequently underscored (Faure 2003; Baldwin 1976). Location is one of the determinants of negotiating contexts that influences the negotiating pattern. Terrorists' preference, therefore, is to hold hostages in a friendly and familiar location, falling within the territorial jurisdiction of their patrons, sympathizers or accomplices, which is virtually hostile to its adversary. Location has a strong built-in factor of power that plays a significant role in negotiations. Generally, in a hostage crisis taking place in a terrorist-friendly location, strong pressure is mounted on the targeted government to free the hostages, by paying the price demanded by the other side, since it cannot "control the negotiation environment" and, at the same time, is faced with severe constraints in maneuvering. If one party is secure and the other is vulnerable, the power balance in negotiations is difficult to maintain (Faure 2003: 477). If a hostage crisis unfolds in a location neutral or hostile to terrorists, they tend to feel insecure and vulnerable more or less than their counterpart. A third country that hosts the crisis may try to limit the power and maneuverability of hostage-takers, and the targeted government can hopefully have more options and maintain the upper hand in negotiations. Thus, though both parties depend on the third (host) country, it tends to be sympathetic to the targeted government resulting in a definite tilt in the power balance to its side. Yet terrorists may still be left with sufficient power to exercise their veto over a deal or oppose a decision by virtue of their continued act of hostage-taking and threat to the hostages' life.

Kandahar was an ominous choice for the Indian government, severely limiting its power, means, and options. The friendship and cooperation between Pakistan and Afghanistan under the Taliban regime coupled with the HuA's traditional ideological and military links with the Taliban warlords gave the hostage-takers a distinct advantage over the Indian government. By all means therefore the Afghan territory was a safe and secure heaven for them. Generally Pakistan had exercised tremendous influence over the Taliban regime virtually on all policy matters. It took special interest and played a dominant role on issues involving India. The ISI's indirect involvement in the hostage crisis testified to this policy (Dixit 2002). Thus the Kandahar hostage crisis typified the prominent Afghan–Pakistan–Kashmir *jihadi* linkages to the protracted Kashmir conflict. What accentuated India's difficulties further was its broken relationship with Afghanistan. India not only refused to recognize the Taliban regime but also supported international economic sanctions on Afghanistan.[10] Realizing its weakness, India was forced to be realistic in dealing with the hostage crisis. It gave up the military option in favor of negotiating with the terrorists as the only practical way out of the hostage crisis – a choice it exercised with much hesitation.

Launching an armed attack to rescue the hostages was not possible because of the logistical constraints imposed by the absence of diplomatic reasons between

India and Afghanistan and also the Afghan–Pakistan nexus. In order to transport its commandos and equipment, India needed the Taliban authorities' permission for its plane to land in Kandahar. Since the Indian rescue aircraft would use the Pakistani air space, the Pakistani government's approval was also a legal necessity. Both permissions were impossible to obtain, given their strong patron–client relations with the hostage-takers. Pointing out the absence of diplomatic relations, the Taliban regime forthrightly rejected India's plea for a rescue plan. It also did not want to risk bloodshed. On India's suggestion out of desperation that Afghan commandos could storm the aircraft, with New Delhi assuming responsibility for its outcome, the Taliban said that they had neither the inclination nor the technical capability to undertake the task (Swami 2000: 4).

Public sentiment

Generally there is no room for sympathy (defined as one's sharing of another's feelings out of emotion, compassion or commiseration) in a negotiation process, though the parties may be empathetic (one's ability to identity and understand another's views or problems) to each other (Zartman and Berman 1982: 33). In hostage negotiations, however, neither sympathy nor empathy has any direct relevance and role. Since hostage-taking by itself is a seriously inhuman act, it is indeed unrealistic to expect hostage-takers to have compassion toward hostages. Nor can they afford to identify with government or hostages' families; such an act will amount to self-defeating their goals and subjecting their lives to a grave risk. Similarly governments do not sympathize or empathize with terrorists for the simple reason that they have committed a crime that cannot be condoned. Lack of empathy *for each other* is one of the hurdles for a smooth process of negotiations over hostages.

Nevertheless public sentiment tends to influence the negotiating position of governments. As innocent human beings are used as pawns in a hostage crisis, it attains a serious emotive dimension that no democratic leadership interested in regime survival, electoral victory, and popularity can simply overlook. They easily succumb to public pressure, particularly that mounted by the hostages' families, by giving up their tough negotiating position in favor of a compromise settlement. It requires the acceptance of some or most of the demands of the terrorists. A government that bows to sustained public pressure and shows its sympathy to hostages cannot be tough in negotiating with terrorists who, knowing their opponent's political compulsions and predicament, try to exploit its moral commitment to protect the lives of its citizens while effectively bargaining for a deal.

The public pressure and emotional appeals of the affected people formed one of the major factors to limit India's negotiating power. The government could not ignore the anger and despair expressed in public by the hostages' families.[11] They first wanted the government to send a team of negotiators fast to Kandahar. On seeing its utter reluctance and delaying tactics, they became an angry mob. When the terrorists set a deadline to begin negotiations and threatened to kill all the hostages one by one if the Indian government's response was negative they turned hostile, particularly against the Prime Minister. They threatened to hang all 540 elected Members of Parliament if any hostage was killed (Machida 1999). When the government initially refused to accept the terrorists' demands, the angry public criticized it as being insensitive and callous. At the end the Indian leadership succumbed to public pressure as it accepted the swap-deal to save the lives of the hostages (see below).

Negotiation analysis

The structural elements largely influence negotiations and their final outcomes. A process of negotiations entails formal bargaining interactions directly between the parties with an intention of converting their "conflicting positions" into "a common outcome" (Zartman 1989: 249). Generally, bargaining in a hostage crisis tends to be tough, since it is over and about human lives. Stalemate and breakdown are therefore not unexpected. Ripeness marked by a mutually hurting stalemate (Zartman 1989) in a hostage crisis as an essential precondition for its eventual termination under an agreement is extremely hard to come about. It is in this context that a third party's role as facilitator or mediator assumes greater relevance and importance.

Negotiation as a process is somewhat structured and progresses in integrated stages. The three-stage integrative model, incorporating pre-negotiation (diagnostic phase), defining solutions (formula phase) and reaching agreement (detail phase), developed by Zartman and Berman (1982), is pertinent to hostage negotiations. Though each phase stands out to be separate in view of the differing tasks to be accomplished, all three are interconnected. Progress in each phase is necessary to take the other forward without which negotiations tend to receive a temporary setback or permanent breakdown. This can happen in any of the phases of a negotiation process.

Pre-negotiation

In hostage negotiations pre-negotiation is all about accepting and then integrating the idea of negotiation into the crisis structure while making preparations for a tough bargaining process that seeks to change the parties' perception, behavior and attitudes. Cumulatively, the parties transform the nature and pattern of their relationship. Since the idea of negotiating is an integral part of the terrorists' larger hostage-taking strategy, governments are expected to change their "no negotiation" position by abandoning their coercive approach to crisis termination. However, the latter need to overcome many obstacles before accepting the idea of and preparing for negotiations.

One of the major problems facing governments is related to the issue of legitimacy. This is a "delicate, embarrassing and thorny" problem (Faure 2003: 476) that they need to resolve in the pre-negotiation phase. Their compulsions are twofold, occurring in the same time-context: At one level, they like to reject the offer or demand for negotiations and at another they experience sustained pressure for negotiations. Often the former tends to outweigh the latter until and otherwise a reverse happens, resulting in gradual breaking of governments' hardened position to accept negotiations as the most realistic option. For governments, being realistic means that they accept by all means the onus of saving the life of hostages and seek a negotiated end of the crisis. In this context Faure (2003: 477) observes that the "moral disqualification of the counterpart on both sides may authorize behaviors that would otherwise not be present in a negotiation, such as lying, playing tricks, manipulating, or using deceptive devices." This implies that there may be a serious credibility gap between what one party promises and what it ultimately delivers to the other. More than governments, it is terrorists who resort to such behavior if the deal they have entered into fails to meet their expectations or fulfill their demands. This, however, does not mean that all governments will maintain a high level of credibility by adhering to the agreed formula and deal reached with hostage-takers.

The issue of legitimacy has twofold dimensions. For many governments, the very idea of accepting negotiations with terrorists is considered to be an act of according legitimacy to the criminals. For others, accepting terrorists' demands tends to be more damaging than engaging them in tactical negotiations. It is necessary that both positions are changed in the pre-negotiation phase. Since the issue may cause political dissension, hard-liners and dissenters should be convinced of the urgent need to negotiate and concede to some of the demands of terrorists in the interest of hostages. If the government leaders are unable to win them over by political means, they resort to the tactics of deception by maintaining secrecy.

The search for "terms of trade" is another activity in the pre-negotiation phase (Zartman 1990). Since terrorists alone propose them even as the crisis is stabilized, governments merely respond. The latter consider, revise or propose an alternative trading formula. The lesser the terms of trade, the greater is the chance for governments to accept negotiations. But terrorists invariably pitch their demands high in order to have enough room for hard bargaining. In the absence of lesser terms of trade governments prefer camouflaged ones. Their aim is to minimize the negative impact of negotiating with terrorists on the polity. No government wants to spoil its national and international image or create an impression that terrorists have virtually defeated it at the negotiating table. Nor does it want its hard-line policies related to counter-terrorism to receive a setback or lose its credibility in the eyes of terrorists and the larger public. Governments therefore always prefer terms of trade that give them a face-saving mechanism in the event of reaching a deal with their opponents.

Concomitant to a critical assessment of the terms of trade proposed by hostage-takers and their behavior is an examination of third parties' role and international responses. This is mainly necessitated by the criticality of third parties in hostage negotiations, especially if the crisis location is adverse to governments and, at the same time, friendly to terrorists. The concerns of government are related to the third parties' behavior and positions. The questions bothering it are: Whom will they support or cooperate with? Will they be impartial or partial? Will they be sympathetic toward hostages or terrorists' cause? Will they implement the deal in letter and spirit? While seeking third parties' cooperation and support, governments expect them to be covertly partial toward them to undermine or weaken their opponent's negotiating position. This is presumably sought on the moral high ground that terrorism and hostage-taking are criminal acts which civilized nations cannot condone. It is therefore not an amoral act if third parties covertly work to favor governments in negotiations. Earning third parties' sympathy and assurance of their support will quicken the process of completing the pre-negotiation phase as governments prepare themselves to select a strong team of negotiators, brief them on the negotiating position to be taken and devise the negotiating tactics. Reliable and fast communication links are established both with third parties and, through them, hostage-takers. Logistical issues are sorted out to take the negotiation process to the next phase.

In the Kandahar hostage crisis the pre-negotiation phase consumed about four days. The Indian government had to overcome political difficulties, resolve the problems related to logistics and make a correct assessment of all actors in the hostage crisis before accepting the idea of negotiating. It did so at its own pace, causing anger and desperation among the terrorists, who as early as December 26 spelt out their core demand, viz. the release of Mastoid Zahra and initiation of negotiations. The foremost task before the government was to change its position from *no*-to-negotiation to *yes*-to-negotiation. The day after the hi-jacking, Prime Minister Vajpayee declared that his government would not "bend before such a show of terrorism" (Frontline, January 21, 2000, p. 10) and ruled out any compromise with the terrorists. Thus, for at least three days, there was no decision taken on sending a negotiating team to Kandahar.

The issue of legitimacy was paramount in the Indian leadership's thinking and decision. Having suffered from and fought terrorism for several years, the government did not want to give legitimacy to the hostage-takers by engaging them in negotiations and accepting their demands. On this issue the Indian Cabinet was seemingly divided.[12] In arriving at the decision on December 27 to send a team of negotiators the government was influenced by two incidents – an ultimatum issued by the Taliban[13] and the terrorists' threat to kill the hostages by 1.40 PM (IST) the same day. Thus the pre-negotiation phase saw a complete revision of India's response to the crisis in that the "threat" – whether real or incredible – formed a significant factor.

India began the pre-negotiation process with a quick on-the-spot assessment of the crisis and the Taliban's role. Before sending its own representative the government preferred to gather information from the UN representative Erik de Mull who visited Kandahar on December 26 and interacted with the Taliban authorities and the hostage-takers. His five rounds of talks with the latter revealed their interests (in negotiations) and expectation (of major concessions from India). The first-hand information that he gathered helped create both a sense of urgency and confidence in the Indian government's mind in dealing with the crisis. Taking cognizance of the terrorists' deadline the government sent on December 27 its diplomat, A. R. Ghanashyam, posted at the Indian embassy in Islamabad. Reaching Kandahar at the last hour of the deadline, he convinced the hostage-takers of the Indian government's desire to negotiate.[14] This signaled the formal acceptance of the terrorists' demand for negotiations as a political means to end the hostage crisis.

An important task before the India government was to assess the Taliban's position in the crisis. It did not want, in the words of Minister Singh (2000), any "misjudgment" of the Taliban at "this critical juncture." It expected the Taliban authorities not only to support its cause but also oppose the terrorists' demands. In view of the fact that the Taliban pursued an orthodox ideology, enjoyed close relations with Pakistan, adopted vigorously an anti-India stand on the Kashmir conflict and extended support to fundamentalist organizations in South Asia, initially India was skeptical about their support. However, its diplomat's meetings with the Taliban leaders – best considered as an exercise in confidence and mutual trust-building – helped clear the negative impressions. The Indian government felt that at a time it was faced with extreme challenges and difficulties, it found a crucial source of support from a regime it had refused to recognize earlier. Encouraged by Ghanashyam's positive field report, it took a decision to send negotiators to Kandahar on the evening of December 27.

For the government, terms of trade, spelt in a hostages-for-terrorists swap, were too high. Given the fact that a section of the Indian leadership remained opposed to negotiations, it was required to lower the trading terms to match its high expectations. This set a stage for a hard bargaining process aimed at lowering the hostage-takers' expectations. Besides, on India's part, the issue of logistics was also to be addressed in the pre-negotiation phase.[15]

Formulation

Direct bargaining between parties marks the formulation phase. This dynamic phase in a negotiation process is significant for a wide range of activities involving adversaries as definers (of problems), bargainers (for better terms of trade) and deal makers (agreeing to a formula). In hostage negotiations the search for a formula tends to be tough, requiring both parties to change their incompatible position on defining the problem and work out a compromise formula. The terms of trade proposed in the pre-negotiation phase constitute an agenda for talks. Considering government's acceptance of negotiations, rather under intense pressure, as their first victory, terrorists try to increase the terms of trade. At the same time, government maintains that its decision to negotiate does not imply that it has accepted its opponent's terms of trade. Lowering them by all means is its major objective. Thus, both parties keep the level of their expectations high, providing a framework and context for a tough bargaining process.

India agreed to negotiate under compulsion without accepting the terms of trade spelt out by the hostage-takers. Its three major objectives in negotiating were early termination of the crisis, safe return of the hostages, and protection of the nation's security (Singh 2000). Ruling out any deal based on the higher trading terms, the government sought to revise them. It appeared to be willing to trade at the most the terrorists' security for exchange of hostages. In the event of its failure to achieve such a deal, its preference was to break the talks and launch a commando attack. This was apparently proposed to the Taliban leaders when the negotiations became tough (Jaggia and Shula 2000: 136). But their rejection instantaneously of this left the Indian government with no viable choice except changing its original position on the trading terms.[16]

In searching for a formula to resolve their problem the parties take a composite or piecemeal approach. A composite formula-making process tends to be lengthy and time-consuming, but its advantage lies in ensuring a balanced distribution of pay-offs by avoiding a winner-takes-all situation (Zartman and Berman 1982: 179). On the contrary a piecemeal approach provides opportunities for gradual accumulation of pay-offs in each party and in the final counting one tends to obtain more benefits than the other. Thus the advantages are shared between the parties in a disproportionate way. Knowing this full well, the hostage-takers in Kandahar preferred a piecemeal approach. When the negotiations began on the night of December 27, they demanded the release of Mastoid Zahra in exchange for ten Indian, five foreign and some other hostages of their choice. This was a paltry sum given the fact that over 155 hostages were on the plane. Calculating that at this rate the terrorists would ask for freeing a large number of their comrades from jail, the Indian negotiators urged them to make their entire demands together. Simultaneously, in a way of engaging the hostage-takers in a bargaining process, the Indian negotiators wanted them to release the wife of the murdered hostage whose body was dumped in Dubai. Rejecting this demand, the terrorists made Azhar's release a precondition to any concession on their side. On their part the Indian negotiators were equally tough and asked their opponents to show greater flexibility in their position so as to enable the government to consider the terrorists' demands. Thus both parties were testing each other's resoluteness and flexibility while formulating their strategies and responses.

Expectedly, therefore, two preliminary rounds of negotiations ended on a discordant note. When the talks resumed on the morning of December 28, both sides continued to maintain contrasting positions on the approach (composite versus piecemeal) to formula-making. Modifying their earlier offer slightly without changing their chosen piecemeal approach, the terrorist proposed now to release thirty-five hostages in exchange for Zahra. The government asked its negotiators to reject the offer and told both the hostage-takers and Taliban that there would not be any talks until the former changed their approach and made a "formal, full and unambiguous" detailing of demands in a composite manner (Singh 2000). The hostage-takers relented for the first time under the Taliban's pressure as they accepted the composite approach. They took about twenty minutes to prepare their exorbitant wish-list scribbled on a paper and dropped from the plane. The package contained names of thirty-six terrorists including Zahra whose release from Indian jails topped their demands; payment of US$200 million and return of the coffin of Sajjad Afghani after exhuming it from the burial site in J&K.[17]

These demands were not only in tune with the higher terms of trade that the terrorists set earlier but also comprehensive both in terms of the number of their comrades sought to be exchanged for the hostages and the number of demands contained in the package. The last demand was peculiar, indicating the hostage-takers' strong emotional attachment to their cause, ideology, organization and leadership. The government was surprised. It had to lower its expectations or use its negotiating skills and the influence of the Taliban to lower its opponent's expectations. The terrorists made one thing very clear, i.e. they could match the skills of professional negotiators and knew how to do a profitable business with the Indians. They sat pretty well, calling the shots, to which the Indian negotiators responded with equal toughness, but from a position of weakness. However, as the days passed, the hostage-takers began to lose their confidence and consequently became desperate too.

In this context the negotiation strategies of both parties assume greater importance. Unlike in other types of negotiations, a hostage negotiation process is known for the employment of deception tactics wilfully by both parties. These are accepted methods in any negotiation process. In the Kandahar negotiations both sides employed the following strategy aimed at pinning each other down:

- *Stressing and mutual denial.* Both the Indian negotiators and terrorists used this hard bargaining strategy by relentlessly insisting on their respective demands and position amidst their persisting mutual denial. The issues they stressed and denied were both core and peripheral. In the beginning the Indian side, for instance, kept insisting on the release of the wife of a deceased hostage in order to create an impression that the other side was forced to give concessions. The hostage-takers, on their part, insisted on Azhar's release, while rejecting their counterpart's demands, with an objective of creating a structure of pressure on it and making interlinkages between the demands of both sides. In so doing their calculation and expectation was that the emotion-ridden hostages' families would turn against their own government and exert pressure on their leaders to accept the terrorists' demands. In addition, by employing this strategy one side wanted to prove or project the other being weak in the negotiation process.
- *Keeping on track.* Despite their mutually incompatible goals and interests both the negotiating parties had a common objective and desire in avoiding a breakdown of the negotiations. This was however, not openly declared for the reasons connected with their bargaining strategies. Yet, that they worked toward ensuring a sustainable negotiation process was undoubtedly clear. When the negotiations became tough and deadlocked, the chosen method adopted by both parties was to postpone the talks on the pretext of holding their internal consultations. Often the Indian negotiators gave a reason that they needed to consult their government on the issues raised. By this they made their counterpart understand that the actual decision-making authority on the crisis was located in New Delhi and that their status was merely one of interlocutors. Hence the hostage-takers were told every time to wait for

the government's response to their demands. In the meantime, to keep the terrorists engaged in negotiations, the government negotiators used to ask for more information or details about their demands – specific names and background of their jailed comrades, for example. This was in a way to create a positive impression among the terrorists that their demands were being considered by the government and that the negotiation process was not broken. Thus continuing the talk without conceding to the demands is the main thrust of this strategy.

- *Beating about the bush.* The Indian negotiators adopted this strategy the most. In making their demands the terrorists expected a categorical response in unambiguous terms from their adversary. Such responses tend to provide the necessary context for defining the formula of solution. Once a party makes its position clear and definite, it may not be able to easily backtrack. Doing so would not only undermine the mutual trust between the adversaries but also undercut the whole negotiation process. Given such adverse implications, the government negotiators were extremely careful not to commit themselves by giving a definite response to their opponent's firm demands and queries. Instead they invariably gave lengthy rhetorical answers to short and precise demands and questions. Cunning, shrewd and intelligent as they were, the hostage-takers asked the Indian negotiators on many occasions not to act smart and advised them to be short in their reply.
- *Creating guilt.* Since the terrorists were religious-minded, and belonged to a group that based its ideology on religious orthodoxy, the government negotiators tried to use religion as an instrument to moderate their behavior. There were occasions when the chief Indian negotiator, Doval, passionately argued with the terrorist leader that the tenets of Islam prohibited people from causing agony and harming the innocent human beings. He told the hostage-takers that their very act was against their religion and that there were other ways and means to fight for their cause. When they retorted, the government negotiators tried to reason out in a soft tone that many hostages were quite unwell and might even die and, if that happened, "you would be blamed." "Do you want to take the blame?" "The blame will be on your government," the reply came from the terrorists (Jaggia and Shula 2000: 146).
- *Buying time.* In hostage negotiations both sides operate in contrasting directions. The government seeks to prolong negotiations with an objective of lowering the terms of trade set by its opponent who, in contrast, wants to conclude the whole process at a quick pace. "Since reorientation of expectations and lessened or redefined terms of trade are the major goals of bargaining with terrorists, early substantive concessions or concession-behavior in general is not only counter productive but is contrary to the appropriate approach to the problem" (Zartman (1990: 180). What it essentially implies is that the longer the duration of a negotiation process, the greater will be the chance for the government to lower the terms. The shorter the process, the more substantive will be the concessions achieved by terrorists. It

became clear that the Indian government negotiators were keen to continue the negotiation process as long as possible – until the terrorists' resolve was weakened, reflecting in their willingness to show greater flexibility in lowering and reorienting the terms of trade.

Besides some of the above-mentioned methods, the government's chief negotiator occasionally provoked his counterpart to speak for an extended period of about twenty minutes. To this, the response from the government side used to be equally long. Subjects for exchange were generally related to the situation in Kashmir and India's position on the conflict. When the terrorist chief would launch a diatribe against the Indian government by pointing out human rights violations, the government negotiator would reply that "excess of hi-jacking could not be condoned as a gesture of redressing perceived excesses in Kashmir" (Baruah 2000: 12). This would provoke further the terrorist chief, who would give a long reply; the exchange would continue thus. The terrorists joined this exercise without realizing the fact that this was their opponent's ploy to buy time and deflect their attention from the main issues.

- *Burn-out*. This strategy should be seen in conjunction with the above stated one. In a prolonged hostage crisis and protracted negotiations over hostages, exhaustion and debility become a serious problem for terrorists. Being hostages themselves, beyond a point and time-frame, they may find it extremely difficult to keep up their pressure on their adversary, maintain a foolproof security system for themselves, bargain hard all the time with their opponent and push for a deal of their choice. Their spirit dwindles constantly, forcing them to be keener than ever before in getting a deal struck and ending the crisis. Unlike tired and fatigued terrorists, government negotiators are fresh and keyed up all the time. They enjoy freedom to do things and relax like any other ordinary person. They are left with a huge reserve of energy and a strong interest in continuing negotiations. While being largely free from the problem of negotiation-weariness, they surely want to see their opponent totally burning out. The Indian negotiators tried to do this to the hostage-takers in Kandahar. Their slow and calibrated steps and responses caused so much irritation in the terrorists' mind, who in turn often expressed their utter frustration and anger by issuing threats and deadlines that the Indian government by and large ignored (see below). In all, the crew became the immediate target.[18]

In five days there were about a dozen rounds of intense and long negotiations, with each session lasting for several hours at a stretch. Negotiations were direct at best but not face-to-face. Both sides were hiding their faces; it was a hiding-face-to-face negotiation. This is typical of a hostage negotiation process. An important feature of the bargaining process was that behavior of both parties remained by and large constant. Until they reached the last phase of the hostage crisis there was not any significant change in their orientations, strategies, demands and responses. The terrorists began the bargaining according to their higher terms of trade (*high expectations*), to which the government negotiators' response was one of total rejection (*low acceptance*). Toward the end, while keeping the terms of trade still high, the former showed its inclination to make concessions (*low expectations*). To this the latter responded in a positive way (*high acceptance*). In the intervening period the negotiations were deadlocked and the hostage crisis escalated marked by the issuance of threats almost every day by the terrorists to kill the hostages[19] – the latter stemmed from the former. It was an expression of the hostage-takers' utter frustration and deep sense of disappointment over the outcomes of talks.

The Indian government found the threats quite incredible. Yet it did not want to give an impression to the hostage-takers that it was prepared to ignore them. Its negotiators often pointed out the need to sort out the legal hurdles facing the government in accepting their demands. The terrorists were not prepared to buy this argument. Yet they could not make the threat credible, partly due to their determination to achieve their stated goal and partly because the Taliban authorities opposed killing of any hostages lest they would have been blamed for the act. Having deterred the hostage-takers and moderated their behavior, the Taliban took up their cause by exerting pressure on the Indian government to negotiate a deal quickly.

In playing an intermediary role, the Taliban leaders adopted a twin strategy of incentives and punishment. It was applied to both the parties, albeit disproportionately. They began pressing the Indian government from the beginning of the hostage crisis to send a negotiating team. Subsequently, rejecting its military plan for a rescue operation and suspecting that it would undertake such an action unilaterally, the Taliban provided an open military cover to the terrorists under the guise of preventing them from attacking or killing the hostages.[20] By taking this measure when the negotiations were stalemated, the Taliban sought to send a tough message to the Indian government that it should expedite the negotiation process by agreeing to some of the demands of the terrorists. In return it was assured of the safety and security of the hostages. In the same vein, they asked the terrorists to scale down their demands and make them acceptable. In return they were assured of their security (by preventing a storming operation), acceptance of their demands by their opponent (under pressure on the Indian government) and also safe passage (in the post-deal phase). Disapproving the Indians' intransigence, the Taliban authorities issued a threat of action periodically against both parties, by asking the hi-jacked aircraft to leave Afghanistan for another destination (obviously of the terrorists' choice) (Baruah 2000: 12).

Thus the Taliban were a biased intermediary. Participating in the negotiation process, they played a crucial role in terminating the crisis.[21] The Indian government did not have any other choice except to rely on them for this. Left to the Indian negotiators themselves, it would have been difficult for them to change the terrorists' demands and behavior. The Taliban made the first successful intervention in the bargaining process on December 29, when they prevailed upon the terrorists to drop two of their demands – $200 million as ransom and the coffin of Sajad Afghani – on the ground that they were un-Islamic. At the same time they rejected the Indian government's contention that a demand for the release of terrorists was also un-Islamic (Singh 2000). Having agreed to reduce their demands under pressure, the terrorists now sought to compensate for the loss by insisting on the piecemeal approach again. They wanted the release of Zahra in exchange for fifteen hostages and such others as they might choose to free (Singh 2000). The government negotiators rejected their demand. At this stage the Taliban counseled both parties to work for a compromise formula. Within two days of its engagement with the terrorists in negotiations, the Indian government realized the difficulty of changing or reorienting the terms of trade and was therefore prepared to accept a formula within their ambit. Obviously the formula was to be based on the hostages-for-terrorists swap. On this India could merely try to maneuver a little. Through a hard bargaining in the third phase it sought to extract from its opponent some concessions on the number of terrorists to be released.

The deal

The third phase is largely concerned with evolving a mutually acceptable set of specific principles of a proposed deal. This is the detail phase in the sense that it involves "a long, tense search for agreement on details to implement the general framework set out in the previous phase" (Zartman and Berman 1982: 199). Both parties bargain hard to maximize their gains and minimize their losses. In a hostage crisis terrorists and government define the maximum–minimum gains in terms of the number of demands accepted or rejected. While the former strive to have a maximum number of their demands accepted by the latter that seeks to minimize its losses by agreeing only to a few of its opponent's demands. In addition, they address issues such as implementation of the deal, modalities of executing the swap and the role of guarantor.

Having scaled down from its position to accept the terms of trade set by the terrorists, the Indian negotiators sought to fix the number of terrorists to be released at a bare minimum. This turned out to be a major ticklish issue on which both parties held intense bargaining. Until the morning of December 30 the hostage-takers remained very rigid; they stuck to their original demand of thirty-six. Only in the same noon, under the Taliban pressure, did they agree to scale down to fifteen. This figure was still high for the Indian government, whose negotiators urged the Taliban to intervene again to bring down the number on the ground that it was legally and politically difficult to release a large number of terrorists from Indian jails at the same time. Responding to the Indian plea, Muttawakil talked tough with the terrorists, resulting in further reduction of the number to five and ultimately to just three men. On the whole, the Indian negotiators were happy at reaching this figure.

Though the Indian government representatives and the hostage-takers were the principal negotiators, the Taliban's participation in the bargaining process made it a triadic affair. The latter's powerful intermediary role encompassed a crucial task of moderating the behavior and influencing the negotiating position of the terrorists by limiting their total demands to a scale that was acceptable to the Indians. The government has acknowledged the Taliban's crucial role in goading the negotiations on the hostage-takers (Singh 2006: 233) and controlling the entire process until a settlement was reached. Indeed, its reliance on the Taliban became total, since its negotiators could not break the intransigence of the hostage-takers and therefore made an equally tough bargaining posture, demonstrated in their rejection of the opponent's demands. In doing so, they did not offer any alternative formula, which was essentially done by the Taliban according to the expressed desire and interest of the Indian government.

However, on two issues the Indians had a difference with both the Taliban and terrorists. First, the Indian negotiators insisted that their government should be allowed to release any three terrorists of its choice, which the hostage-takers categorically rejected. The idea behind such an Indian position, in a manner of partially diluting the terms of trade in the last stage of negotiations, was to oppose the demand for Azhar's release. At this juncture, the Taliban intervened and forced the Indian negotiators to agree to all three names given by the hostage-takers; Zahra topped the list. The second issue was related to the status of the hostage-takers after the end of the hostage crisis. The Indian government wanted them to be arrested and tried in Afghanistan for the crime they had committed or handed over to it. External Affairs Minister Singh took up this matter with his Afghan counterpart. But the Taliban authorities took a firm position in favor of the terrorists' undisturbed freedom. In demonstrating his power mediation, Muttawakil emphatically asked the Indians to abide by his decision (Jaggia and Shula 2000: 183). The Indian government had no choice but to accept the Taliban's arbitration. A deal on terms (freeing the hostages in exchange for three terrorists) that were available on December 25 was concluded.

The deal was between the Indians and the terrorists, with the Taliban playing the role of guarantor. The need for a third-party guarantor in a hostage crisis assumes significance in view of mutual antagonism and suspicion between the parties. Since their bilateral deal lacks legal sanction, governments and terrorists tend to mistrust each other's commitment to implement it. In order to avoid deception and backtracking both parties share a view on engaging a third-party guarantor. Having participated in the entire negotiation process the Taliban became the obvious choice. They were called upon to sort out a last-minute hitch in implementing the deal; the issue was about the process by which the swap was to be carried out. The Indian government wanted the hostages to be deplaned soon after verification of the jailed terrorists' identity and thereafter the latter would be handed over to the hostage-takers. It claimed that this plan had the Taliban's consent (Singh 2006: 241–242). Since the issue did not figure in the negotiations, it seemed to be an afterthought occurring in the hostage-takers' mind during the stage of implementation of the deal. Rejecting the Indian plan, the hostage-takers insisted that freeing their comrades should precede the release of the hostages. On this issue the Taliban sided with the terrorists, who ultimately prevailed upon the Indians. In the process the Taliban became typical "bag men" (Zartman 1990: 187–188) who, having let the culprits flee with their booty – three released terrorists – were condemned for their complicity in ending the crisis in the hostage-takers' favor.

The grand swap was made on the evening of December 31 in the presence of Indian and Afghan Ministers, Singh and Muttawakil.[22] The implementation of the deal was completed in a few minutes. First, a Taliban vehicle took the terrorists, released from Indian jails, close to the hi-jacked plane. One hostage-taker climbed down first and identified them before asking his comrades to dismount.[23] All of them were given ten hours to leave the Afghan border. Muttawakil wanted Singh to announce this at a Kandahar media conference, with a view to winning "a stamp of bilateral approval" for the "sordidness and illegality" of allowing the terrorists "to go scot-free" (editorial of Frontline, January 21, 2000, p. 11). Thus the safe passage for the terrorists included in the deal was implemented smoothly. Nevertheless they appeared insecure. They took a Taliban hostage and made him travel with them till they reached the Afghan–Pakistan border. Their final destination was Pakistan.

It is not necessary to know the winner and loser in the Kandahar crisis. Indeed, this is not an easy task, given the fact that a definition of success and failure of hostage negotiations is subjective and outcome is interpreted according to one party's interest and preference. A government likes to assess outcomes positively while it is possible that opposition parties consider them negative. Terrorists will have their own way of evaluating their deal with a government. Interpretations of hostages and their families may be different from opinions of the general public and media. This suggests that a composite definition encompassing all shades of interests and opinions is hard to evolve. The current literature is not helpful, either. Definition of "negotiated success as the achievement of some, but not all, of the terrorist groups' demands," offered by a group of authors (referred to in Hayes 1991: 369), is questionable. Measuring success or failure in quantitative terms (number of demands accepted or rejected) may not make a good sense if we take into account terrorists' tough bargaining strategies. Faure (2003: 490) therefore lays emphasis on the hostage-takers' "real, not the stated, objectives."

I argue that a definition should take cognizance of one side's accomplishment of a broad array of objectives in a given hostage crisis and the cumulative cost it pays for the same. Is the concerned government able to get hostages released? Has it paid any ransom? Has it captured the hostage-takers? Has it made any substantive concessions in terms of, for example, release of terrorists in a trade-off? A success may be "absolute" and "partial"; a failure must also be seen in the same gradational terms. A government tends to claim an absolute success in a hostage negotiation if it is able to free hostages and arrest terrorists, but refused to make any trade-off. A partial success involves the release of hostages for a huge ransom and safe passage to terrorists. From the standpoint of opposition parties, any significant trade-off and concessions amount to be a failure. The same may be the view of the media. A government, in its opinion, is said to have failed if it has agreed under a deal both to exchange terrorists for hostages and grant safe passage to hostage-takers. Such a deal is rather difficult to sell in countries suffering from scourge of terrorism. At the same time, in hostage-takers' opinion, success is defined in terms of a highly profitable trade-off, and failure implies that they are arrested or killed and hostages are freed.

Though the Kandahar negotiations produced a mixed outcome, people in India were divided along the official and unofficial lines. In the absence of camouflaged principles and a face-saving formula, the government became very defensive, arguing that the deal offered "the best possible solution in a basket of worse alternatives" (Singh 2000).[24] Its post-crisis managers tried to project the negotiations a success in two ways: first, the hostages were saved and, second, the government's hard bargaining helped bring down the terrorists' demands. This claim was, however, rejected by the Opposition and media. They characterized the swap deal as the most "humiliating and deeply damaging defeat for the Indian state, its pro-active anti-terrorism stance, and its vital interest in Kashmir" (Frontline, January 21, 2000, p. 10). One analyst went further to say that "The government emerged from this grave crisis with its incompetence exposed and its credibility in the mud. The nation has suffered grievously for the misdemeanors of the momentary stewards of its affairs" (Noorani 2000: 18). Describing the Indian state as soft, the Hindu nationalists questioned its power and capability (Dixit 2002: 32). Understandably the deal was disapproved mainly because the Indian government agreed to release three terrorists. Had it limited the concession-making merely to providing safe passage to the hostage-takers, the criticisms against the deal would have been significantly muted, if not totally absent.

Assessment

The analysis of Kandahar hostage negotiations provides some useful insights in the realm of crisis bargaining and termination. As this case study reveals, negotiating with terrorists entails a complex process in which difficulties occur at all phases – beginning, middle and end. Negotiation does not begin easily as governments resist and even reject, at the first instance, terrorists' demands to this effect and it is only after a careful weighing of options and assessing the cost-effectiveness of the available strategies that the former accepts the idea of political talks. This raises a basic question: when does actual negotiation begin? If negotiations between a government and terrorists are a mutually accepted political engagement, it is necessary that they develop a common perception or sort of a shared view, either out of choice or compulsion, on the negotiability of the crisis and reaching a solution through a joint problem-solving exercise. Thus both acknowledge each other's interests without, at the same time, recognizing or accepting them. Changing government response and position – from "no to negotiations" to "yes to negotiations" – occurring rather incrementally is an indication of its changed mind out of pragmatism. The greater the asymmetry of power characterizing a government position *vis-à-vis* hostage-takers due to its disadvantages caused by an inaccessible location of the crisis, inability to neutralize hostage-takers' threat, third-party pressure and public sympathy for hostages, the greater are its compulsions to accept negotiations as a viable way out of a crisis situation.

Table 7.1 The negotiation process

Critical tasks	Process questions	Factors/incentives/motives
Initiating negotiations	When does negotiation begin?	Development of common perception Government's inability to alter its asymmetrical power position
	Why do parties negotiate?	Exploration of perception and power
	How do parties negotiate?	Formulation of demands and responses
Sustaining negotiations	When is a negotiation process sustained?	Development of commitment to talks Negotiation crossed the threshold level Military option closed Development of rapport between negotiators
	Why is a negotiation process sustained?	Non-availability of other options External and internal pressures
	How is a negotiation process sustained?	Endless discussions/bargaining on terms of trade Manifold queries and lengthy clarifications Expression of shared feeling and reassurance of a political settlement
Concluding negotiations	When do parties make a deal?	Mutually hurting stalemate
	Why do parties make a deal?	Escape from pain and ending torture
	How do parties make a deal?	Active role of intermediary in formulating and implementing the deal

Acceptance of political engagement by both adversaries does not in any way indicate that they are prepared to accommodate each other's vital interests and demands. For terrorists, negotiation is a continuation of the hostage crisis (until their core demands are accepted) by other (political) means. It is indeed a terrorist tactic. Similarly, when the use of force tends to become an undesirable or unfeasible option, government treats negotiation as a tactical (non-violent) move to buy time or create fatigue or finally reject their demands. Tactical negotiations are possible mainly at the beginning when one or both parties lack commitment to a political solution and accordingly seek to pursue silently contradictory objectives through their open political engagement. Each tries to win the other to its side, which amounts to be weakening of one party at the negotiating table and at the same time emboldening of another – a sort of zero-sum game. Resultantly, the issue of developing a common formula takes a back seat, until both parties realize the imperative of protecting their interests and promoting their goals. Particularly, the weaker side should understand its limitations arising of an asymmetrical power position in order to change the pattern of negotiations.

Tactical negotiations become truly strategic under a changed situation brought about by a combination of factors. It implies a changed relationship between parties marked by their mutual recognition of each other as an interested partner of peacemaking. If a change in government's perception is fundamental to this altered relationship, terrorists' behavior also matters in this regard. Government tends to change its perception and resultantly its position when it finds all other options are closed or too costly, when terrorists correctly understands their adversary's tactical negotiations as a political ploy and therefore put pressure by issuing threats and setting deadlines for accepting their demands, and when third party becomes a dominant factor in negotiations and uses its leverage *vis-à-vis* both parties to push them to find a political settlement. Hostage negotiations are characterized by asymmetry of power between parties or symmetry of power in an asymmetrical power situation, but their principal goals are numerically equal. For a government, freeing all hostages without any harm to them constitutes its only goal. Similarly, terrorists want to ensure their safety while trying to achieve their demands.

A hostage negotiation process has some peculiar features. Both parties tend to be keen on exploring initially each other's perception, strengths, and weaknesses before assessing its negotiating position. It means that even when they are said to be engaged in a substantive negotiation, they are still actually involved in mere exploratory talks. On this government is found to be more keenly interested than terrorists who always seek a much quicker and shorter negotiation to achieve their goals. At the same time, government prefers a lengthy negotiation process with a view to changing its adversary's position by altering its terms of trade. Its assumption therefore is that the longer the duration of negotiations the greater the chance of changing terrorists' trading terms. Duration of negotiations therefore forms an important element of their negotiating strategy. Exploratory talks, however, cannot be stretched for long. Under hostage-takers' pressure, government is forced to respond to their demands; it is compelled to take a negotiating position. Interestingly, terrorists formulate proposals and government merely responds by seeking to lower their terms of trade. Its rejection of their proposals therefore should simply mean asking their total revision and not their total abandonment. In responding to government's stand terrorists reiterate their trading terms, the process continues until a significant change is incrementally brought in their stand by a third-party intermediary. Correspondingly changes occur in both parties' negotiating position. Government tends to climb up from a lower-end (low acceptability level to higher) and hostage-takers walk down from a higher-end (higher demand level to lower) in that a third party's role as a moderator becomes decisive, which in government's interpretation and perception amounts to be favoring or siding with terrorists.

The task of sustaining negotiation is as challenging as initiating it. For negotiations to be a durable process, favorable conditions should exist. First, parties should be convinced of each other's unwavering commitment to negotiations as a joint problem-solving exercise. The level of their mutual confidence should be high enough to take the process forward. Second, negotiations should have crossed the threshold level characterized by extreme fragility, potential breakdown and possible backtracking by parties. Third, having given up its military approach, government redesigns its strategy to maneuver at the negotiating table;

its objective is to minimize the cost of a deal. At the same time, terrorists seek to increase their opponent's cost while lowering theirs by reiterating their terms of trade. A competitive dimension is thus given to negotiations. To these, rapport developed between negotiators over the days can also be added as an incentive for sustaining negotiations.

Parties keep negotiations on track for mutual benefit. Besides it being the only way out since other options are closed or considered costly and self-destructive, they face external and internal pressures for continuing political dialogue. The third party is a major source of external pressure. Its interest in sustaining negotiations is borne out of its commitment to find a political end of crisis or desire to support one of the parties in achieving its goal. In all it has its self-interest to promote. Being an interested third party with leverage over parties, it seeks to garner some rewards for its intermediary role. Negotiation is therefore as important for itself as for parties themselves who, having been pressurized to abandon their violent means, are forced to remain engaged politically until a settlement is reached.

External pressure may also come from interested stakeholders (governments of foreign hostages) and the international community, whose sole interest in sustaining negotiations is to avoid bloodshed and free the hostages. Internal sources of pressure, exerted mainly on government, are political parties, media, general public, and hostages' families. They tend to develop a unanimous view on the issue of continuing negotiations to release hostages; disagreements are likely to arise over concession-making to terrorists. Serious negotiation prevents one side from issuing threat and fixing deadlines for accepting its core demands, or helps both parties to manage threat and deadline. It also prevents escalation of crisis by making terrorists abjure violence against hostages. Stalemate in negotiation is not ruled out, and both parties show interest in averting its breakdown. They accept the proposition of sustaining negotiation, but prolonging it tends to invite terrorists' wrath. In their view, prolongation without progress is a deception tactic by government. Its consequences are escalation of crisis, issuance of threats and setting deadlines.

Often hostage negotiation is sustained against heavy odds. It proceeds despite contrasting pressures: government wants it to be longer as against terrorists' desire to make it shorter. In the end what determines negotiation duration are parties' bargaining strategies and third party's role. Endless discussions, manifold queries, and lengthy clarifications mark a sustained negotiation process. Though government use these as buying-time tactics and terrorists dislike them the latter may feel assured of reaching a political end of crisis since their terms of trade are brought in for discussion. At this stage negotiators' language tends to change. While being formal and hard-hitting often, they intermittently display a sense of shared feeling, express concern and reassure each other of their total commitment to a negotiated settlement. However, use of soft language does not necessarily imply softening of a dominant party's position. It increases the durability of negotiation – an important precondition for it success. The lengthier the negotiation process, the greater the chance of reaching a political end of hostage crisis. But it is difficult for a government to drastically change or reject terrorists' terms of trade even if both parties are engaged in long-drawn-out negotiations in a situation in which the latter, with the support of an intermediary and patrons, has significantly tilted the power balance against their adversary. Therefore, wining patrons and weaning patrons away from its adversary form an important task of government's negotiating strategy. Also, terrorists' threats and deadlines becoming incredible does not necessarily make them soften their position or lessen the likelihood of reaching a negotiated end of the hostage crisis; nor does it increase government's chance of significantly changing its opponent's terms of trade.

Deal-making is a positive outcome of a successful negotiation process that builds on ripe moments centering on both parties' perception of a mutually hurting stalemate (Zartman 1989). Ripeness develops gradually as parties, attaching greater importance to their goals, resist all pressures and withstand stresses and strains while involving tough bargaining until each side realizes that it cannot secure a decisive victory for itself or defeat the other at the negotiating table. Deadlock becomes painful to both parties. For terrorists, as days pass, being hostages themselves while involved in a hostage-taking act is an excruciating experience from which they want to escape. Similarly, government likes to regain the lost freedom for hostages. More delays not only mean continuing the torture to hostages and causing anxiety among their families but also bringing more pressure on government and questioning its capability. Thus ripeness develops *during* the talks, which become full-fledged negotiations only when the parties see their painful stalemated position. As the cost of breaking negotiations or failure of making a deal is prohibitive, both parties are forced to find an alternative way out with the help of an intermediary which uses carrot and stick strategies in pursuit of a political settlement. Importantly, its leverage over both parties increases when negotiations reach a mutually hurting stalemate. Correspondingly, its role expands so much that it effectively guides the negotiation process, influences and presses both parties to change their demands and responses, contributes to the formula-making, and guarantees implementation of a deal reached between government and terrorists. In the process intermediary emerges to be the most significant factor in hostage negotiations and crisis termination.

Lessons

Notwithstanding their declaratory counter-terrorism policy, in practice governments not only negotiate with terrorists but also do deals with them to save lives. The Kandahar hostage crisis showed a democratic government's predicament and compulsion to engage terrorists in negotiations even while adopting a policy of hot pursuit in conflict areas like Kashmir. The deal, resembling the one to end the 1985 TWA jetliner hi-jacking,[25] was of course less than desirable but truly a practical way out. Yet it has become unpopular in Indian politics and the government of the day stands condemned.

1 *Terrorists leverage their political demands for maximum utility.* The case shows how difficult it is for a democratic polity to accept the idea of political engagement with terrorists even if a concerned government prefers it under pressure or as a pragmatic step. When a hostage deal is politicized, governments become defensive by giving credence even to terrorists' incredible threats. This is what the Indian leadership has consciously chosen to do in the post-crisis period.[26]

2 *Concessions to terrorists can be either the first or the last.* The question of legitimacy that deters governments from negotiating with terrorists is not a permanent factor. It loses its salience when parties agree to negotiate. Governments find it easier to compromise on their stated position on legitimacy to terrorists than rewarding them under a deal. A reward for their terrorist act can potentially be a large political stick for the opposition to beat the government with. It is assumed that countries with a history of making concessions to terrorists are particularly vulnerable at the negotiating table as they are reminded of their past responses and pressed to repeat the same every time. It was for this reason that the Indian government resisted till the end the terrorists' pressure for a swap deal. Having finally acquiesced in the deal, India has now taken a stand that it will never reward terrorists in the future. It is possible that such a peacetime declaratory position becomes unintentionally violable when a government, as in the past, faces grave terrorist challenges.

Notes

1 The identity of all the hi-jackers was established after four of their accomplices were arrested in Mumbai, India's commercial capital. They were identified as: Ibrahim Attar, Shahid Akhtar Sayeed, Sunny Ahmed Qazi, Mistri Zahoor Ibrahim and Shakir Ahmed, alias Rajesh Gopal Verma. However, during the hostage crisis they were known to the passengers and crew as Red Cap (Chief), Doctor, Burger, Bhola and Shankar. Since they wore masks all the time, no one could get to see their faces. Nevertheless their identity as hard-core terrorists was quite revealing.

2 The CMG is a permanent body of officials, set up in 1996, to deal with emergency situations. Its members are the Cabinet Secretary (chairman), Principal Secretary to the Prime Minister, Foreign Secretary, Defense Secretary, Home Secretary, Secretary of Civil Aviation, Secretary (Research and Analyses Wing) in the Cabinet Secretariat, Director of Intelligence Bureau (IB), Director General of National Security Guard, and Additional Secretary in the Cabinet Secretariat (convener).

3 It must be noted that the Indian government kept a National Security Guard (NSG) task force ready for operation in Kandahar. Even the relief aircraft sent to Kandahar with the negotiators and a relief team (doctors, nurses, and technicians) had twenty commandos of the Special Action Group, whose presence, however, was not known to the Taliban.

4 On December 25 1999 the Indian government had asked the United Nations in writing not to get involved in the negotiations with the hi-jackers (Noorani 2000: 22). It seemed to be paranoid because any external role in the hostage crisis at its official invitation would set an undesirable precedent for mediating the Kashmir conflict.

5 In total compliance with India's desire, UN Secretary General Kofi Annan declared that the UN team's role would be limited to providing humanitarian assistance to the hi-jacked passengers (Malhotra 1999).

6 Being one of the three countries (others were the UAE and Saudi Arabia) which accorded diplomatic recognition to the Taliban-led government in Afghanistan (named the "Islamic emirate") after they had replaced the Rabbani regime on September 27 1996 in a bloody *coup*, and having extended crucial support in their battle for power and supremacy in the civil war-torn country, Pakistan enjoyed leverage over the Taliban. Indeed, they were very much an ISI creation. Pakistan's aim in supporting a medieval-minded group in establishing a fundamentalist regime was to regain its control and influence over Afghanistan. Since Kabul was very much a dependent ally of Islamabad, the countries which had approached Pakistan for help hoped that they would be able to earn the Taliban's goodwill toward the hostages through their patron next door.

7 Governments of Switzerland, Spain, Italy, Belgium, France, Canada, and Australia sent representatives to Kandahar (to ascertain the welfare of their nationals and facilitate the process of ending the hostage crisis) where they came in contact with the Taliban authorities.

8 The US behind-the-scenes role included placing, at India's request, a point person who kept in constant touch with Indian and Pakistani governments and the United Nations. He was to decide and respond to any help sought from the United States (Gupta 2000). Despite the high level of cooperation and interaction between New Delhi and Washington during the hostage crisis, some Indian commentators felt that the US help was far below what they had expected (Cherian 2000: 15–16).

9 The hostage crisis gave the Taliban regime an unexpected opportunity to engage the world. Their crucial role in reaching a negotiated end of the crisis on its eight day earned them enough international publicity and attention at a time when the whole world condemned and isolated them for their policies of religious extremism, cultural oppression, authoritarianism, and denial of human rights. The United Nations sanctioned international embargo since October 1999 created severe economic problems for the country.

10 Describing the Taliban's policies as "medieval malevolence," New Delhi was openly critical of their "increasing political excesses and religious extremism" and often condemned in the strongest possible terms their policies and actions to brutalize women and religious minorities (Foreign Office statements, quoted in Cherian 2000: 20).

11 During the hostage crisis Delhi witnessed emotional scenes which all television channels and print media captured and presented to the entire country. In this process they kindled emotions of Indians who were deeply sympathetic to the victims and their families. The public expressed its anger by resorting to violence. They broke gates of the CMG office, fought with policemen, abused government officials, blocked traffic and threatened many times to break all the barriers and surge inside the Prime Minister's residence. There were incidents of agitators being beaten by the police during demonstrations, which damaged the government's image.

12 One section, led by Home Minister L. K. Advani, seemed to have taken a hard-line position on the ground that any concessions to the hostage-takers would be politically damaging to the government and, therefore, preferred a rescue military operation. Some others like External Affairs Minister Singh argued that Indian public opinion would turn against the government if its rescue mission resulted in killing of hostages. He also convinced the Cabinet that the Taliban would cooperate with the government since they were desperate to gain international recognition.

13 Disappointed with India's reluctance to negotiate, the Taliban warned that they would ask the hi-jacked aircraft to leave Kandahar unless India sent its representatives by the morning of December 27. They defended their ultimatum on the ground that the hi-jackers decided to blow up the plane if their demand for negotiation was not met. Foreign Minister Wakil Ahmed Muttawakil ventilated his feeling of frustration when he said that Indians were not taking interest in the hostages (ENS 1999).

14 Shortly before Ghanashyam's arrival, the hostage-takers tied two foreign hostages up and threatened to kill them. The Taliban moved their forces around the aircraft with a strong message that they would storm the plane if the threat issued by the terrorists was carried out. This seemed to be a tactical step on the Taliban's part to prove their *bona fides* to the Indian government which suspected their role in the hostage crisis.
15 A communication link between New Delhi and Kandahar was established. Kandahar ATC tower was the venue for Indians to hold talks with the hostage-takers, who operated from the plane's cockpit. In the absence of face-to-face negotiations both sides used radio phones and walkie-talkies. It was difficult to maintain uninterrupted power in the aircraft. Often power broke down due to lack of facilities to recharge batteries. It was in such an adverse environment that the Kandahar negotiations were conducted.
16 India's earlier stand rejecting the hostage-takers' terms could be attributed to the lack of correct information on their real strength and power. The intelligence reports suggested that they possessed a pistol, a hand grenade, and a penknife. It was hardly known to the government authorities that the day before negotiators reached Kandahar and in the wake of implementing their first deadline, the terrorists took out from the aircraft's cargo compartment a bag full of weapons (which included automatic guns, hand grenades, and RDX) and brought them inside the plane. The negotiators were virtually jolted when they came to know of this.
17 Sajjad Khan, better known as Sajjad Afghani, was the HuA's supreme commander in the Kashmir valley. He masterminded and led many successful terrorist operations in the Kashmir valley until he was arrested, along with Maulana Mastoid Zahra, on February 11, 1994, and killed by the police in a jailbreak incident in September 1999.
18 One incident took place on the night of December 29, when the terrorist chief told the pilots, "Your government is crazy. They think that they are the hi-jackers and we are the hostages. They believe just the opposite of what's happening on the ground. How can this dialogue go on? How can these talks progress?" (Jaggia and Shula 2000: 152).
19 The first threat was issued on December 27, asking the government to send its negotiators. The deadline passed without any incident even though the negotiators reached Kandahar three hours late.
20 On December 30 the Taliban deployed a contingent of their crack troops and a multi-barrel rocket on the Kandahar airport tarmac. The barrel of a rocket launcher was pointed toward the Indian relief aircraft; the tanks took up vantage positions overlooking it (Baruah 2000: 12–13). On the Indian government's proposal for a rescue operation, Afghan Foreign Minister Wakil Ahmad Muttawakil categorically declared that their *Amir* (ruler) did not want the blood of innocent people to be shed on their own soil (Agencies 1999).
21 Muttawakil was metaphorically at best when he described the negotiation process and position of all three parties (India, terrorists, and Taliban) thus: "the Indians have one key and the hi-jackers have one, while the Taliban are holding the lock firmly and urging them to open it. We wish and are eager to see the lock opened" (Agencies 1999).
22 Singh travelled to Kandahar, taking with him all the three terrorists named for freeing, to see that the end game was smooth and there was no last-minute hitch in termination of the hostage crisis. In the wake of scathing criticism by the opposition in India, he defended his decision in this regard. See Singh (2006: 230–243).
23 Singh (2006: 243) said that the issue of identification of released terrorists was another "give-away of the ISI hand." He maintained that the ISI brought friends/relatives of them from Pakistan with a purpose of confirming their identity; only after that the hostage-takers were assured that a "trick was not being played upon by the wily Indians."

24 Rajesh Mishap, who actively took part in the decision-making, said that the Indian government had the option of releasing three terrorists or collecting about 170 bodies with a wreckage of the hi-jacked aircraft (Gupta 2000).
25 Apart from getting about 300 Shiite prisoners released by Israel in exchange for 153 passengers and crew, the hi-jackers negotiated for their safe retreat.
26 External Affairs Singh (2006: 238), one of the prominent defenders of the swap deal, used the argument of threat. He said that "The threat was real, it could not be brushed off: what if the aeroplane is blown up?"

Conclusion
Lessons for action

Guy Olivier Faure and I. William Zartman

The major objection to negotiation with terrorists is that it encourages them to repeat their tactics. However, it is not the negotiation per se that encourages terrorism but rather the degree to which they are able to achieve their demands by negotiation. If negotiating leads to a purely symbolic result – a radio appeal or a newspaper ad – the terrorists are likely to decide that the result is not worth another try. Or, if negotiating leads them to a bargain for their escape but totally bypasses their original demands, they are not likely to feel encouraged to have another try. But if negotiation leads to prisoners' release or to ransom payments, it sets the precedent for future negotiations and in addition it materially feeds the terrorist organization. Thus, encouragement comes from the results, not from the act of negotiating itself. Nor does it come from talking – as opposed to actually negotiating – with the terrorists. Contact and communication are absolutely necessary to find out the terrorists' goals and expectations, as well as to obtain operational intelligence. The answer of the negotiator to his public's fears of appeasing and legitimizing terrorism lies in the deal he is able to extract from the terrorists and in the necessity to focus on the fate of the victims, and in this constraint, the negotiator and the terrorist are each other's hostage.

Step 1, identifying the actors: types of terrorists

The analysis begins by separating *absolute* from *contingent* terrorists, i.e. those with no interest in negotiation versus those who act with the purpose of negotiating. These categories are not divided by a sharp line; they may overlap and, more important, they are mobile: The challenge of negotiation is to turn *total absolutes* into *conditionals*, and to work on the *contingents'* need for negotiation.

Absolute terrorists are those whose action is non-instrumentalist, who commit a self-contained act that is completed when it has occurred and is not a step to a second action. Absolute terrorism is the demonstrative act of the weak; it expresses the suicide's frustration with the situation and his inability to change it by any other means. Absolute terrorists do not want society to be whole again; they want it wounded and bleeding. To be able to commit terror, they must believe in their own rectitude, whether the sense of justice that counterbalances their asymmetrical power position comes from revelation (as in the case of fundamentalists), from revolution (as in the case of social revolutionaries), or from revulsion against a world they feel owes them this right as a result of its own basic discrimination or corruption (nationalists and criminals, respectively). It is not only the suicidal tactics (means) but the unlimited cause (ends) that makes for truly absolute terrorism. Both revolutionaries and fundamentalists want to overthrow the given social system and build a new world in the image of their dreams, and are willing both to kill others and die themselves to achieve their goal.

Within the absolute category, however, *total* (or revolutionary) absolutes can be distinguished from *conditional* absolutes. Total absolutes have nothing to negotiate about; they have nothing to negotiate with, and any attempt to negotiate with them only encourages them, as is often noted. As contact and communication are basic conditions of negotiation, inaccessibility is another component of absolute terrorists. It is notoriously difficult even to contact them and to talk them out of their act while they are up in the air or even on the street heading toward their target.

Contingent or instrumental terrorism involves mainly hostage-taking and kidnapping, the primary focus of this study. Its violence is not definitive or absolute; it is accomplished only in part by the act of hostage-taking and is a threat or contingency for the rest, as in the fate promised for the hostages if the demands are not met. Contingent terrorists seek negotiations, to exchange their victims for something – publicity, ransom, release of their own people. They use others' lives as currency for other goals and want to get the full price for their hostages; for the most part, live hostages are better bargaining material than dead ones. Hostages are capital or, more precisely, bargaining chips, that is, items of no intrinsic value to the bargainer but created for the purpose of being bargained away. Contingent terrorists try to overcome their essentially weak position by appropriating a part of the other side and trying to get the best deal out of the other side's efforts to get that part back, to make itself whole again and stick to their fundamental values.

All terrorists are hostage-takers and all are their own victims. The standard hostage-taking terrorist takes identifiable hostages; the suicidal terrorist holds the people around him hostage, adding to the terror itself by the fact that they never know when they will become his chosen victims. Fear makes the whole population hostage to the terrorist, and some of the population is victim at any specific time. But the terrorists are all their own victims. The suicide bomber kills himself along with his victims, just as the hostage-taker has taken himself hostage; he cannot escape from the barricade, kidnap hideout, or hi-jacked plane any more than his captives can.

The problem in the case of contingent terrorists is not that they are not interested in negotiating but that the world does not accept their deal. But that is merely an extreme case of a typical negotiating situation. In that situation there are two appropriate negotiating strategies – either *reduce* or *change* their terms. Negotiators need to construct legitimacy and acceptability for a negotiated agreement. They have to build the terrorists' independent decision-making capabilities to think in terms of lowered expectations and thus of *lowered demands*.

Treatment as equals, development of the legitimacy and acceptability of a solution, and expansion of options are all ways of moving the hostage-takers off positional bargaining and opening up the possibility of a fruitful search for mutually satisfactory solutions by newly defined standards.

Negotiators can also *change demands* or terrorists' terms of trade – the price demanded for hostage release – from their demands to their fate. Terrorists tend to focus on their original terms of trade – release of hostages in exchange for fulfillment of demands – and are not looking for alternatives, in other words, options that need to be developed if negotiations are to succeed. They need to be shown that there is no chance of their original demands being met but that their future personal situation is open for discussion; innumerable details then become available for negotiation. The two messages must be delivered in tandem, indicating that while one is closed to discussion, the other is open and personally more compelling, giving them the prospect of something real and attainable. As in any negotiations, when the terrorists become convinced that a search for a solution is legitimate and acceptable to both sides, they become joint searchers for a solution to a problem rather than adversaries. To entice them into this common pursuit, they need to be convinced that the other side is willing to consider their interests, and not just their actions, strategies, and tactics.

Both strategies depend on removing obstacles to creative negotiating, indicating the legitimacy and interest of both parties in finding a solution, and developing a range of options. At this point, the problem returns to the other side, to *the official negotiator, who needs to lead the terrorist against his will into the give-and-take of negotiation*. There is room for a wide range of tactics; at some point, take-it-or-leave-it offers are useful, whereas at other times invitations to further refinement and creative thinking are appropriate; at some points firmness in the subject of negotiations is in order, whereas at other points parties can explore alternatives and options. Structurally, at the beginning of the process, *time is on the side of the negotiator*, a point that the terrorist may seek to reverse by either killing or releasing some of his hostages, or playing with public opinion.

Similarly, the negotiator needs to offer the conditional absolute terrorist concessions to his demands as the payment for abandoning his violent terrorism, not concessions following the terrorist's line itself. If the negotiator should make concessions to the terrorist part of the negotiation process, so too must the terrorist, and even the absolute terrorist does have something to offer as payment – his choice of terrorist tactics.

Step 2, identifying the strategy: dealing with absolutes

The principal purpose when dealing with absolute terrorists in a strategic/political situation is always to separate the conditional terrorists from the total absolutes. By definition, *total absolutes are beyond any negotiation* and attempts to deal with them directly are pointless, usually only confirming the flabbiness of the negotiators. But it is an error to assume that all absolutes are totals, beyond negotiation, or that the category "total" is fixed and immutable. It is an equal error to assume that all totals are fixed in that attitude. The point is to identify potential conditionals and then encourage them to see the hopelessness of their situation and the potential hopefulness in responding to negotiations.

One of Gandhi's three mantras on the subject is *Address the issues behind the terrorism*. This can be overextended: terrorism is ultimately related to such structural issues as globalization, poverty, and inequality, which, for all their cosmic importance, are far beyond any immediate – or perhaps even distant – remedy. Nevertheless, along with the sense of frustration they entail, there are related issues of importance to the potential supporters of/acquiescers in terrorism where steady attention would *Climb to the moral high ground and cling to it*, another of Gandhi's maxims. These include the Arab–Israeli dispute, where the Peace Process after all is a US invention that has returned only Arab land to Arab states, a fact not always recognized.

Although strategic/political negotiations occur in a highly charged issue-laden context, one does *not negotiate a belief system*. Perhaps, in the course of implementing the outcome of the negotiations, one can sow doubt about the bases of the motivating beliefs, but the negotiation needs to focus on specific items and will at best result in an agreement between enemies. Then, it places the next challenge on implementation, not a coming together between new partners. At best, that comes later.

Any attempt to negotiate strategic/political situations must be seen within a larger context and used as part of a larger strategy. Unlike many hostage/kidnapping situations, such terrorist acts are not self-contained events, so negotiation is *not an autonomous subject or policy*. It is a long process and can only be discussed in the context of complex events and a wide-ranging policy to handle them. Other policy actions are needed as a support for attempts at negotiation. Three groups of principles are involved.

General contextual policies involve respect, ripeness and mediation. Probably the most difficult aspect of negotiation in political/strategic situations is the need for *respect* toward the terrorist(s). Respect is the basic condition of any negotiation. The opponent must be recognized as a party with standing, a negotiating partner and formal equal because of its ability to veto any agreement and an actor with identifiable reasons behind its actions. Creating a sense of equality and enhancing the opponent's sense of its ability to make independent decisions are crucial elements in a positive negotiation setting.

Respect is a personal relation, not a status recognition, and needs to be conveyed through formal gestures and personal politeness. Regardless of public relations with the state the negotiator represents, the negotiator needs to be interested and appear understanding in his contacts with the terrorist representative. Both sides have an interest in keeping the contacts out of the public eye, facilitating equality and respect. Respect does not mean sympathizing with the terrorists' aims and goals or even recognizing their legitimacy. Indeed part of the negotiating process is to show how the terrorists' fears and concerns are unfounded and their goals unattainable as conceived. So it does mean *understanding* where the terrorist comes from, mentally and experientially.

Respect rests on a paradox. It has already been noted that terrorism is a response to power asymmetry: government is stronger, and one theme of government negotiators is to have the terrorist understand the ultimate unproductivity of his tactic. On the other hand, "one down" approaches which seek to impart a sense of inferiority are unproductive in negotiation. Here and now, the equality of the parties is important to convey; in the broader sense, the hopelessness of the tactic needs to be made clear. Respect carries with it entrapment dangers. A negotiator can become so attuned to the terrorist's point of view that the original aim of negotiation becomes obscured. This creates the common *re-entry problem*, making it difficult for negotiators to bring their achievements back to their home authorities and find acceptance.

Parties do not negotiate unless the situation is *ripe*, meaning that they find themselves in a *mutually hurting stalemate* (MHS) and see the possibility of a *way out* (WO) through negotiation. In a word, authorities must have a two-handed strategy, using both sticks and carrots, blocking the terrorists with force and offering them something in exchange for their agreement to end terror. These two sets of tools are complementary and not mutually exclusive or alternatives. Both sets are perceptional and subjective, although objective evidence can help orient perceptions mightily.

There is no point getting around the fact that as long as the parties (authorities as well as terrorists) feel they can achieve their ends without negotiations, they have no incentive to negotiate. In a terrorist situation, the authorities must decide whether they are stalemated and hurting and therefore interested in negotiation. Thereafter, the challenge is to put the terrorists into a *hurting stalemate* too, so the painful impasse can be mutual. Terrorists must be made to see that their tactics will get them nowhere and will lose them any hope of moving even part way to their goal. Military pressure must be maintained, but displaying force does not constitute an impediment to parallel negotiations.

Authorities must also show, however, that terrorists have *something to gain* from negotiation, i.e. a way out of their stalemate. Blocking with force without enticing them into an agreement merely drives them underground. The WO may be the achievement of lessened aims, or it may merely be a chance to cut losses by avoiding elimination. Terrorists are not going to give up their weapons of the weak without getting something in exchange. This can be done through *conditional promises*: if you do something, we would consider doing something else in return. The government can indicate its willingness to listen and negotiate if terrorist tactics are dropped ("negotiate with ex-terrorists") without compromising its announced no-negotiation policy.

Direct negotiations and agreements are the most efficient and the most difficult; *mediation* is often necessary. Parties in conflict need help, if only because of the difficulties noted under Respect. Ultimately the parties may have to be in direct contact, depending on the breadth and formality of the agreement, but even then, mediation is crucial. Mediation can take two forms, depending on the obstacle to direct negotiations: *communication* and *formulation*. (A third form, Manipulation, is less common in the case of mediation in terrorist negotiations.)

The mediator as communicator is needed as a telephone line when the parties cannot talk directly, either because direct talks are compromising or because they simply can find each other. The mediator as formulator is necessary as a source of ideas when the parties cannot think beyond their conflict to find a solution. The mediator generally begins by building contacts and confidence with the terrorists and then approaches the government with his estimate of the "negotiability."

The mediator's prime function is as *a bridge of trust*. Neither party trusts the other but both must trust the mediator for the mediation to work. As such, the mediator can become a cover for concessions, the parties making compromises for the sake of good relations with the mediator that they could not make directly to each other. However, in the end the terrorist negotiator must be able to take responsibility for the agreement, which cannot be seen as having been forced on him by the mediator.

Particularly in regard to religion-based terrorists, external authorities can be useful in attempting to clarify religious precepts. This is a role that secular authorities can absolutely not fill, and indeed any perceived link between the secular and religious authorities can weaken the latter. Often, the effect of the *religious authorities* on the terrorists is indirect; religious statements condemning terrorism can work to de-legitimize it in the eyes of the potentially sympathizing public and thus weaken public support for terror. However, the effect can also be direct, sowing doubt in the terrorist's mind about the legitimacy and productivity of his tactics. Since terrorism involves a mixture of ends and means, the mediator may well be more sympathetic toward the terrorists' ends than the government, giving himself an entry that allows him to work on reducing the means. Government should be prepared for such divergence and accept it, since it is the means that is the target of his efforts.

General aims in strategic/political negotiations with terrorists include *identification, separation* and *moderation*, all involving crucial contradictions and dilemmas. The first step on the way to negotiating with absolute terrorists is the *identification* of members of the group (or the sub-group) who seem to be open to talks. *Intelligence* of all sorts is useful in this regard. An individual may simply feel that the conflict has gone on too long, that terrorist tactics are unproductive, that terrorism is not as clearly condoned by the motivating ideology as he once thought, or that terrorism is distasteful. Behind these attitudes may lay other, often very personal, causes: aging of the individual, maturing of his children, whom he would like to see lead a normal life, opportunity to spring to leadership over more radical rivals, need to hold on to leadership against more radical rivals, and personality differences.

Such individuals may not be immediately available, but rather simply pose potentialities that need *cultivation*. Again, third parties can be of particular use in this regard, since direct contacts at this point may be suspect and rejected. However, mediators of the second type, the formulator type, are particularly useful in floating "what if" ideas that might attract attention and set individuals thinking For this, the authorities need to indicate potential rewards that they would be willing to consider (WO) and even float trial balloons. Cultivation is a long-term process, caught between the need to act rapidly and the dangers of impatience.

Like time, *openness* is a dilemma of identification. At some point the potential negotiator will have to come out into the open, yet if too early a public position will make him vulnerable to his radical rivals, while holding back impedes the process. The cultivated individual(s) will have a delicate job of his own in bringing key colleagues along with his developing position.

Selection is the other side of the identification dilemma. Government is tempted – if only for the sake of effective communication – to indicate its preferred interlocutors, yet it must stay out and let the moderates emerge on their own. Again, intelligence and mediation are helpful. The government can "meet" them as they emerge but must be careful not to compromise them, since their eventual participation in negotiation is useful only if they carry some of their colleagues along with them.

Separation of the potential negotiators from the spoilers is a key point to opening negotiations and closing agreements. From the beginning until deep into the process, the potential partner to negotiations among the terrorists is not going to carry his whole group but rather will cause a split. Negotiations occur when a faction either wins adherents and carries a crucial vote or else breaks away from the main group; in either case a split within the group is involved. Negotiators need to encourage such a split by separating ends from means and emphasizing alternative means available to the moderates at a lower cost than the use of terror.

Separation confronts the group's sacred value of *unity*, which de-legitimizes and delays it, but also enables the potential negotiating terrorists to appeal to their colleagues to rally around the new option. Unity operates as a tipping point effect: it inhibits the potential negotiator from declaring his new option but it also makes it possible for him to gain backing once his option has begun to attract attention and interest.

Separation can also refer to *goals*. As with hostages and kidnappings, terrorists usually come with a long laundry list of demands. Negotiation involves paring them down but also separating out those that can be handled while leaving aside other demands "for later on." Postponing, packaging, and unpackaging are as much a part of negotiation as raising and lowering, as parties seek to match acceptable terms of trade. Such matters make up the initial phase of the negotiation process, to decide what the negotiation is about and what could be potential *formulas* for the agreement.

Separation means that authorities need to provide something toward which to separate. Like a trapeze artist, the negotiating terrorist needs to see a new perch swinging toward him, an *opportunity*, before he lets go of the old one. The potential negotiating faction needs to show that it is not selling out but rather is seizing the occasion to achieve some goals, and that it is the spoilers who are losing the opportunity. The authorities need to show that there is a better way for the terrorist to reach (some of) their goals than through violence or that there are better goals to be achieved through negotiation than those currently claimed.

Moderation is a process, not a condition. Negotiation depends on some sort of sign of moderation but it can also itself promote the moderating of the terrorists. Normally, absolute terrorists will not negotiate by definition; at most, they will see negotiation as a sign of surrender by the authorities. By definition, true negotiation implies a change in the terrorists' attitude toward the means of the struggle, and eventually toward its ends. The challenge lies in discerning how much moderation is necessary as a precondition and how much is likely to occur as a result of negotiations.

Strict preconditions are generally excuses for non-negotiation. *Cease-fire or no-violence negotiations can be useful steps to larger agreements but should not be taken as absolutes.* Terrorists are usually so decentrally organized that a leader's agreement to a cease-fire is often broken by uncontrolled splinter groups. Governments need to show that they will not be derailed by spoilers. Paradoxically, incidents of violence can often be signs of serious interest in negotiation, as terrorists make last-minute moves to strengthen their position before signing an agreement.

Changes in means and then ends are impelled by blockage and bought by incentives.

Moderation is not irreversible if incentives and stalemates are removed. Moderation and aggression are brought about by the same condition – frustration in the current course impelling a search for alternative paths. The challenge is to turn this blockage to moderation rather than to explosive, expressive violence. The feeling that there is no WO leads to aggression; the perception of real alternatives provides incentive to moderation. The chance to have a constructive role in society can offer such an alternative, but it has to overcome alienation and distrust in governments' promises. Hence the need to practice patience and to emphasize good faith is essential on the part of government negotiators.

The immediate aim of negotiation is to change the means, but the *means of terrorist violence are justified by the ends* of the terrorist. Changing goals is deeper and more difficult than changing from a violent to a political path to get there. Moderation of means is only superficial without moderation of goals, yet it is usually all that can be accomplished in a round of negotiation, the deeper change having to await several rounds on several instances of terrorism.

Engagement in negotiation and the new situation it creates can gradually produce deeper changes. The conditions of negotiation – compromise, persuasion, positive-sum outcomes – and of democracy – legitimacy of all parties, need to appeal widely, acceptance of popular judgment – themselves impose limitations on terrorists that can mark the beginning of the socialization process toward inclusion. However, such a process may take time, years or even decades.

General means of negotiation with terrorists include *investigation, contact, and communication.* In diagnosing the situation, it is important to know the *background* of the terrorists. Terrorists' motives are a complex bundle of antecedents and perceptions, and will not be addressed in a negotiation. Still, they are useful for understanding the basis of demands and devising counter-offers and arguments. Perceived past wrongs and future dangers can be handled by costless promises and assurances, although they must not be seen as admissions of guilt. Doubts about religious revelation can be introduced by external religious authorities. Exasperation with domestic corruption or foreign policy failures can be turned to more productive means of expression.

Negotiations need to be prepared by broad inquiry into terrorists' past actions, life histories, group affiliations, and experiences, since the path to their participation in negotiation may be straightened by small events as well as broad backgrounds and contexts. Former friends, family and colleagues are also a potential source of information and understanding of terrorists' motives and perceptions.

Feelings of powerlessness are a major motivator of terrorists and terrorist movements; an important element in negotiation is to induce a sense of independent decision-making power. Powerlessness is part fact and part perception. As a weapon of the weak, terrorism is a compensating action for this powerlessness. Yet negotiators can point to alternate sources of power, even among the supposed weakest, and can highlight alternative goals that are attainable. Powerlessness is often a function of goals; parties unable to attain one goal are often able to attain alternatives.

Talking is not negotiating. It is important to establish and maintain contact for purposes of investigation and to be able to communicate when parties feel negotiation is possible. Talking provides intelligence and understanding, and eventually provides opportunities for playing the "What if?" game, which is a crucial tactic for opening possibilities in any negotiation through conditional offers. *Contacts* will doubtless begin in secret and through third parties, but they need to be backed by public statements indicating openness to negotiate under whatever conditions are appropriate. Such statements have the added advantage of maintaining the high ground.

A negotiation is *pact-making between parties who represent sides*. Authorities need to assure that the party to whom they are talking represents the part of the opposing side with whom they want to make a pact. They need to know they are facing a representative spokesman for the terrorists, one who speaks for at least a part of the other side with whom they can work as the negotiation and formula for agreement evolve. That party needs to be strong enough to overcome any de-legitimization incurred by talking with the authorities. They need to know that any potential spoilers excluded from the negotiations are not strong enough to upset any ensuing agreement. At some point in the opening contacts, both sides will want to know that they are speaking – even if indirectly – to authorized representatives who will be able to deliver on any agreement that might be reached. Such assurance can take the form of a public statement or some other prearranged signal; this can be one of the functions of a cease-fire or of a no-violence pledge.

Although there are specific times when public statements are useful, as indicated, such *statements must be used carefully and judiciously*. They must not be used to trap the terrorist negotiators still working on an agreement nor to de-legitimize them, intentionally or unintentionally. Pulling terrorists into a conventional agreement is pulling them out of a dark hole, where they are unsure of the broad daylight and need time to get used to it.

Communication is an ongoing process, like moderation. For these reasons among others, terrorist negotiations are best advanced by *step-by-step* agreement. Successive agreements allow issues to be handled seriatim, permit checkpoints along the way, engage the parties in a familiarization and moderation process, and build trust. Incremental negotiations also avoid major crises posed by a large take-it-or-leave-it proposal, which may be too much to swallow all at once and therefore cause breakdowns.

Negotiation is mainly a matter *of giving something to get something*. The negotiator needs to offer the terrorist concessions to his demands as the payment for his abandonment of his violent action, not as concessions to the pressure of the action itself. If the negotiator should make concessions to the terrorist as part of the negotiation process, so must the terrorist too. In addition, the absolute terrorist does have something to offer as payment – his choice of terrorist tactics.

Negotiation, as noted, is a matter of pact-making, *not demanding surrender or suicide*. The agreement needs to specify a reduction in the means of violence and, if possible, in the goals of violence, thus it will also bring the (former) terrorists into legitimate politics, under conditions which the agreement can specify.

It is not the matter of negotiation *per se* that encourages terrorism but rather the degree of their demands that they are able to achieve by negotiation. The answer of the negotiator to his public's fears of appeasing and legitimizing terrorism lies in the deal he is able to extract from the terrorist and in his need to focus on the fate of the victims. Any encouragement would come from the results but not from the act of negotiating itself.

Step 3, identifying the tactics: dealing with contingents

Contingent terrorists are those whose actions are predicated on negotiation. The basic situation of hostage-takers is to appropriate the lives of other people by force and create a situation enabling them to issue a credible threat to a target that may be a government, a company, sometimes a family. Contingent terrorists' demands vary a lot. They do not necessarily raise issues such as having the whole country adopting Islam, or implementing the Shari'a, or radically modifying women's status, or changing the lifestyle of a population. If they address issues such as money, freedom for prisoners, access to media, then negotiation can take place. Hostage-taking, kidnapping, and hostage-barricade situations call by definition for negotiation, for the hostage is an exchange currency.

Preparatory policies involve *analysis* of *context, demands, hostage-takers* and *stakeholders. Context analysis* is the first step in action – not to act but to get a clear understanding of the situation. What is the global context of the hostage-taking? What is the history of the problem? How deep is the conflict? Sometimes, hostage-takers play for the show rather than to really get anything in return for the hostages. Do parties to the conflict know each other? What type of relation did they have before this event? Are hostage-takers acting in a context friendly to them or hostile?

If the hostage-taker operates in a *hostile environment* such as hostage-barricade situations – in an embassy, a school, a hotel, a bank, an airplane, a train, even a bus, the fishbowl principle applies. The hostage-taker faces a high risk and usually tends to put more pressure on the negotiators. The take-over may be protracted and the risks for the hostages increased. The terrorists' dependence on the outside world makes them quite vulnerable. Supply of water, food, electricity, medicine can be used as bargaining chips. Anxiety, fatigue, isolation play a crucial role. One of the hostage-takers' answers to such an unfavorable situation is to move the place of detention to a more welcoming environment such as an accomplice state.

If the hostage-takers hold the captives in *a context they control*, the negotiators are deprived of many means of action such as resorting to technical devices to gather data. They cannot use optical probes, high-sensitivity microphones, micro-lasers, bugs introduced during the negotiation process. These are classical techniques to drill a hole in the psychological shell the terrorist uses to protect himself when hearing his hesitations, his dilemmas, his angers, his feelings.

Demand analysis will be the real starting point to devise a strategy for negotiating and for defining possible trade-offs. The motivations behind the demands – recognition, reputation, compensation, recruitment, resources – will condition the first strategic choice. Will the negotiation be carried out to come to an agreement or will the negotiation be just used as a toll to prepare an assault? Among the most common terrorists demands are: release of jailed terrorists, money, weapons, access to media, safe conduct for themselves, presence of a mediator during the negotiation, means of transportation, public apologies, and change in politics. Some of these demands are quite negotiable.

Agent analysis is the next step for the real interaction with the hostage-taker to start.

One has to be sure that there is *someone to negotiate with*, making sure that the negotiation counterpart is the real hostage-taker. In kidnappings, it is not unusual that once the event is known publicly, many people pretend to be the kidnapper to reap the benefits of the action without having had the trouble to capture the hostage or the constraints attached to keeping him. Who do the terrorists represent? Work for? Do they just operate for themselves? How many are they? What kind of weapons do they have? Do they have equipment such as radio, mobile phone, television? Could they have among the various onlookers accomplices pretending to be journalists? Did they introduce a mole among the hostages?

Stakeholder analysis is also important. Besides the hostage-takers, the hostages and the negotiation team, there may be a number of parties, visible or invisible, directly or indirectly involved in the situation and likely to influence the negotiation process. Among them are the wider group to which the perpetrators belong, the media, the hostages families, the public opinion, militant groups, governments, public and private organizations, terrorists' relatives. This complex web of stakeholders has to be managed in parallel during the discussions, especially in the case of protracted negotiations. Some of them may play an ambiguous role such as the hostages' families or the media when smartly manipulated by the hostage-takers. Authorities may have infiltrated agents into the terrorist group, as it was the case in Colombia with the FARC.

Operational policies involve organization, objectives, management, and closure.

Organization of negotiations with terrorists begins with the strict application of the principle *of separation between the negotiators and the decision-makers*. The negotiator in contact with the terrorists may develop some empathy toward them, thus may be influenced by them and should not make strategic decisions. Being the decision-maker means assessing the overall current situation and making strategic choices that go beyond the negotiation process.

At the head of the negotiation team should be a person in charge of coordinating these various functions and of reporting to the decision-maker. The primary negotiator in contact with the terrorist leads the discussion and assumes a role of mediator between the legal authorities and the terrorists. He can be helped by a secondary negotiator who possibly will take over if it is useful. Some basic qualities are required to be able to stand the contact with the terrorists such as not being emotional, being patient, looking credible, able to control carefully his wording during the discussions, and being a good listener.

Two other people may play an important role. One is the referent, usually a psychologist who follows the entire process and provides analysis and insights with enough methodological distance to bring added value to the capacities of the team. The other is an intelligence officer, who is in charge of gathering information relevant to the situation and analyzes it. For instance, collecting details about the number of terrorists, their state of mind, the degree of homogeneity of the group, where they stand in the building or in the airplane, where and when do they sleep. If necessary, the negotiator may also resort to experts in a precise domain where specific knowledge is required such as on technical, psychiatric, or cultural matters.

There is no effective negotiation without having *set up precise objectives*. "There is no favorable wind for those who know not where they want to go," wrote Seneca. Objectives have to be defined before starting to negotiate. The first objective is to preserve human life, especially that of defenseless hostages. The second objective is often to deter other terrorists from doing the same. Therefore, concessions must be put to the minimum and some kind of punishment has to be carried out after the end of the hostage-taking. The second objective is to avoid dangerous terms of trade, such as giving weapons, avoiding trading weapons, avoiding enabling terrorists to escape, deter rogue states to back them or to offer them a shelter. The third objective is to avoid outcomes that can encourage the repetition of terrorist acts.

The negotiation *process needs to be managed* in its three stages, each one having its own rationale. The first stage is a kind of *pre-negotiation* in which conditions for discussions are met. Among them: establishing a communication channel such as a telephone line; organizing the negotiation team, collecting intelligence; analyzing the initial demand. The first hour of a hostage-taking is usually the most dangerous for the hostages. Terrorists are unfamiliar with the place and such a situation; they are extremely nervous, anxious and aggressive.

Hostages can be subjects to panic reactions or may do something misinterpreted. When the situation has become more stable, the risk of having to face unexpected events diminishes for both sides. Then, the real negotiation may start.

The second stage consists in elaborating a *formula* for agreement. This is a most difficult phase because negotiators are often confronted with exorbitant demands form the terrorists. It can be the release of hundreds of prisoners, to obtain highly sophisticated weapons or means of communication, to receive huge amounts of money that can be equivalent to the annual budget of an average country, to get access to international television networks, to get the resignation of a government.

During these lengthy discussions a number of basic principles for effectiveness should be followed. Among them, to only make statements that are meaningful within the frame of reference of the terrorists, to establish enough of a relationship too gain insights into the personality of the counterpart, to resort systematically to tactics that defuses the dramatic character of the hostage-taking, to minimize the damage done and its consequences, to build enough trust to be heard and considered credible, to avoid unilateral breaks and negative wordings. Hostages should not be called as such or referred to by names. Promises that cannot be kept or do not seem credible should absolutely be avoided. Escalating stress, threats, and strong criticisms should be avoided, as well as challenging the terrorists, getting into a row or setting up a deadline. Any concession made by the negotiators should be reciprocated – for instance, food, drinking water, electricity – against one hostage. The negotiation team should keep a record of all that has been said and done.

The third phase deals with the *details* of the transaction. The point at this stage is to agree on concrete figures for each of the issues previously put on the agenda. This fine-tuning stage can be quite competitive as again negotiators are involved in a zero–sum rationale. In addition each side may try to compensate quantitatively what has been conceded qualitatively in the previous phase. Everyone may fear the worst as interests again strictly oppose both sides. Uncertainty about the possibility of reaching the agreement remains and escalation, tricks, deception may still be part of the game.

Closure is a psychological moment to catch to conclude the deal. Every negotiation must end. There are no mathematics that can tell when. One must have a sense of it, a sort of intuition. However, there are some signs that may indicate that the situation is soon ready for the final settlement. For instance, when the terrorist keeps talking longer than necessary to the negotiator, when he speaks about something other than the debated issues, when the content of his discourse gets less violent, when no more threats are used, when he starts considering the future.

The negotiator must at that time stress that the counterpart had his point made, his demands heard, his cause understood. He must convince the terrorist that the authorities have reached the extreme limits of what is conceivable in terms of concessions. He must show that going any further, keeping the hostages longer, would discredit him and his cause in the eyes of public opinion. On occasions, initiatives such as reading verses of the Koran have been quite effective to trigger the final will to come to terms (Miller 1980).

Implementation and *review* are final steps. *Implementation* of the agreement can be a very difficult moment because the context may change if the hostage-taker leaves the place of the siege and anxiety and suspicion rise again at their highest level. Are the hostages all alive? In the case of Aldo Moro, a former Italian Prime Minister, the Red Brigades had killed him. Are the authorities going to carry out the agreement or are they going to launch an assault?

Kidnappings often end up with the murder of the hostage. As the police do not know where the kidnappers are, it can be quite instrumental to suppress an essential source of information that could ultimately lead to them. In the case of a state sponsored hostage-taking, there is a better guarantee that the agreement will be respected for reasons of reputation and future credibility for that state. In the case of a hostage – barricade situation, the storming of the place remains an option, discussed below under *force*.

Review is meant to prepare for the next case. Every negotiation is unique but brings something to the general case in several ways. Understanding the situation; finding out the paradigm governing it; improving the bargaining methods; developing an awareness of unexpected events; lessons for the future.

Every negotiation has to end with a double debriefing:

- A chronology of the events of the negotiation.
- A focus on themes that can be considered as essential such as *risk, timing, culture, trust, sympathy, media, families* and *force*.

No negotiation entails more *risks* than dealing with hostage-takers. At every stage of the process one has to assess the level of risk attached to the lives of the hostages. In other words for the negotiator, how far one can go without going too far? Uncertainty and threat govern that type of negotiation. Behaviors are not easily predictable; arguments used are not always rational and leave room for a wide range of interpretations; conflicting values can hardly lead to consensus; variations in the context may introduce more uncertainty in goals, strategies; emotional outbursts can trigger dramatic consequences.

Time is a resource, a condition for being effective until it turns counterproductive through the pressure it puts on the negotiators. At the beginning of the process, negotiators need time to organize themselves, understand the situation, gather information, establish a relation with the hostage-taker. Later on, pressure comes from the hostages families, the public opinion complaining that legal authorities do not do what they should to free the hostages.

In a hostile context, time runs against the terrorist. The longer the negotiation, the more risk of a storming of the place. The terrorists realize that they have been turned into prisoners. Problems such as the Stockholm syndrome (hostages siding with their captors) or the Lima syndrome (terrorists developing empathy toward the hostages) may occur.

In hostage negotiations often two national *cultures* meet with their different mind sets and communication codes. In addition, terrorists have developed a culture of their own with a very particular set of values making it quite incompatible with global cultures. As most of the people in jail, terrorists consider themselves not as culprits but as victims. The solution can be found in having local people, those sharing the same culture, joining the negotiation team. On the substance of the discussions, it is highly recommended to avoid putting values in the foreground because there is no way to negotiate over values. One constant concern should also be to only make statements that are relevant within the frame of references of the terrorist.

Building trust may seem quite impossible as values and representations of the other are so far apart. In fact some trust can be established if the negotiation lasts long enough. For this purpose wordings have to be put positive when remaining realistic and credible. Some level of empathy should be expressed, and promises should be kept. Sometimes it may be wise to ask relatives of the hostage-taker, prominent and respected personalities to join the negotiation. In Latin America, for instance, priests are often involved.

Although not as common as the media suggest, the *Stockholm syndrome* is not unusual, as hostages identify themselves with the terrorists and side with them. The case of Patricia Hearst, daughter of a press tycoon, first abducted, then adopting the cause of her captors and going as far as attacking banks at gunpoint, illustrates such a psychological process. Sometimes, negotiators themselves may be subjected to that syndrome. When such a phenomenon occurs, the latter should be replaced in the job. In all cases, both hostages and negotiators should be debriefed by psychologists to help them come back to a more realistic state of mind.

The media usually have a special interest in the terrorists' activities because of their dramatic and spectacular dimensions. They should be kept informed but in such a way that does not harm the hostages or the room for maneuver of the negotiators.

Friends and relatives of the hostages gradually tend to shift the blame on to the negotiators and legal authorities for not doing enough to have the hostages freed. Although it is quite understandable, their attitude should not be taken into consideration to impact the negotiation strategy of the authorities, for it is exactly what the terrorists expect. However, they should not be ignored and regular briefings and explanations should be delivered to them.

The "tactical option," a so-called neutral wording, simply means an *assault* on the place where the hostages are kept and free them by usually killing the captors. Then, the negotiation is of no more use and is replaced by a *fait accompli*. However, Rambo-style storming of the place entails quite a few risks with the lives of the hostages, of the intervening squad, and on people around. Even if not harmed, hostages may be strongly traumatized by the view of so much violence displayed.

Two types of actions can be distinguished. The first has to be decided from the very beginning of the hostage-taking because, for instance, deterrence has been considered as the first priority, as is the case with Israeli policy. Other reasons for resorting to the "tactical option" could be that the site offers favorable conditions, that the terrorists are a very small number, or that there is nothing to expect from the terrorists. In such a case the negotiation does not serve to reach an agreement but to prepare the storming of the place by collecting information, exhausting the captors, and reducing their level of vigilance. A typical illustration was the Lima hostage-taking that lasted four months and during which the terrorists asked for games to relax and keep people busy. Chess games were provided but bugs had been inserted inside some of the pieces.

The second decision on force is process-generated. Sometimes during the negotiation process an opportunity for intervening by force becomes available because the hostage-takers are getting negligent, because of tiredness, because of an unexpected event coming to disturb their organization. Another reason can be because terrorists deliberately start killing hostages and urgent action becomes necessary.

In sum

"Terrorist" is a concept that too broad to be useful as such regarding negotiation possibilities. The first task is to distinguish between different types of terrorists and then devise different approaches according to the type involved in the situation. Only the absolute terrorists cannot be expected to be willing to negotiate, as long as they remain absolute.. They do not take hostages but take revenge, punish people, and spread fear by doing so. Their basic means are bombs or suicide bombers. The September 11, 2001, drama is another type of illustration of their methods. The challenge for negotiators is to find conditionals among the absolutes and prise them away from their unnegotiability.

By contrast, contingent terrorists take hostages with the only purpose of negotiating, which makes the negotiation likely although very uncertain in terms of achieving an effective agreement and determining its content. Conditional absolute terrorists take hostages but with no intention to negotiate as they present their demand as an ultimatum. The second challenge for the negotiators is first to find a way out of the "take it or leave it" option.

Then, both categories of terrorists, contingents and conditionals absolutes, correspond to distinctive characteristics and require implementing strategies that are different and specific. Dealing with contingent terrorists is a short-time matter, but patience and persistence are the key points. Dealing with conditionals is a longer-time affair, involving many surrounding contextual conditions, but patience and persistence are even more key essentials. The major initial objective is not to define terms of agreement in the classical sense but to reformulate the problem/situation in such a way that the negotiation option starts to make sense. In such a short time, there is no point to try to modify the values of the terrorists but, within this constraint, to work at reconstructing the problem differently. This means that the changes will be expected in the vision the terrorists have of the relation between the object (the goal) and the method to reach it.

Then, the negotiation to come may open itself to a new domain of discussion allowing changes in both means and ends.

Considering the overall situation, the first crucial challenge to meet for negotiators is to sense who are the conditionals among the absolutes. Then, the second crucial challenge will be to convert them to negotiability by showing that negotiation as a means of action is worth a try, while not betraying their values. In the longer run, it might be the only realistic way to reduce terror by reducing tactical goals and hopefully innocent deaths. In these ways, the negotiator can wrest free from the hostage situation that the hostage-taker has imposed, while freeing the hostage-taker from his own constraining concept of his own situation, imposed by his own ends and means.

References

Agencies. 1999. Demands Soar, Hopes Crash, Agony Prolongs, www.indianexpress.com/res/web/ple/ie/daily/19991229/ina29041.html.

Alani, Mustafa 2004. *Political Kidnapping: An Operational Methodology*. Dubai: Gulf Research Center.

Alonso, Rogelio, and Reinares, Fernando. 2005. "Terrorism, Human Rights and Law Enforcement in Spain," *Terrorism and Political Violence* 17 1: 265–278.

Amado, Gilles and Guittet, André. 2005. *Dynamique des communications dans les groupes*. Paris: Armand Colin.

Amuzegar, Jahangir. 1997. "Iran's Economy and the US Sanctions," *Middle East Journal* 51 2: 185–199.

Anderson, Jack. 1999. *Peace, War and Politics*. New York: Forge.

Antokol, Norman and Nudell, Mayer. 1990. *No one a Neutral: Political Hostage Taking in the Modern World*. Medina, OH: Alpha.

Arblaster, Anthony. 1977. "Terrorism, Myths, Meanings and Morals," *Political Studies* 25 3: 413–424.

Arena, M. P. and Arrigo, B. A. 2006. *The Terrorist Identity: Explaining the Terrorist Threat*. New York: New York University Press.

Arendt, H. 1962. *The Origin of Totalitarianism*. New York: Meridian.

Arnson, Cynthia and Zartman, I. William, eds. 2005. *Rethinking the Economics of War: The Intersection of Need, Creed and Greed*. Baltimore, MD: Woodrow Wilson Center Press/Johns Hopkins University Press.

Asencio, Diego and Nancy. 1982. *Our Man is Inside*. Boston, MA: Atlantic/Little Brown.

Aslakhanov. 2004. RFE/RL "Basaev Claims Beslan Attacks," September 17.

Aston, C. C. 1984. *Political Hostage Taking in Western Europe*. London: Institute for the Study of Conflict.

Atkinson, Scott E., Sandler, Todd, and Tschirhart, John. 1987. "Terrorism in a Bargaining Framework," *Journal of Law and Economics* 30 1: 1–21.

Avenhaus, Rudolf and Sjöstedt, Gunnar, eds. 2009. *Negotiated Risk*. New York: Springer.

Baer, Robert. 2002. *See No Evil: The True Story of a Ground Solder in the CIA's War on Terrorism*. New York: Crown.

Baer, Robert, 2002. PBS Frontline interview, www.pbs.org/wgbh/pages/frontline/shows/tehran/interviews/baer (last accessed April 7 2006).

Bailey, William G., ed. 1995. *The Encyclopedia of Police Science*, 2nd edn. New York: Garland.

Baldwin, David A. 1976. "Bargaining with Airline Hi-jackers," in I. William Zartman (ed.) *The Fifty Percent Solution*. New York: Doubleday.

Baldwin, David A. 1998. "Exchange Theory and International Relations," *International Negotiation* 3 2: 121–149.

Bapat, Navin A. n.d. "Deals with Devils: State Bargaining with Terrorist Groups." Paper, Houston, TX: Department of Political Science, Rice University.

Bapat, Navin A. 2006. "State Bargaining with Transnational Terrorist Groups," *International Studies Quarterly* 50: 213–229.

Barayev, Mosvar. 2003. Cited in Nedkov, Vesselin and Wilson, Paul. *Fifty-seven Hours: a Survivor's Account of the Moscow Hostage Drama*. Toronto: Viking.

Baruah, Amit. 2000. "Warning Signals," Frontline, January 21.

Bass, Gail, Jenkins, Brian, Kellen, Konrad, and Ronfeldt, David. 2005. *Options for US Policy on Terrorism*. Santa Monica, CA: Rand.

Beeman, William O. 2005. *The "Great Satan" versus the "Mad Mullahs."* Westport, CT: Praeger.

Ben-Menashe, Ari. 1992. *Profits of War: Inside the Secret US–Israeli Arms Network*. New York: Sheridan Square Press.

Besayev, Shamil. 2002. Statement of Chief of the Military Council of State Defense Council "Majlis al-Shura" of Chechen Republic of Ichkeria Abdullah Shamil Abu-Idris concerning the Events of October 23–26, 2002, in Moscow, http://62.212.121.113/www.kavkazcenter.com/eng/articlebe27.html?id=605.

Besayev, Shamil. 2005. Kavkaz Center: Transcript of Shamil Basayev Interview for Channel 4 News, http://kavkazcenter.com/eng/article.php?id=3500 (last accessed on August 4 2005).

Bill, James A. 1988. *The Eagle and the Lion: The Tragedy of American–Iranian Relations*. New Haven, CT: Yale University Press.

Bolz, Frank and Hershey, E. 1980. *Hostage Cop: The Story of the New York City Police Hostage Negotiating Team and the Man who Leads it*. New York: Rawson Wade.

Bolz, Frank, Jr., Dudonis, Kenneth J., and David P. Schulz. 1990. *The Counter-terrorism Handbook: Tactics, Procedures and Techniques*. Amsterdam: Elsevier.

Bonn, Keith and Baker, Anthony E. 2000. *Guide to Military Operations other than War*. Mechanicsburg, PA: Stackpole.

Boot, Max. 2003. The End of Appeasement: Bush's Opportunity to redeem America's Past Failure in the Middle East. New York: Council on Foreign Relations Publications on line, *Weekly Standard*, February 10, www.cfr.org/publications (last accessed April 7 2006).

Buhite, Russell D. 1995. *Lives at Risk: Hostages and Victims in American Foreign Policy*. Wilmington, DE: Scholarly Resources.

Burton, John. 1979. *Deviance, Terrorism, and War: The Process of Solving Unsolved Social and Political Problems*. Oxford: Martin Robertson.

Carswell, Robert and Davis, Richard J. 1985. "The Economic and Financial Pressures: Freeze and Sanctions" and "Crafting the Financial Settlement," in Warren Christopher et al. (eds.) *American Hostages in Iran: The Conduct of a Crisis*. New Haven, CT: Yale University Press, pp. 173–200, 201–234.

Cave, George. 1994. "Why Secret 1986 US–Iran 'Arms for Hostages' Negotiations Failed," *Washington Report on Middle East Affairs*, September–October.

Chechnya Weekly. 2005. "Kulayev Trial provides New Beslan Details," 6 23 (16 June 2005).

Cherian, John. 2000a. "Failure of Diplomacy," Frontline, January 21.

Cherian, John. 2000b. "Megaphone Diplomacy," Frontline, February 4.
Clutterbuck, Richard. 1978. *Kidnap and Ransom: the Response*. London: Faber.
Clutterbuck, Richard. 1987. *Kidnap, Hi-jack and Extortion: The Response*. New York: St. Martin's Press.
CNN. 1999. UN won't Negotiate for India in hi-jacking, Minister says, www. archives. cnn.com/1999/ASIANOW/south/12/26/india.hi-jack.02/index.html.
Cobban, Helena. 1999. *The Israeli–Syrian Peace Talks 1991–1996 and Beyond*. Washington, DC: US Institute of Peace Press.
Cockburn, Leslie. 1987. *Out of Control: The Story of the Reagan Administration's Secret War in Nicaragua, the Illegal Arms Pipeline, and the Contra Drug Connection*. New York: Atlantic Monthly Press.
Collelo, Thomas. 1989. *Lebanon: A Country Study*. Washington, DC: US Government Headquarters, Department of the Army.
Cooper, H. H. 1981. *The Hostage Takers*. Boulder, CO: Paladin Press.
Crelinsten, R. et al. 1978. *Terrorism and Criminal Justice*. Lexington, MA: Lexington Books.
Crenshaw, Martha. 1988. "The Subjective Reality of the Terrorist: Ideological and Psychological Factors in Terrorism," in R. O. Slater and M. Stohl (eds.) *Current Perspectives on International Terrorism*. London: Macmillan.
Crenshaw, Martha. 2000. "The Psychology of Terrorism: an Agenda for the Twenty-first Century," *Political Psychology* 21 2: 405–420.
Cristal, M. 2006. "Negotiating under the Cross: The Story of the Thirty-day Siege of the Church of the Nativity," in I. William Zartman (ed.) *Negotiating with Terrorists*. Leiden: Nijhoff, pp. 103–130, reprinted from the journal *International Negotiation* 8 3 (2003).
Crocker, Chester A., Hampson, Olser Fen, and Aall, Pamela. 2005. Introduction in Chester A. Crocker, Olser Fen Hampson and Pamela Aall (eds.) *Grasping the Nettle: Analyzing Cases of Intractable Conflict*. Washington, DC: US Institute of Peace Press.
Crowell and Moring LLP. 2006. www.crowell.com/content/Expertise/VictimsofTerrorism/High.... (last accessed April 5 2006).
Dixit, J. N. 2002. *India–Pakistan in War and Peace*. New Delhi: Books Today.
Docherty, Jayne Seminare. 2001. *Learning Lessons from Waco: When the Parties bring their Gods to the Negotiating Table*. Syracuse, NY: Syracuse University Press.
Dolnik, Adam. 2003. "Contrasting Dynamics of Crisis Negotiations: Barricade versus Kidnapping Incidents," *International Negotiation* 8 3: 495–526.
Dolnik, Adam. 2006. *The Beslan Code*, RUSI Whitehall Papers. London: Royal United Services Institute.
Dolnik, Adam and Fitzgerald, K. 2007. *Negotiating Hostage Crises with the New Terrorists*. Westport, CT: Praeger.
Dominus, Susan. 2006. "The Peacemaker of Flight 847," *New York Times Magazine*, December 25.
Donohue, William and Taylor, Paul J. 2003. "Testing the Role Effect in Terrorist Negotiations," *International Negotiation* 8: 527–547.
Dupont, Christophe. 2006. *La Négociation postmoderne: bilan des connaissances, acquis et lacunes, perspectives*. Paris: Publibook.
Elliott, J. and L. Gibson, eds. 1978. *Contemporary Terrorism: Selected Readings*. Gaithersburg, MD: IACP.
Elster, Jon. 2004. "Kidnappings in Civil Wars." Prepared for the Workshop on Techniques of Violence, Oslo, Norway, August 20–21.

Enders, Walter and Todd, Sandler. 1993. "The Effectiveness of Anti-terrorism Policies: Vector–Autoregression–Intervention Analysis," *American Political Science Review* 87: 829–844.

ENS. 1999. Plane Grounded but Hopes Rise, www.indianexpress.com/res/web/ple/ie/daily/19991228/ina28016.html.

Faure, Guy Olivier. 1995. "Conflict Formulation: The Cross-cultural Challenge," in B. Bunker and J. Rubin (eds.) *Conflict, Cooperation and Justice.* San Francisco: Jossey Bass.

Faure, Guy Olivier, with Shakun, M. F. 1988. "Negotiating to Free Hostages: A Challenge for Negotiation Support Systems," in M. F. Shakun (ed.) *Evolutionary Systems Design: Policy Making under Complexity.* Oakland, CA: Holden-Day, pp. 219–246.

Faure, Guy Olivier. 2002. "Negotiating with Terrorists," *PIN Points* (Laxenburg), 18: 6–7.

Faure, Guy Olivier. 2003. "Negotiation with Terrorists: The Hostage Case," *International Negotiation* 8 3: 469–494.

Faure, Guy Olivier. 2007. "Demonizing," *PIN Points* (Laxenburg), 29: 7–10.

Faure, Guy Olivier. 2008. "Negotiating with Terrorists: A discrete Form of Diplomacy," *Hague Journal of Diplomacy* 3: 179–200.

Faure, Guy Olivier and Kahn, Maha. 2010. "Negotiation in Terrorism's Life Cycle" I "Growing up in Groups," in I. William Zartman and Guy Olivier Faure (eds.) *Engaging Extremists: Negotiating Ends and Means.* Washington, DC: USIP.

Faure, Guy Olivier and Sjostedt, Gunnar. 1993. "Culture and Negotiation: An Introduction," in Guy Olivier Faure and Jeffrey Z. Rubin (eds.) *Culture and Negotiation: The Resolution of Water Disputes.* Newbury Park, CA: Sage.

Faure, Guy Olivier and Rubin, J. Z., eds. 1993. *Culture and Negotiation*, Newbury Park, CA: Sage.

Fayazmanesh, Sasan. 2003. "The Politics of the US Economic Sanctions against Iran," *Review of Radical Political Economics* 35 3: 221–240.

Fisher, Roger, Ury, William and Patton, Bruce. 1982. *Getting to Yes.* New York: Penguin.

Fitzgerald, V. 2004. "Global Financial Information, Compliance Incentives and Terrorist Funding," *European Journal of Political Economy* 20: 387–401.

G-8. 1999. G-7 Guidelines: International "Best Practices" in Dealing with Hostage Situations. G8 Ad-hoc Group on Security, June.

Galula, D. 1964. *Counterinsurgency Warfare: Theory and Practice.* New York: Praeger.

Gama'a Islamiya. 2002: *Initiative of Stopping Violence*, Cairo: Islamic Turath Books.

Ganguly, Sumit. 1997. *The Crisis in Kashmir: Portents of War, Hopes of Peace.* Cambridge: Cambridge University Press.

Ganor, Boaz. 2005. *The Counter-terrorism Puzzle.* London: Transaction.

Ganor, Boaz. 2006. *Postmodern Terrorism.* London: Transaction.

Goldaber, Irvin. 1979. "A Typology of Hostage Takers," *Police Chief*, June, pp. 21–23.

Gongol, Brian. 2004. When to Negotiate with Terrorists, Hi-jackers, and Kidnappers, www.gongol.com/research/negotiationwithterrorists/ (last accessed February 24 2006).

Goodenough, Patrick. 1999. "Was Iran behind Lockerbie?" *Conservative News Service*, April 6, www.conservativenews.net/InDepth/archive/199904/IND199 (last accessed April 19 2006).

Goodenough, Patrick. 2005. German Trade-off Suspected in Release of Terrorist Killer. CNS News.Com: Cybercast News Service, December 22, www.cnsnews.com/ViewForeignBureaus.asp (last accessed April 4 2006).

Goodwin, Deborah. 2001. *Negotiation in International Conflict.* London: Cass.

Goodwin, Deborah. 2005. *The Military and Negotiation: the Role of the Soldier-Diplomat*. Abingdon: Cass.
Goodwin, Deborah. 2007. "The Negotiation Precipice: the Attraction of the Aggressive BATNA in Modern Conflict," in *Negociation et transformations du monde*. Paris: Negocia.
Gupta, Harish. 2000. US played Key Role in resolving Crisis, www.indianexpress.com/res/web/ple/ie/daily/20000101/ian01040.html.
Hafez, Mohammed M. 2003. *Why Muslims Rebel*. Boulder, CO: Lynne Rienner.
Hammel, Eric. 1985. *The Root: The Marines in Beirut, August 1982–February 1984*. New York: Harcourt Brace Jovanovich.
Hammer, M. 2007. *Saving Lives: The SAFE Model for Resolving Hostage and Crisis Incidents*. Westport, CT: Praeger Security International.
Hammer, M., Rogan R. and Van Zandt, C. 1997. *Dynamic Processes of Crisis Negotiation: Theory, Research and Practice*. Westport, CT: Praeger.
Hampson, Fen Osler. 2006. "The Risks of Peace: Implications for International Mediation," *Negotiation Journal*, January, pp. 13–30.
Hampson, Fen Osler and Zartman, I. William. 2010. *Word Power: Enhancing the Role of Diplomacy*, forthcoming.
Harmon, Christopher, C. 2001. *Terrorism Today*. London: Cass.
Harwood, Charles Judson. 2003. Beirut 1983–1984: Judicial Theft? http://homepage.ntlworld.com/jksonc/Beirut-1980s.html (last accessed February 5 2005).
Hayes, Richard E. 2002. "Negotiations with Terrorists," in Victor A. Kremenyuk (ed.) *International Negotiation: Analysis, Approaches, Issues*. San Francisco: Jossey-Bass.
Hayes, Richard E., Kaminski, S. R., and Beres, S. M. 2003. "Negotiating the Non-negotiable: Dealing with Absolute Terrorists," *International Negotiation* 8 3: 9–25.
Hersh, Seymour M. 2006 "The Iran Plans: Would President Bush go to War to stop Teheran from getting the Bomb?" *New Yorker*, April 17, pp. 30–38.
Herz, Martin. 1982. *Dilomats and Terrorists: What Works, What Doesn't*. Washington, DC: Institute for the Study of Diplomacy, Georgetown University.
Hewitt, Gavin. 1991. *Terry Waite and Ollie North: The Untold Story of the Kidnapping and the Release*. Boston, MA: Little Brown.
Hiro, Dilip. 1991. *The Longest War: The Iran–Iraq Military Conflict*. New York: Routledge.
Hoffman, Bruce. 1989. "World Taken Hostage," *Los Angeles Herald Examiner*, August 6.
Hoffman, Bruce. 2001. "Change and Continuity in Terrorism," *Studies in Conflict and Terrorism* 24, 417–428.
Hoffman, Bruce. 2004a. Foreword in A. Silke (ed.) *Research on Terrorism: Trends, Achievements and Failures*. London: Cass.
Hoffman, Bruce. 2004. "The Changing face of al-Qaeda and the Global War on Terrorism," *Studies in Conflict and Terrorism* 37: 549–560.
Hoffman, Bruce. 2006. *Inside Terrorism*. New York: Columbia University Press.
Hoffman, Bruce. 2007. "The Logic of Suicide Terrorism," *Atlantic Monthly*, June, www.theatlantic.com/doc/200306/hoffman (last accessed December 2007).
Homans, Charles. 1961. *Social Behaviour: its Elementary Forms*. New York: Harcourt Brace.
Horgan, John. 2003. "Leaving Terrorism Behind: An Individual Perspective," in Andrew Silke (ed.) *Terrorists, Victims and Society: Psychological Perspectives on Terrorism and its Consequences*. New York: Wiley.
Horgan, John. 2009. *Walking away from Terrorism*. New York: Routledge.

Hughes, Martin. 1990. "Terror and Negotiation," *Terrorism and Political Violence* 2 1: 79–80, 82.
Ikle, Fred Charles. 1971. *Every War Must End.* New York: Columbia University Press.
Innes, Martin, 2006. "Policing Uncertainty: Countering Terror through Community Intelligence and Democratic Policing," *Annals of the American Academy* 605 (May): 1–20.
Institute of International Economics. 1984. "Case Studies in Sanctions and Terrorism," Case 84, 1 US v. Iran (1984–: Terrorism, Proliferation), www.iie.com/research/topics/sanctions/iran.htm (last accessed February 5 2005).
International Crises Group. 2006. "Palestinians, Israel, and the Quartet: Pulling Back from the Brink," Middle East Report 54, June 13. Jerusalem, Amman and Brussels: ICG.
Irvin, Cynthia 1999. *Militant Nationalism.* Minneapolis, MN: University of Minnesota Press,
Jacobsen, David. 1993. *My Life as a Hostage: The Nightmare in Beirut.* New York: Shapolsky.
Jaggia, Anil K. and Shula, Saurabh. 2000. *IC814 Hi-jacked: The Inside Story.* New Delhi: Roli.
Jajanpour, Farhang. 1992. "The Roots of the Hostage Crisis," *World Today* 40: 2. London: Royal Institute of International Affairs.
Karmon, Ely. 2002. The Risk of Terrorism against Oil and Gas Pipelines in Central Asia, www.ict.org.il/articles/articledet.cfm?articleid=426 (last accessed April 26 2006).
Karoui, Hichem. 2002. "Iskandar Safa and the French Hostage Scandal," *Middle East Intelligence Bulletin* 4 2:
Katzman, Kenneth. 2000. "Iran: US Policy and Options," CRS Report for Congress. Washington, DC: Congressional Research Service, January 14.
Katzman, Kenneth. 2002. "Terrorism: New Eastern Groups and State Sponsors, 2002," CRS Report for Congress. Washington, DC: Congressional Research Service, February 13.
Katzman, Kenneth. 2006. "Iran: US Concerns and Policy Responses." CRS Report for Congress. Washington, DC: Congressional Research Service, April 6.
Kaufmann, Johan. 1989. "Toward an Integral Analysis of International Negotiations," in Frances Mautner-Markhof (ed.) *Processes of International Negotiations.* Boulder, CO: Westview Press.
Kennedy, Gavin. 1997. *Pocket Negotiator.* London: *The Economist.*
Khuzmieva, Madina. 2005. Testimony in court. The Kulayev trial, July 19.
Kim, Chae-Han. 2005. "Reciprocity in Asymmetry: When does Reciprocity Work?" *International Interactions* 31 1: 1–14.
Kissinger, Henry. 1982. *Years of Upheaval.* Boston, MA: Little Brown.
Kissinger, Henry. 1989. "The System of International Negotiations and its Impact on the Processes of Negotiation" in Frances Mautner-Markhof (ed.) *Processes of International Negotiation.* Boulder, CO: Westview Press.
Kitson, F. 1971. *Low Intensity Operations: Subversion, Insurgency and Peacekeeping.* London: Faber.
Kitson, F. 1977. *Bunch of Five.* London: Faber.
Kremenyuk, Victor, ed. 2002. *International Negotiation: Issues, Approaches, Analysis.* Jossey-Bass, 2nd. ed.
Kremenyuk, Victor. 2004. "War on Terrorism: Search for Focus," in R. Ragaini (ed.) *International Seminar on Nuclear War and Planetary Emergencies, Thirtieth Session.* London: World Scientific.
Kushner, Harvey W. 2003. *Encyclopedia of Terrorism.* Thousand Oaks, CA: Sage.

Kydd, Andrew and Walter, Barbara. 2002. "Sabotaging the Peace: The Politics of Extremist Violence," *International Organization* 55 2: 263–296.

Lake, David A. 2003. "Interview with David Lewis: Negotiating with Hezbollah." PBS Frontline, June, www.pbs.org/frontlineworld/stories/lebanon (last accessed April 6 2006).

Lake, David A. and Powell, Robert. 1999. "International Relations: a Strategic Choice Approach," in David A. Lake and Robert Powell (eds.) *Strategic Choice and International Relations*. Princeton, NJ: Princeton University Press.

Lake, David A. and Donald Rothchild, eds. 1998. *The International Spread of Ethnic Conflict*. Princeton, NJ: Princeton University Press.

Lanceley F. J. 1999. *On-scene Guide for Crisis Negotiators*. New York: CRC Press.

Lapan, Harvey E. and Todd Sandler. 1988. "To Bargain or Not to Bargain: That is the Question," *American Economic Review* 78 2: 16–21.

Laqueur, Walter. 1987. *The Age of Terrorism*. Boston, MA: Little Brown.

Laqueur, Walter. 1999. *The New Terrorism*. New York: Oxford University Press.

Laqueur, Walter. 2004. *Voices of Terror*. London: Reed Publishing.

Leeds, Brett Ashley. 1999. "Domestic Political Institutions, Credible Commitments, and International Cooperation," *American Journal of Political Science* 43 4: 979–1002.

Lehany, David. 1989. "US Policy Options in the Hostage Crisis in Lebanon." Rand Corporation Report P-7585. Santa Monica, CA: Rand Corporation.

Lehany, David. 1999. *Inside Terrorism*. New York: Columbia University Press.

Lehany, David. 2005. "Terrorism, Social Movements, and International Security: How Al Qaeda affects Southeast Asia," *Japanese Journal of Political Science* 6 1: 87–109.

Lehany, David. 2007. "The Logic of Suicide Terrorism," *Atlantic Monthly*, June, www.theatlantic.com/doc/200306/hoffman (last accessed December 2007).

Lum, Cynthia, Leslie W. Kennedy, and Alison J. Sherley (2006). *The Effectiveness of Counter-terrorism Strategies: A Campbell Systematic Review*. New Brunswick, NJ: Rutgers University School of Criminal Justice and Center for the Study of Public Security.

MacWillson. A. C. 1992. *Hostage-taking Terrorism: Incident-response Strategy*. New York: St. Martin's Press.

Malhotra, Jyoti. 1999. India appreciates Taliban's role in Hi-jacking Drama, www.indianexpress.com/res/web/ple/ie/daily/19991229/ian29037.html.

Machida, Sonal. 1999. Angry Relatives clash with Cops, www.indianexpress.com/res/web/ple/ie/daily/19991228/ifr28019.html.

Maddi, Salvador. 1989. *Psychological Theories: A Comparative Analysis*. Pacific Grove: Brooks/Cole.

Mark, Clyde R. 1992. *Lebanon: US Hostages, an Overview and Chronology, February 10, 1984–December 27, 1991*. CRS Report for Congress, April 7.

Marston, D. and Malkasian, M., eds. 2008. *Counterinsurgency in Modern Warfare*. New York: Osprey.

Martin, G. ed. 2004. *The New Era of Terrorism: Selected Readings*, Thousand Oaks, CA: Sage.

Martinez, Michael L., and Stuart H. Newberger. 2002. "Combating State-sponsored Terrorism with Civil Lawsuits: Anderson v. Islamic Republic of Iran and other Cases," *Victim Advocate: Journal of the National Crime Victim Bar Association* 3 4: 5–8.

McMains, Michael J. and Mullins, Wayman C. 2001. *Crisis Negotiations: Managing Critical Incidents and Hostage Situations in Law Enforcement and Corrections*, 2nd edn. Cincinnati, OH: Anderson.

Mickolus, E. F. 1980. *Transnational Terrorism: A Chronology of Events, 1968–1979.* London: Aldwych.

Mickolus, Edward, Todd Sandler, Jean Murdock, and Peter Fleming. 2000. *International Terrorism: Attributes of Terrorist Events.* Dunn Loring, VA: Vinyard Software.

Mickolus, Edward, Todd Sandler, Jean Murdock, and Peter Fleming. 2006. *ITERATE: International Terrorism: Attributes of Terrorist Events 1968–2005.* Dunn Loring, VA: Vinyard Software.

Miller, Abraham H. 1980. *Terrorism and Hostage Negotiations.* Boulder, CO: Westview Press.

Miller, Gregory D. 2007. "Confronting Terrorisms: Group Motivation and Successful State Policies," *Terrorism and Political Violence* 19 3: 331–350.

Miller, R. 1995. "The Bangkok Solution: Peaceful Resolution of Hostage-taking," *Intelligence and National Security 1743–1990* 10 2: 306–326.

National Commission on Terrorism Attacks upon the United States. 2004. *The 9/11 Commission Report: Authorized Edition.* London: Norton.

National Commission on Terrorism Attacks upon the United States. 2009. *Report on Terrorism 2008.* Washington, DC: National Intelligence, National Counter-terrorism Center.

Nelson, Dean. 2009. "Taliban were paid £20,000 for Sham Truce, claim Diplomats," *Daily Telegraph*, July 28.

Nesser, P. 2006. "Jihadism in Western Europe after the Invasion of Iraq: Tracing Motivational Influences from the Iraq War on Jihadist Terrorism in Western Europe," *Studies in Conflict and Terrorism* 29 4: 323–342.

Noorani, A. G. 2000. "A Tale of Shattered Credibility," *Frontline*, February 4.

Oberdorfer, Don. 1992. "Iran paid for Release of Hostages: Tehran gave Captors up to $2 million for each, Officials say," *Washington Post*, January 19.

O'Brien, Brendan. 1999. *The Long War: The IRA and Sinn Féin.* Dublin: O'Brien Press.

O'Brien, Sean P. 1996. "Foreign Policy Crises and the Resort to Terrorism: A Time-series Analysis of Conflict Linkages," *Journal of Conflict Resolution* 40 2: 320–335.

Ochberg, F. 1980. "Victims of Terrorism," *Journal of Clinical Psychiatry* 41: 73–74.

Oettgen W. and Spinazzola, B. 1987. *La négociation lors de la prise d'ôtages terroristes.* Paris : Sorbonne, René Descartes, mémoire de maîtrise de sociologie.

Opall, Barbara. 1998. "US May Owe Iran Billions in Penalties," *Defense News*, February 22–26.

Pape, Robert. 2005. *Dying to Win: The Strategic Logic of Suicide Terrorism.* New York: Random House.

Pargeter, A. 2009. Conference organized by the Centre for Defence Studies at King's College and the Norwegian Defence Research Establishment, London.

PBS Frontline/World. 2001. Terrorist Attacks on Americans 1979–1988, www.pbs.org/wgbh/pages/frontline/shows/taraget/etc/cron.html (last accessed February 5 2005).

PBS Frontline/World 2001. 2002. Interview: Robert Baer, March 22, www.pbs.org/wgbh/pages/frontline/shows/tehran/interviews/baer (last accessed April 7 2006).

PBS Frontline/World 2001. 2003. Lebanon Party of God, May, www.pbs.org/frontline-world/stories/lebanon (last accessed 16 April 2006).

Pearson, C. and E. Radli. 1999. *Negotiate! Manage! Survive! Hostage Situations: From Crisis Intervention to Dealing with Terrorists.* San Clemente, CA: Law Tech.

Pepper, C. B. 1977. "Kidnapped," *New York Times Magazine*, November 20.

Perl, Raphael F. 2006. "Terrorism and National Security: Issues and Trends." CRS Issue Brief for Congress. Washington, DC: Congressional Research Service.

Pervin, Lawrence A. 1984. *Personality: Theory and Research.* New York: Wiley.

Picco, Giandomenico. 1999. *Man without a Gun: One Diplomat's Secret Struggle to Free the Hostages, Fight Terrorism, and End a War.* New York: Random House.

Poland, J. M. and McCrystle, M. J. 1999. *Practical, Tactical, and Legal Perspectives of Terrorism and Hostage-taking.* Lewiston, NY: Edwin Mellon Press.

Post, Jerrold. M. 1990. "Terrorism Psycho-logic: Terrorist Behaviour as a Product of Psychological Forces," in Walter Reich (ed.) *The Origins of Terrorism: Psychological, Ideologies, Theologies, State of Mind.* Cambridge: Cambridge University Press.

Post, Jerrold M. 2005. "Psychological Operations and Counterterrorism," *Joint Force Quarterly* 37: 105–110.

Post, Jerrold M. 2006, "Countering Islamist Militancy: An Epidemiologic Approach," in C. Timmerman, D. Hutsebault, S. Mels, W. Nonneman and W. Van Herck (eds) *Faith-based Radicalism:Christianity, Islam and Judaism between Constructive Activism and Destructive Fanaticism.* Brussels, etc.: Peter Lang.

Post, Jerrold M., Ruby, K. G., and Shaw, E. D. 2002. "The Radical Group in Context" 2 "Identification of Critical Elements in the Analysis of Risk for Terrorism by Radical Group Type," *Studies in Conflict and Terrorism* 25: 101–126.

Post, Jerrold M., Sprinzak, E., and Denny, L. M. 2003. "The Terrorists in their Own Worlds: Interviews with Thirty-five Incarcerated Middle Eastern Terrorists," *Terrorism and Political Violence* 15 1: 171–184.

Pruitt, Dean G. 2006. "Negotiation with Terrorists," *International Negotiation* 11 2: 370–394

Quandt, William B. 2005. *Peace Process: American Diplomacy and the Arab–Israeli Conflict since 1967*, 3rd edn. Washington, DC: Brookings Institution.

Qutb, Sayyid. 1964. *Milestones of Negotiations.* Background Paper, PIN Task Force Meeting, December.

Ragaini, R., ed. 2004. *International Seminar on Nuclear War and Planetary Emergencies, Thirtieth Session.* London: World Scientific.

Rainwater, Janette. 1997. Afghanistan, "Terrorism" and Blowback: A Chronology, www.janwainwater.com/hdocs/afghan2p9.htm (last accessed April 19 2006).

Randal, Jonathan C. 1983. *Going all the Way: Christian Warlords, Israeli Adventurers, and the War in Lebanon.* New York: Viking.

Ranstorp, Magnus and Xhudo, Gus. 1997. *Hizb'allah in Lebanon: The Politics of the Western Hostage Crisis.* New York: St. Martin's Press.

Rapoport, Anatol. 1960. *Fights, Games and Debates.* Ann Arbor, MI: University of Michigan Press.

Rapoport, David. 1984. "Fear and Trembling: Terrorism in Three Religious Traditions," *American Political Science Review* 78 3: 658–657.

Rapoport, David. 2006. *Four Waves of Modern Terrorism.* Los Angeles: Burkle Center for International Relations, UCLA.

Reich, W. 1998. *Origins of Terrorism: Psychologies, Ideologies, Theologies, States of Mind.* Washington, DC: Woodrow Wilson Center Press.

RIA. 2005. Russian Official Reveals Evidence Uncovered by Beslan Investigation, February 4.

Ricigliano, Robert. 2005. *Choosing to Engage: Armed Groups and Peace Processes.* London: Conciliation Resources.

Rodman, Peter W. 1981. "The Hostage Crisis: How not to Negotiate," *Washington Quarterly* 4 3: 9–24.

Sageman, Marc. 2004. *Understanding Terror Networks.* Philadelphia: University of Pennsylvania Press.

Samii, A. William. 2002. "Tehran, Washington, and Terror: No Agreement to Differ," *MERIA: Middle East Review of International Affairs* 6 3: 1–15.

Sandler, Todd. 2005. "Collective versus Unilateral Responses to Terrorism," *Public Choice* 124: 75–93.

Sandler, Todd and Enders, Walter. 2002. "An Economic Perspective on Transnational Terrorism," working paper, Department of Economics, Finance and Legal Studies University of Alabama, Working Paper series Index, www.cha.ua.edu.

Sandler, Todd and Scott, John. 1987. "Terrorist Success in Hostage Taking Incidents: An Empirical Study," *Journal of Conflict Resolution* 31 1: 35–53.

Schiff, Ze'ev and Ya'ari, Ejid. 1984. *Israel's Lebanon War.* New York: Simon & Schuster.

Schimmelfenning, Frank. 2005. "Strategic Calculation and International Socialization: Membership Incentives, Party Constellations, and Sustained Compliance in Central and Eastern Europe," *International Organization* 59 4: 827–860.

Schmid, A. P. 1988. *Political Terrorism*. Amsterdam: North Holland.

Schmid, A. P. 2000. *Thesaurus and Glossary of Early Warning and Conflict Prevention Terms*. London: FEWER.

Schmid, A. P. 2004. "Magnitudes of Terrorist Victimization," in E. Vetere and P. David (eds.) *Victims of Crime and Abuse of Power: Festschrift in honour of Irene Melup*. Bangkok: Eleventh UN Congress on Crime Prevention and Criminal Justice.

Schmid, A. P. and Crelinsten, R. D., ed. 1993. *Western Responses to Terrorism.* London: Cass.

Shoumikhin, Andrei. 2004. *Deterring Terrorism: Russian Views*. Fairfax, VA: National Institute for Public Policy.

Shulimson, Jack. 1958. *Marines in Lebanon 1958: A Report to the Department of the Navy, Headquarters United States Marine Corps.* Washington, DC, www.au.af.mil/au/awc/awcgate/usmchist/lebanon.txt (accessed April 17 2006).

Seale, Patrick. 1992. *Abu Nidal: A Gun For Hire*. New York: Random House.

Sharf, Michael. 2001. "The Broader Meaning of the Lockerbie Trial and the Future of International Counter-terrorism." Presentation at the fall 2001 symposium "International Terrorism, Victims' Rights and the Lockerbie Criminal Trial," *Syracuse Journal of International Law and Commerce* 29 1: 50–62.

Sick, Gary. 1991. *October Surprise: America's Hostages in Iran and the Election of Ronald Reagan*. New York: Random House.

Silke, A. 2003. "Becoming a terrorist," in A. Silke (ed.) *Terrorists, Victims and Society: Psychological Perspectives on Terrorism and its Consequences*. Chichester: Wiley.

Singh, Jessant. 2006. *A Call to Honour: In Service of Emergent India*. New Delhi: Rupa.

Singh, Jessant. 2000. Suo Motu Statement by the Minister of External Affairs in Parliament on the Hi-jacking of Indian Airlines Flight IC-814, www.indianembassy.org/policy/Terrorism/jsingh_parliament_03_13_2000.html.

Sofaer, Abraham. 1999. "Government-to-Government Cases and Settlement of the Small Claims," in Andreas F. Lowenfeld, Lawrence W. Newman and John M. Walker (eds.) *Revolutionary Days: The Iran Hostage Crisis and the Hague Claims Tribunal: A Look Back*. Huntington, NM: Juris.

Sutherland, Tom and Jean. 1996. *At Your Own Risk: An American Chronicle of Crisis and Captivity in the Middle East*. Golden, CO: Fulcrum.

Swami, Praveen. 2000a. "Bowing to Terrorism," *Frontline*, January 21.

Swami, Praveen. 2000b. "Of theology and Terrorism," *Frontline*, January 21.

Taylor, Peter and Donohue, W. 2006. "Hostage Negotiation opens up," in Kupfer-Schneider, A. and Honeyman, C. (eds.) *The Negotiator's Fieldbook: The Desk Reference for the Experienced Negotiator.* Chicago: Section of Dispute Resolution, American Bar Association.

Thompson, Sir Robert. 1966. *Defeating Communist Insurgency: Experience from Malaya and Vietnam.* New York: Praeger.

Thomson, L. 2001. *Hostage Rescue Manual.* London: Greenhills Books.

The Times (London). 2006, May 22.

Touval, Saadia and Zartman, I. William. 1985, "Conclusion. Mediation in Theory and Practice," in Saadia Touval and I. William Zartman (eds.) *International Mediation in Theory and Practice*, Vol. VI. Boulder, CO: Westview Press.

Tower Commission Report. 1987. *The Full Text of the President's Special Review Board.* New York: Random House Bantam.

US Government. 2003. *Guide to Surviving Terrorism, complied from Official US Government Documents.* New York: Barnes & Noble.

United Nations Assistance Mission to Afghanistan (UNAMA). 2007. *Suicide Attacks in Afghanistan 2001–2007*, www.unama-afg.org/docs.

UNODC. 2006. *Counter-kidnapping Manual.* New York: United Nations Office on Drugs and Crime.

US Department of Defense. 1983. *Report of the Commission on Beirut International Airport Terrorist Act, October 23, 1983.* December 20. Washington, DC: Department of Defense.

US Department of State. 2006. State Sponsors of Terrorism, www.state.gov/s/ct/c14151.htm (last accessed April 17 2006).

US–Iran Relations. 2005. Washington, DC: Atlantic Council, www.acus.org/InternationalSecurity/policy_updates.htm (last accessed February 9 2005).

Vasey, Michael C. 1985. "Hostage Negotiations: Policies, Procedures and Attitudes." Doctoral dissertation, University of Oregon.

Vetter, Harold J. and Perlstein, Gary R. 1991. *Perspectives on Terrorism.* Pacific Grove, CA: Brooks-Cole.

Victoroff, Jeff. 2005. "The Mind of the Terrorist: A Review and Critique of Psychological approaches," *Journal of Conflict Resolution* 49 3: 3–42.

Victoroff, Jeff. 2006. *Tangled Roots: Social and Psychological Factors in the Genesis of Terrorism.* Amsterdam: IOS Press.

v. d. Feltz, Baron, W. n.d. "Dealing with Hostage Situations." Confidential note by W., Attorney General, The Hague.

Voss, Christopher T. 2004. "Crisis Negotiation: A Counter-intuitive Method to Disrupt Terrorism," *Studies in Conflict and Terrorism* 27: 455–459.

Waas, Murray and Unger, Craig. 2002. "In the Loop: Bush's Secret Mission," *New Yorker*, November 14.

Walker, Stephen G. 2004. "The Management and Resolution of International Conflict in a 'Single' Case: American and North Vietnamese Exchanges during the Vietnam War," in Zeev Maoz, Alex Mintz, T. Clifton Morgan, Glenn Palmer and Richard Stoll (eds.) *Multiple Paths to Knowledge in International Relations: Methodology in the Study of Conflict Management and Conflict Resolution.* Lanham, MD: Lexington Books.

Walter, Barbara F. 1997. "The Critical Barrier to Civil War Settlement," *International Organization* 51 3: 335–364.

Wanis-St. John, Anthony. 2006. "Back-channel Negotiation: International Bargaining in the Shadows," *Negotiation Journal* 22 2: 119–144.

Waugh W. L. 1982. *International Terrorism.* Salisbury, NC: Documentary Publications.

Weinberg, Leonard. 2008. *Global Terrorism*. Oxford: Oneword.
Wilkinson, P. 2006. *Terrorism versus Democracy: the Liberal State Response*, 2nd edn. London: Routledge.
Wilson, M. A. 2000. "Toward a Model of Terrorist Behavior in Hostage-taking Incidents," *Journal of Conflict Resolution* 34 3: 403–424.
Wilson, M. A. 2002. "The Psychology of Hostage-taking," in Silke A. (ed.) *Terrorists, Victims and Society*. New York: Wiley.
Wright., Stuart A. 1999. "Anatomy of a Massacre," *Terrorism and Political Violence* 11 2: 39–68.
Zakaria, Fareed. 1989. "Make Hostages' Lives the Second Goal," *Wall Street Journal*, August 10.
Zartman, I. William. 1989a. *Ripe for Resolution*. New York: Oxford University Press.
Zartman, I. William. 1989b. "Prenegotiation: Phases and Functions," *International Journal* 44 3: 237–253.
Zartman, I. William. 1989c. "In Search of Common Elements in the Analysis of the Negotiation Process," in Frances Mautner-Markhof (ed.) *Processes of International Negotiations*. Boulder, CO: Westview Press.
Zartman, I. William. 1990. "Negotiating Effectively with Terrorists," in Barry Rubin (ed.) *The Politics of Counterterrorism: The Ordeal of Democratic States*. Washington, DC: Foreign Policy Institute, Paul H. Nitze School of Advanced International Studies, Johns Hopkins University.
Zartman, I. William. 2000. "The Structure of Negotiation" and "Regional Conflict," in Victor A. Kremenyuk (ed.) *International Negotiation: Analysis, Approaches, Issues*. San Francisco: Jossey-Bass.
Zartman, I. William and Berman, Maureen R. 1982. *The Practical Negotiator*. New Haven, CT: Yale University Press.
Zartman, I. William and Touval, Saadia. 2007. "International Mediation," in Chester A. Crocker, Fen Osler Hampson and Pamela Aall (eds.) *Leashing the Dogs of War: Conflict Management in a Divided World*, Washington, DC: US Institute of Peace Press.
Zartman, I. William and Alfredson, Tanya. 2008. "Negotiating with Terrorists and the Tactical Question," Baltimore, MD: School of Advanced International Studies, Johns Hopkins University.
Zartman, I. William, ed. 1995. *Elusive Peace: Negotiating an End to Civil War*. Washington, DC: Brookings Institution.
Zartman, I. William and Rubin, Jeffry Z., eds. 2000. *Power and Negotiation*. Ann Arbor: University of Michigan Press.
Zartman, I. William, ed. 2006. *Negotiating with Terrorists*. Dordrecht: Nijhoff.
Zartman, I. William, ed. 2001. *Preventive Negotiation: Avoiding Conflict Escalation*. Lanham, MD: Rowman & Littlefield
Zartman, I. William and Faure, Guy Olivier, eds. 2005. *Escalation and Negotiation in International Conflicts*. Cambridge: Cambridge University Press.
Zartman, I. William and Faure, Guy Olivier, eds., 2010. *Engaging Extremists*. Vienna, International Institute of Applied Systems Analysis.
Zartman, I. William and Kremenyuk, V., eds. 2005. *Peace versus Justice. Negotiating Forward and Backward-looking Outcomes*. Lanham, MD: Rowman & Littlefield.

Index

Note: Page numbers in *italics* denote tables.

9/11 5, 16, 27, 125, 212

Abu Sayyaf 8
Advani, L.K. 194n12
Afghani, Sajjad 180, 184, 195n17
Afghanistan: Kandahar Hostage Crisis *see* Kandahar Hostage Crisis; Swat Valley 82; terrorist incidents in 4, 5; U.S. involvement *see* United States
Aguinaldo, Emiliano 74
Ahmadinejad, Mahmoud 88
Ahmed, Shakir 193n1
Air France hi-jacking 1994 20, 25
Air France hi-jacking 1976 *see* Entebbe Hostage Crisis
Air India hi-jacking 1985 125
al Muqrin, Abdul Aziz 144, 145n1
Al Shiraa 101
Al-Aqsa Martyrs Brigade 6, 7
Algeria 8, 81, 89, 92
Algiers Accord 1981 91–2, 102, 106, *109*, 111
al-Qaeda: demands 4, 12; online manual 85, 144, 145n1; policies 19; training manual 21, 85; typologies of 8, 9, 75–6; U.S. embassy attacks 119
Al-Shabab al-Islamiya 5
Al-Sharq al-Awsat 115
Amin Dada, Idi 14
Anderson, Terry *98*, 105, *112*, *114*, 118
Angry Brigade 69
Annan, Kofi 193n5
Arab–Israeli War 1967 94
Arafat, Yasir 4
Aslakhanov, Aslanbek 130, 143
Attar, Ibrahim 168, 193n1
Aubenas, Florence *54*
Aum Shinrikyo 8

Aushev, Ruslan 129–31, 140, 143, 146n19
Azhar 180, 181, 186

Baader-Meinhof gang 69
Bangkok Solution 18, 19, 24, 51, *56*
Basayev, Shamil 129–30, 132–4, 143–4, 146n30, 147n35
BATNA 127, 132, 171
Begley, Kenneth *54*
Beslan Hostage Crisis 13, 20, *51*, 79: chronology of events 127–32; de-escalation 140; negotiations 141–4; terrorist goals 132–4; terrorist backgrounds 134–5; volatility 135–40
Betancourt, Ingrid 13
Black September (event) 153
Black September (organization) 18, 77
Bojinka Plot 16
Bosnia 76, 119
Braunlich, Rene *54*
Brazil 52
Brigate Rosse 70
Britain *see* United Kingdom
Brzezinsky, Zbigniew *107*
Buckley, William 96, *98*, 105, 111, *112*
Bush, George H.W. 104

Carlos 17
Carter, Jimmy 87, 92, *108*
Casey, William 120
Castro, Fidel 80
Chechnya 125, 129–31, 133–4, 136, 141–4, 152–3
Chernomyrdin, Viktor 146n30
Chesnot, Christian *54*
China 17
Church of the Nativity Hostage Situation 23–4

Index 227

Cicippio, Joseph 99, *112*, *114*
Cold War 8, 73, 75
Collins, Michael 73
Colombia: FARC see FARC; kidnappings 13–14, 53, 89; and M-19 80; negotiation policy 25; Operation Jaque 25–6
Congo, Democratic Republic of 4, 118
Crowell & Moring 118
Cuba 73, 80, 118

Dastigir, Malawi 82
Dawah, the 94
de Mull, Erik 172, 178
Democratic Front for the Liberation of Palestine 125
Dodge, David *98*, 102, 111, 118
Doval, Ajit 168, 182
Dzosokhov, Alexander 128, 143, 146n19

Egypt: ancient 12; modern 18, 118
Entebbe Hostage Crisis 14, 20, 23, 25, 51
Euskadi Ta Askatasuna (ETA) 7, 70

FARC 12, 13–14, 17, 25–6
Fatah 7
FBI 43, 63, 68n4, 126
France: Air France hi-jacking 1994 see Air France hi-jacking 1994; deals for hostages 17, 53, *54*, 116; French Revolution 12; German occupation of 12; and Kandahar Hostage Crisis 194n7; and Lebanon 88

Gaddafi, Muammar *114*, 116
Gaza 13
Gemayyil, Bashir 94
Germany: deals for hostages 17, 53, *54*, 116; GSG-9 20; and Lebanon 88; occupation of France 12; von Spreti, Count see von Spreti, Count
Ghanashyam, A.R. 179, 195n14
Glass, Charles 99, 111
Greeks 12
Group Islamique Armé (GIA) 9, 20
Guatemala *52*
Gutseriev, Mikhail 128

Harkat-ul Mujahideen (HuM) 167
Hassan, Margaret *54*
Hearst, Partricia 211
Hezbollah: American hostages in Lebanon 50, 89, 96–7, 104–5; conflict with Israel 88; and Iran 88, 94, 96, 105, 116, 118, 122; politics 118; typology of 8, 9

Higgins, William 99, 111, *113*
hostage negotiations: crisis negotiations 31–3; literature on 1–2; and media 23–4; paradigms 15; strategies see hostage-taking negotiation strategies; risk 33–4
hostage typologies: involuntary 12; voluntary 12
hostage-taking negotiation strategies: no negotiation 14–15; secret negotiation 14–15; regular negotiation 14–15; negotiation to prepare for assault 15
hostage-taking typologies: *barricade* 13; *kidnapping* 13; *sky-jacking* 14
hostage-taking: definition *51*, 90; hostage-taker typologies *61*; negotiation strategies see hostage-taking negotiation strategies; phases of *63*; typologies see hostage-taking typologies
Hukbalapaps 74
Husayn Suicide Commandos 94
Harkat-ul Ansar (HuA) 166–7, 170, 174
Hamas 4, 5, 9, 13, 76
Habib, Philip 94–5

Ibrahim, Mistri Zahoor 193n1
India 4, 5; Air India hi-jacking see Air India hi-jacking 1985; Kandahar Hostage Crisis see Kandahar Hostage Crisis
Ingushetia 125, 128, 129, 134, 136, 144, 146n26
Inter-American Human Rights Commission 80
International Emergency Economics Power Act (IEEPA) *107*–8
Iran: dealing with the United States see Iran-Contra Affair; and Hezbollah see Hezbollah; Shah 91, 100, 102, *107*, *114*, 120; Tehran Embassy hostage-taking 14, 53, 91–2; war with Iraq see Iran–Iraq War
Iran Air flight 655, 105, *110*, 111, *113*–14
Iran–Contra Affair: context 88–93; generally 17, 24, 50, 73; lessons 123–4; negotiation analysis 105–18; negotiation history 97–105
Iran–Iraq War 95–6, 97, 105, 115
Iran–U.S. Claims Tribunal 103, 106, *109*, 116–17, 119, 120–1
Iraq: *coup* against monarchy 93; foreign occupation 4, 18; war with Iran see Iran–Iraq War kidnappings 12, 13–14, 17, 24, 53, *54*, 89, 116, 119; sponsor of terrorism 118; attacks in 4
Iraq–Iran War see Iran–Iraq War

Ireland 17, 72–3, 88, 116: Irish Republican Army *see* Irish Republican Army (IRA)
Irish Republican Army (IRA) 17, 70, 71, 72–3, 76
Islamic Holy War for the Liberation of Palestine 105
Islamic Jihad 5, 94, 97, 105
Israel: Arab–Israeli conflict 76, 88, 94, 200; Bangkok embassy attack 18; Church of the Nativity Hostage Situation *see* Church of the Nativity Hostage Situation; Entebbe Hostage Crisis *see* Entebbe Hostage Crisis; and Iran–U.S. arms deal 100–2, 106, 116, 120; and Lebanon 94–6, 118; Ma'a lot 125; Munich Olympic attack *see* Munich Olympic Games; negotiation policy 14, 50, 212; release of prisoners 51, 196n25; suicide bombings 119; Yamam and Saveret Matkal 20
Italian Red Brigades 8, 19, *51*, 210
Italy 10, 16, 17, 53, *54*, 78, 81, 88, 194n7: Italian Red Brigades *see* Italian Red Brigades

Jacobsen, David *98*, 101, 105, 106, *112*
Jama'a al-Islamiyh al-Musallaha *see* Group Islamique Armé
Japan: Aum Shinrikyo *see* Aum Shinrikyo; exchange for consul general *52*; and Iraq 18; storming of ambassador's residence in Lima *see* Lima hostage-taking
Jenco, Lawrence Martin *98*, 100, 105, *112*
Jourdain, M. 31, 38
Jundallah 94

Kaczynski, Theodore 75
Kandahar Hostage Crisis 86: assessment of negotiations 188–92; chronology of events 164–7; context 167–76; the deal 185–8; formulation phase 179–85; lessons from 192–3; prenegotiation 176–9
Kashmir 164, 166–7, 169, 174, 179, 183, 188, 192, 193n4, 195n17
Katipunan 74
Katju, Vivek 168
Kenya 74, 119
Kerr, Malcolm *98*, *112*
Khalid, Facular Raman 170
Khan, Sajjad *see* Afghani, Sajjad
Khasavyurt Agreement 1996 154
Khodov, Vladimir 138–9, 147n54
Khubayeva, Marina 139

Khuchbarov, Ruslan 128–31, 138–40, 143, 146n8
kidnapping, definition of *51*
Kilburn, Peter *98*, 111, 112, *114*, 118
Koran 19, 210
Koresh, David 68n4
Kudzyeva, Larisa 131, 133, 147n55
Kurdistan Workers' Party (PKK) 5–6, 7
Kuwait 95–6, *98*, 115

Lamberth, Royce 118
Lebanon: and foreign intervention 88; Iran *see* Iran; kidnappings in 88–91, 96–9, 106, 115, 118–19, 121; U.S. Marine Barracks attack 87, 96, *98*, 102, 106, *110*, 111, 118; war and instability 88, 93–7
Ledeen, Michael 102
Levine, Jeremy *98*, 100, *112*
Liberation Tigers of Tamil Eelan (LTTE) 4, 5, 7
Libya 14, 72, 111, *114*, 116, 118, 121, 123
Lima hostage-taking 15, 20, 25, 212
Lima syndrome 210
London suicide attacks 2005 7
Lord's Resistance Army 8

M-19 79–80
McFarlane, Robert 100, 120
McGuiness, Martin 73
McVeigh, Timothy 68n4
Malbrunot, Georges *54*
Mamitova, Larisa 128, 129–31, 138, 139, 147n53
Mamsurov, Taymuroz 130–1
Maskhadov, Aslan 131, 143, 146n19, 153
Mastrogiacomo, Daniele 78
Meloy, Francis *99*
Mexico 13
Mishap, Rajesh 170, 196n24
Moro, Aldo 19, *51*, 210
Moscow theatre hostage-taking 13, 20, 132, 143–4, 153
Mughniyah, Imad 96, 98
Munich Olympic Games 1972 20, 77, 153
Muski, Edmund 101
Muslim Brothers 9
Muttawakil, Wakil Ahmed 185–7, 194n13, 195n20

Naccache, Anis 17
National Counter Terrorism Center 4
National Security Decision Directive 138, 96
Nazran raid 128, 134, 142, 147n35

negotiations: definition of 48–9; terrorist negotiations *see* terrorist negotiations
Nepalese Maoists 9
Netherlands 48, 68n3; school takeover in Bovensmilde 125
Nitzschke, Thomas *54*
'no concessions' policy 10, 11, 49–50, 67, 90
'no negotiations' policy 49, 90–1, 144
North Korea 118
North Ossetia 125, 130, 138, 144
North, Oliver 103
Northern Ireland 71, 76: IRA *see* IRA

Oklahoma City bombing 68n4
Oman 165
OPEC hostage crisis 1975 17
Organization for the Oppressed on Earth 97
Ostloff, Susanne *54*
Ottoman Empire, terrorism in 2–3
Owen, Roberts 92

PACIFICA method of risk management 34–45
Pakistan: and Kandahar Hostage Crisis 165, 167, 170, 173–5, 179, 187, 194n8; and the Taliban 82, 194n6; terrorist incidents in 4, 5
Palestine 2, 4
Palestine Liberation Organization (PLO) 7, 94, 96
Pan Am flight 103 *99*, 111, *113*, 116
Pari, Simona *54*
peacekeeping forces 75, 88, 94, 119
Perez de Cuellar, Xavier 105
Philippines 8, 18, 25, 74
Picco, Giandomenico 89, 93, 105, 116
PKK *see* Kurdistan Workers' Party
Polhill, Robert *99*, 104, *113*, 118
Polkovnik *see* Khuchbarov, Ruslan
Popular Front for the Liberation of Palestine (PFLP) 6, 7, 14, *99*, *113*
Provisional Irish Republican Army (PIRA) 7, 72–3
Putin, Vladimir 129, 130, 132, 140, 141–4

Qazi, Sunny Ahmed 193n1

Rafsanjani, Hashemi 101, 115
Reagan, Ronald 24, 50–1, 53, 87, 96, 102, *110*, 122
Red Cap *see* Attar, Ibrahim
Reed, Frank *99*, 104, *112–13*

Regier, Frank *98*, *112*, 118
Revolutionary Justice Organization 97, 104–5
risk perception, factors of in crisis negotiation 33–4
Riyadus-Salikhin Battalion (RAS) 135
Rogers, Carl 43
Romans 12
Roshal, Leonid 128, 131, 143
Russia nineteenth-century 2, 148, 152; Beslan Hostage Crisis *see* Beslan Hostage Crisis; and Lebanon 88; Moscow theatre hostage-taking *see* Moscow theatre hostage-taking; Pervomayskaya 79
Rwanda 118

Sahay, C.D. 168
Salafist Group for Preaching and Combat in Algeria 8
Sarajevo syndrome 76
Sarkis, Elias *99*
Saudi Arabia 4, 95, 118, 145n1: and Kandahar Hostage Crisis 173; and Mecca Hostage Crisis 25
Sayeed, Shahid Akhtar 193n1
Schultz, George 102, *110*
Scowcroft, Brent 101, 102
Segrena, Giuliana *54*
Shalit, Gilad 13
'Sheikhu' 127–8, 130
Shepel, Nikolai 138
Singh, Jessant 172–3, 179, 186–7, 194n12, 195n22, n23, 196n26
Singhalese, the 4
Sofaer, Abraham 104, 116, 120–1
Somalia 4, 79, 118
Soviet Union 73, 96, 97, 101, 161
Spain 12, 118, 158, 194n7
Sri Lanka 2, 5
Steen, Alann *99*, 105, *113–14*
Stethem, Robert 116
Stockholm syndrome 14, 36, *67*, 138, 210, 211
Sudan 118
Sutherland, Thomas *99*, 105, *112*, *114*, 115, 118
SWAT teams 20, 21, 59
Switzerland *52*, 88, 89, 194n7
Syria 88, 90, 94, 96–7, 101, 106, 111, 116, 118

'tactical solution' 19–20, 24–5
Talbott, Strobe 165–6

Taliban: attacks 5; and Kandahar Hostage Crisis *see* Kandahar Hostage Crisis; negotiations with Pakistan 82; possibility of agreement 83
Tamil Tigers *see* Liberation Tigers of Tamil Eelan (LTTE)
Tanzania 119
terrorism 2008 statistics 4; activity types 5; definitions of 3, 48, 92–3; distinction from freedom fighters and guerilla warfare 4; distinction from insurgency 69; and globalization 2, 200; and poverty 6, 200; types of members 6
terrorist events: 'demonstration of flag' 153; dual phase incidents 47, 50; political struggle 153; single phase incidents 47, 50
terrorist ideologies: *national separatist* 7–8; *religious fundamentalist* 8; *social revolutionist* 8
terrorist negotiations: complexity 157–61; context 150–4; identifying tactics 206; strategies 199–206; structure 154–7
terrorist situation typologies 32: hostage-takers 32–3; psychotic 32; the 'Tehran Embassy' 32–3
Thailand 18, 51
three phase negotiation model 18–19; *agreement formula* 18; *detail phase* 18–19; *implementation stage* 19; *pre-negotiation* 18
Toretta, Simona *54*
Torshin, Alexander 138, 146n26
Tower Commission 101–2
Tower, John 101
Tracy, Edward *99*, 105, *112*, *114*
Tupac Amaru Revolutionary Movement 20
Turner, Jesse *99*, 105, *113–14*
TWA hijacking 1985 51, *99*, 116, 192
typologies, terrorist group: *absolute* 9, 72, 197–8; *contingent* 9–10, 198, 206
national separatists 7–8; *religious fundamentalist* 8; *social revolutionist* 8

Uganda: Entebbe Hostage Crisis *see* Entebbe Hostage Crisis; Lord's Resistance Army *see* Lord's Resistance Army
UN Counter-Kidnapping Manual 58, 59
UN Security Council Resolution 1373 3
Unabomber *see* Kaczynski, Theodore
United Arab Emirates (UAE) 165–6, 173, 194n6
United Kingdom 22nd Strategic Air Service 20, 79; hostages in Iraq *54*; and the IRA 72; and Lebanon 88, 116; in Malaya, Kenya and Dhofar 74, 81; negotiation policy 50; Operation Nimrod 79
United States: in Afghanistan 72, 73; dealings with Iran *see* Iran–Contra Affair; in Iraq 24, 53, 72, 81; in Latin America 72; in Lebanon 88–96; negotiation policies 11, 50; Oklahoma City bombing *see* Oklahoma City bombing; in the Philippines 74; in Vietnam 72, 81, 82, 124, 161
USS *Vincennes* 99, 105, *110*

Vajpayee, A.B. 170–1, 178
Venezuela 16, 89
von Spreti, Count *52*

Waco hostage incident 63, 68n4
Waite, Terry 52, 77, 89
'war on terror' 5, 83
Waring, Robert *99*
Weir, Benjamin *98*, 100, 105, *112*, 118
West Side Boys in Sierra Leone 75
Williamson, Edwin *114*
World War II 12, 74, 81
Worldwide Incidents Tracking System (WITS) 5

Yazdi, Ibrahim *107*

Zahra, Mastoid 178, 180, 185, 186, 195n17
Zaizikov, Murat 128, 143
Zone of Potential Agreement (ZOPA) 10–11, 16, 29, 164

eBooks – at www.eBookstore.tandf.co.uk

A library at your fingertips!

eBooks are electronic versions of printed books. You can store them on your PC/laptop or browse them online.

They have advantages for anyone needing rapid access to a wide variety of published, copyright information.

eBooks can help your research by enabling you to bookmark chapters, annotate text and use instant searches to find specific words or phrases. Several eBook files would fit on even a small laptop or PDA.

NEW: Save money by eSubscribing: cheap, online access to any eBook for as long as you need it.

Annual subscription packages

We now offer special low-cost bulk subscriptions to packages of eBooks in certain subject areas. These are available to libraries or to individuals.

For more information please contact webmaster.ebooks@tandf.co.uk

We're continually developing the eBook concept, so keep up to date by visiting the website.

www.eBookstore.tandf.co.uk

9780415566292